MW01229810

FIRE
FLURRIES

confessions of a
small town rockstar

by Sandi MarLisa

Printed in the United States of America
First Printing, 2022
ISBN 9798363395840

For more information, write Sandi MarLisa at
SandiMarLisa@gmail.com
www.SandiMarLisa.com

To Sandi MarLisa.
To her past that built her.
To her present that defined her.
To her future that calls her forward.
Because, honestly, it's about damn time that girl gave herself some credit.

Table of Contents

Prologue

Seward, Alaska

The sky over Seward, Alaska is deep blue at 9am, the first light of dawn is about to break.

It snowed yesterday. I watched the flurries dance in front of the wide windows of Resurrect Art Cafe tower.

At this point, you might be wondering why a lifelong Floridian is holed up four thousand miles away in a coastal town in Alaska.

That was me casually mentioning I'm a Floridian. How'd it go?

Anyway.

I'm supposed to be here finishing my book, only I'm experiencing terrible writer's block and anxiety right now.

I gathered what I've written already, the total word count coming up to 90,000 words. But I couldn't make sense of anything, couldn't pull the pieces together for the story I wish to tell.

I was surprised I had written so much. When I left home, I thought I'd be lucky if I found thirty thousand words written. This past year has been such a haze… what with the divorce and 625625all…

You ever get that tingling sensation to blow up your life and start over? That's kinda what I did. Only, I didn't really want to blow up my life, it was just necessary on many counts.

My ex-husband and father of my two children is quite literally a genius, but like magic… it comes with a cost. I was his partner in life for fourteen years and most of it was extraordinary and good.

But I had to leave him, for many reasons. Not because I wanted to, but because it was the better of the options I had.

You may think I'm full of shit, and that's okay. I doubted myself and my decisions all year long so I don't blame you.

Yet, here I sit in… Seward… Alaska. Me. A Florida girl through and through.

I act like I'm so surprised but I planned this trip, much like the one when I initiated the divorce. I needed to get as far away from home as humanly possible so I called up my father who lives in Anchorage. I let my then husband know, who was in France at the time pursuing his PhD in Physics, that I was taking our two children out of school in the middle of the Covid-19 pandemic and flying to Alaska.

Yeah. That happened.

In my defense, at the time my three bedroom home in Lynn Haven, Florida was full of people. My sister, recently divorced, and my two nieces had moved in with the expectation that she would be renting my home from me when I moved to France with my kids. Plus, the godfather of my children was crashing at my house for a few months to get back on his feet after the demise of a terrible relationship.

The godfather dubbed my home… drumroll please…

"Sandi's Sanctuary for Sad Singles."

I think he might have prophesied my impending divorce on the horizon. There were supposed to be T-shirts, we never got to it.

So, I left. I thought about staying gone.

But, like I said. I'm a Florida girl through and through. I prefer the fire to the cold, perhaps because I'm an Aries.

Or maybe just because I love my home so much. My little home in Lynn Haven has seen me through it all… bringing my two children home from the hospital, housing friends and family members in need, protecting my family from category 5 Hurricane Michael, overseeing the pain of taking care of my severely mentally ill spouse, and consequently providing the space for me to heal when it all fell desperately apart.

Plus, I had just started up my music career again. I didn't want to lose the momentum now that I was staying in the States and not moving to France.

Regardless, I returned home from Alaska and threw myself into life. I stopped thinking and just became, saying yes to any and all opportunities to try something new.

I convinced the godfather to quit his job and start a musical duo with me, gigging all around the Panhandle of Florida.

I quit a huge client who treated me like dirt, losing 70% of my income in the process.

I took my newly single introverted self out into the wild of the bar scene in Bay County, Florida; singing and meeting men after having only slept with one person in my entire life.

I traveled. Wrote songs. Screamed into the void and said a final big "fuck you" to living a straight and narrow life.

My life, in short, did a complete 180.

I even found love again… but I'm getting ahead of myself here. And I want to do this right.

I've never been too good at writing things out chronologically. It always got me into trouble in school. My therapist I saw for two years said I may have ADHD. My brain has always worked differently when compared to most.

There is very little distinction to me between past, present and future. I see it altogether, all at once, all the time. I constantly string together patterns and come up with a story that makes it all make sense, even if it seems impossible for it to make sense.

I'm going to try though. There's a fire in my bones today, warming me from the inside out in Seward, Alaska.

The mountains I'm staring at through the old church windows are called Resurrection Peaks… if you can believe it.

I can't help but think of my favorite tree back home in Bay County, Florida as I look at them; a historical oak tree called the Sentry Tree. It's 250 years old and has watched over my town for many generations.

After the Hurricane, my heart filled with joy when I saw it was still standing. The leaves were stripped bare from the branches, but green fern coated the thick arms of the giant.

Curiosity struck me, so I googled the name of the fern.

Resurrection leaves.

The name is not one I can fail to see the symbolism in. I was a Christian minister for a decade, serving in various capacities in the ministry, but mainly as a worship leader. Music is always how I have communed with the divine, something bigger than myself.

I was kicked out of church, and then proceeded to ruffle the feathers of every ministry I attempted to serve in since then. The final hammer came down last year around the divorce when the head honcho found out I was leaving my husband and told me I was, "at risk of endangering the lives of my children if I continued down the path I was on."

I did his holiness a favor and quit on the spot.

But I still haven't been able to shake the core of my spirituality. And as I stare out at the vastness of the Resurrection mountains before me, my sense of connection with the "otherness" I've always believed to be out there… stirs… awakens…

It enchants me.

I wonder if I've made the right decisions. I wonder what I will discover as I pen the final thoughts to complete this particular story, closing one chapter and welcoming a new one.

There is a process of germination that transpires during planting. When a seed is planted in the earth, it has to die in order for the plant to burst through the earth, creating new life.

The seed, essentially, resurrects into its new form... what it was always meant to be.

I've felt like a seed these past years. The process has been painful, but I believe, I hope, I can see the beginning sprouts of growth; much like the resurrection fern coating the bark of my favorite tree.

Or the looming mountains standing as sentries of a different sort in front of me.

Perhaps we are all creatures longing for the hope of resurrection. The concept is in many of our epic tales, from Achilles to Jesus to Harry Potter.

I think my greatest hope in penning this story, is in gaining the understanding of why everything had to happen the way it did. Maybe even finding some justification for the decisions I felt forced to make.

Maybe my greatest fear is in finding no justification at all.

I don't know.

I guess I might as well get started though. To do that, I must start from the beginning. That is, why I ran away to Alaska in the first place.

Dear God. I don't want to go back there. Not to that dark place under the soil when I never thought I'd see light again.

But, I really do think I must. I always have painted my pain with large brushstrokes.

It's a need, really. Maybe even a selfish one.

There's no fighting who you are though. Not unless you choose to kill the part of you that makes you... you.

So, I guess there is no delaying this next part. Go easy on me, reader.

I was fumbling around in the dark after all.

Ah, there it is. The first light of dawn over the Resurrection peaks.

Part One

Chapter 1

Fire Flurries

Sandi is my name.

And I woke up on the couch to the sound of my nieces and children squealing.

My sister took one of my spare bedrooms, the kids all bunked in one room and the godfather had the master.

It felt fair to give him some space in a house full of children.

So I took the couch. I didn't mind. I could pass out anywhere. Plus, the idea of comfort or privacy had been a foreign concept to me for so long.

I blinked a few times and sat up.

My sister opened her door and walked into the living room in her robe.

"Passed out in your gig clothes last night?"

I looked down at the leather skirt I still wore. "You could say that."

Before dawn, I had awakened in a bed that wasn't mine.

A stranger slept next to me.

I knew he was in the military, a Navy diver. I knew he was a former stripper.

And I knew he liked Hallmark movies. That was the Netflix and "chill" part of the escapades the night before.

Only… we actually finished the movie.

The godfather knew where I was. I shared my location with him when I arrived at the house.

You know. The godfather texted. *If I ever don't hear back from you after you send me your locations, at least I know where to send the police when they search for your body.*

Shut up. I texted back. **Are the kids okay?**

I waited in my car for the response.

Yep. He responded. *They fell asleep pretty much as soon as you left for your gig.*

I performed in my 80s synth pop duo that night. The godfather performed babysitting duties for me in exchange for cheap rent.

Great. I'll be back before they wake up.

I slowly moved to get out of the bed, my feet hitting the cold tile floor.

I looked for my leather skirt and found it in the far corner of the room. My high heels next to the door.

The body in the bed stirred.

"You're up early."

I put on a saccharine smile. "Yeah. I have things to do."

The body moved to get out of the bed. "I'll walk you to the door."

I wanted to say, "Don't bother." But I just finished getting dressed and let him walk me to his front door.

"Well, that was fun." He said, reaching for my hand.

"Yeah." I said. I stared at the hand.

"Let's do it again sometime."

"Sure."

He kissed my hand and I turned to walk toward my car.

I never saw him again.

I felt it best that my sister remain oblivious to my late night escapades after my shows. As long as I got home before anyone woke up, no one was the wiser.

No one could judge.

Except the godfather. But he didn't count. He was the ride-or-die.

I walked to the master bedroom and gave a soft knock.

No response.

I slowly opened the door and quickly stepped inside my old room. I still kept my clothes in the closet and showered in the master bathroom.

The godfather was still sleeping, so I tip-toed to the bathroom and quietly shut the door.

I treated the shower like a baptism, washing away all impurities and sins from the night before.

I wished the hot water could warm the ice inside my soul, but I hadn't figured out how to work that magic yet.

If the ministry could see me now.

I had become everything the church had accused me of. I drank. I smoked weed. I had sex out of marriage.

Actually, I had sex while technically still married.

All the things I spent nearly thirty years denying myself from.

I'd be thirty in a few months. April. I'd be officially divorced in a few months, too.

But it was December. 2021 hadn't arrived yet.

My still-husband was away in France for his studies. I tried not to think about the day when I told him I was divorcing him. I tried to block out the repercussions from my mind.

Instead, I thought about the bonfire I was having with my friends that night in my backyard.

It was all part of my plan to reintroduce myself to the outside world. I had worked as a freelance writer for years, and the need for social interaction while caregiving for my husband had long abated.

But I was gonna do it, damn it. I was going to be a creature with friends.

It was for the benefit of the godfather, too. He needed friends as much as I did. I had recently convinced him to quit his job, selling pallets from home, and start gigging with me. He'd start in January.

The man could play multiple instruments. He was a member of the church I got kicked out of (he left eventually, too) and his talents were wasted working for a pallet distributor.

We'd try out our first open mic in January. He'd start off as my guitarist, but his real passion was for the drums.

And he was damn good.

We'd start a four piece band by the end of 2021. That was the plan.

I turned off the shower and stepped out, grabbing a towel. I looked at myself in the mirror.

Dark circles sketched the outline of my dark brown eyes. My wet dark hair hanging limply past my shoulders.

Shit. I forgot to grab my clothes.

The steam from the shower felt like a sauna as I slowly turned the doorknob and stepped into the bedroom.

The godfather was sitting at the desk, two cups of coffee in front of him.

"I see you're not dead." He said, by way of greeting.

"I forgot my clothes." I walked quickly to the closet and shut the door, turning on the light.

"I made coffee." The godfather's voice echoed through the door.

"That's why you're the godfather."

I put on leggings and a loose t-shirt before opening the door again.

"So how was it?"

I paused. "Fine."

"Wow."

"It's a step above mediocre, which is how nights like that usually go."

I remembered back to the first time I ripped the bandaid off and got on with my life.

He was a friend. We randomly came across each other on Tinder.

"Hey."

"Hey."

"Thought you were married?"

"Clearly things have changed."

"Did you swipe right just to see if I swiped right on you?"

"Does it matter?"

We set up a time to meet.

In the hours before the scheduled time, he tried texting me things to make it not so awkward.

It made it more awkward.

Finally, he just said, "Listen. When you get here, climb up the stairs. My room is right in front of the stairway. Open the door, don't say anything. Just climb on top of me and start kissing me."

How romantic.

But that's what I did.

I blasted metal music on the way to his house on the beach to hype myself up. Then I turned on one of my favorite bands from high school. A Plot to Bomb the Panhandle by A Day to Remember blared through the speakers.

When I arrived back home late that night, the godfather was outside beneath my carport smoking a joint with the hood of his jacket over his eyes.

He didn't look at me as I sat down on the concrete next to him.

"How'd it go?"

I didn't speak for a long time. "He wants to see me again."

He blew out a long stream of smoke. "Do you want to see him again?"

I shrugged.

We sat in silence for a long while. Eventually, I stood up and made my way to the side door of the house.

"You know. You didn't do anything wrong. You're doing the best you can with a shitty situation."

He always knew what to say.

I didn't respond. Just walked into the house and headed straight towards the shower.

I grabbed the coffee from the desk in front of the godfather and took a sip.

"I'm making pancakes, eggs and bacon for everyone. You want me to bring your plate to your room?"

"That'd be great." The godfather turned to his computer and picked up his gaming controller.

"Don't forget the bonfire tonight."

He sighed. "Can't I sit this out?"

"And stay a depressed hermit forever?" I rolled my eyes. "How's the dating profile coming along?"

He got out his phone, pulled up the app and handed it to me.

I scrolled through. "Oh my god. This is pathetic."

"Well, thanks."

"We're working on this later." I turned to enter the squealing frenzy of the four children I loved most in the world. Only my godson was missing.

"Can't wait." I heard the godfather say before I shut the door.

I spent the day cooking. First, breakfast for the hungry kid army. And then, dinner for the hungry adult army coming later on.

I gave out my invites selectively, all friends from high school who knew each other. Sierra, my incredible friend who was a local legend tattoo artist building her own shop. Her girlfriend and partner in crime, Lauren. Greg and his girlfriend Michelle. My friend Michael. And then, of course, the godfather.

The festivities would start when the kids were in bed at 8pm.

I made a lot of food, vegetarian options included, keeping it warmed in crockpots.

I took the kids to the park, tiring them out, fed them chicken tenders and mac and cheese for dinner, read them books and put them to bed.

My sister had a date that night.

"You sure you got this?"

"Yep. They'll all be in bed."

"Well. Don't let the party get too crazy."

"Not with the kids here. Of course not."

She left and my friends started arriving. The godfather nowhere to be seen, probably smoking some weed to calm his nerves.

Greg and Michelle arrived first.

"Where's Michael?"

"Ummmm."

I escorted them to the backyard where the godfather had made a fire and put out chairs around the grate.

He finally made an appearance, his hood over his eyes.

"Greg. Michelle. This is the godfather."

We sat for a while before I heard a knock at the door. It was Sierra and Lauren.

Everyone grabbed food and we spent the time laughing, talking about old times, sharing where we were in life now.

I watched the godfather come out of his shell a little bit as he drank more beer. There were plans to help Sierra up at the shop.

Good. Get his ass out of this house.

"Michael's here." Greg said.

"Oh!" I stood up to let him in the front door.

"No." He smiled. "I'll go get him. He's… in his car."

"Oh… everything alright?"

Greg made a movement with his hands and acted like he was blowing out smoke.

I laughed. I remembered Michael had social anxiety, like most of my friends did.

"He'll be alright. I'm just gonna step outside and talk to him."

Michael eventually came out, his hands in his pockets. He loomed over everyone, well over six feet tall.

I got up and gave him a hug. "Hey!"

"Thanks for inviting me." He said, returning my hug.

"Of course!"

At that moment, I saw two little faces that looked like me, peeking from the sliding glass door.

I let my breath out in a loud whoosh. "Aren't you supposed to be in bed?"

"We want to see the fire!" My son said.

I softly rolled my eyes. "You have twenty minutes. And then your butts are going straight back to bed!"

My friends took quickly to my children, laughing with them. My son especially liked talking to Greg. My daughter staying close to me most of the time, staring into the fire.

The godfather added a log and sparks flew out.

"Fire flurries!" My daughter pointed.

"Those are embers, Lorelai." My son said.

"I like fire flurries better." Lorelai stuck her tongue out at her brother, Judah.

I chuckled. "So do I."

And I thought about the book I wanted to write. "Fire Flurries" would make a damn good title.

"So do I." I said again.

Change. Change. Change.

My fear likes to settle in my chest. I like to hold my breath in when fear is near.

So I learned to take deep breaths, riding the fear like an ocean wave, a wave that would pull back in soon, a wave that I could float atop.

My fear also likes to sit in my neck, on my shoulders like a devil.

I roll my shoulders to shake it off. Rolling like the waves.

I breathe. In and out. In and out.

I hold my breath and dive down deep into my fear, getting lost in its vastness.

Just like the ocean.

But I know oceans, too.

My grandparents used to visit us one month a year in Florida and we always went to the beach.

My grandpa is a character. He'd take our hands and lead us into the water.

I was small and the waves would toss me to and fro, to and fro.

But he'd grip my hand, his potbelly spilling over his swim trunks. He'd say, "Plant your feet. One foot forward and one back for balance. Let out a yell!"

And I'd do as he said. Planting my feet and setting my face in determination.

That wave wouldn't knock me down. No current could take me.

And I yelled into the salty air. I yelled with the seagulls and the wind roaring through my ears.

"That's it." He'd say seriously. "Let the Gulf know who's boss!"

Me. I'm the boss.

I make my way to the surface of the ocean of my fear. I take a breath and flip myself over.

Because sometimes, it's best to float, to ride fear like a wave.

At least until you can plant your feet and let out a mighty roar.

Yes. I know fear. I know its mighty grip. I know its choking hand. I know its weight on my shoulders.

I know the very color of its eyes.

It comes in waves. Waves that thunder. Waves that break. Waves that calm.

Waves that change with the tide, ebbing and flowing in response to the moon and the wind.

But change is coming.

Natural Disasters
"So, how are you?" My therapist asked.

"I'm alright. I can't help but see the parallels. I'm getting some tension headaches."

She nodded.

"The whole country is, on a level, going through what I went through in 2018. And I'm watching it happen like a movie."

"That has to be bringing up some memories."

"It does. It really does."

"You've gone through a lot in these past few years. It has to be difficult seeing something like it, on that big scale, happening again."

"I feel well acquainted with grief at this point. You can see it on everyone's face, you can read it in their Facebook posts, you can watch it all happen on the faces of our government officials. Denial. Anger. Bargaining. Depression. Acceptance. I keep watching everyone move through the various stages. So fast. People are hurting like I was hurting."

"But what about you? How are YOU handling it?"

"The only way I can. I acknowledge that I'm probably going through this process of grief again."

"And at this point you've grieved your town. You've grieved your husband."

"Yes."

"So what are you doing now? What's going through your mind?"

I paused. "I think for me, the implications of this virus may feel different."

"How so?"

"Because once you grieve a few times, so much at once, you get quicker at it or at least more aware of it. You sort of say 'hello' to it again and invite it to pull up a chair beside you."

She smiled. "Sort of like a "hello darkness my old friend" kind of scenario."

"Exactly. To love, to embrace this world, is to ultimately lose it."

"So what does that mean for you?"

"I guess it means I'm trying not to fall into cynicism. You know? The past few years have been a pattern of loss. It's easy to just get used to it and stay in grief because, eventually, I'm definitely going to lose something or someone I love again."

"Mmmmm."

"So for me, I'm watching my whole country grieve and I wish I could give them all instructions to feel it. To embrace it. To let it in like a wave so it will eventually pass through. That better times really are ahead. And, yes, there will be bad times again. Everything, everything ends. To love is to lose."

"You're still talking about other people."

"I can't help it. I better understand myself when I understand others."

I took a breath.

"I just keep feeling this weight on my shoulders. Like I have to do something to alleviate the suffering. But that's the trouble with grief. There's nothing anyone can really do besides sit with you in your pain. Just sit without trying to fix. That's sort of what we're all doing across the country. We're choosing to suffer with one another. Most people, anyway. But I fear for some."

"Why is that?"

"This whole idea of positivity. Being positive constantly. It's unsustainable. So many won't let themselves grieve. But grief has a way of showing up in your body anyway."

"You said you were getting tension headaches?"

"Yes. Like I did when I was a teenager. All through my shoulders and neck. I have to remind myself several times a day to breathe. Like I'm holding my breath waiting for better days. Like I don't want to breathe this air."

I took a deep breath, letting it fill me up.

"But this.... this is reality. I don't want to waste my life waiting for better times. I'm going to live it right now. Could you imagine if I waited these whole past 18 months after the hurricane, holding my breath for better days?"

I leaned back in my chair.

"I never would have breathed. I would have wasted 18 months of my life. But you have to wake up every day and choose to live. You have to choose life. Or it will pass you by."

I turned to look out the window, to the summer scene just outside. "You know, I'm grateful. I really am. I'm thankful to be alive. I'm truly, truly grateful."

"But?"

"But... I really wish I didn't have to try so hard to be grateful every day. Every single day I choose it." I shake my head. "I just wish it could be easy. Something I could lean into, not something I fight for and hold on tightly to. Like a lifeline. I make lists in my head. Roof over my head. Food in my children's bellies. Paper for me to write on."

I shook my head. "But that's not always true. I just can't remember a day right now where I didn't have to try so hard to hold on to my sense of self. It's been a long journey these past few years. I keep telling myself if I hang on long enough, there's a light that's coming." I sighed. "But I feel for everyone. I feel for everyone in pain. I truly do."

Tears threatened to spill down my cheeks.

"But I do wonder."

"What do you wonder?"

I swallowed the lump in my throat. "If life is really always like this. Moving from one bad time to the next."

She smiled. "Not always."

I nodded. "Not always."

Sing like you think no one's listening

I glide through the snow, staring down at my feet. My skis gingerly finding the notches someone before me had put there.

A born and raised Florida girl cross country skiing, what madness is this?

My dad told me what he had planned for me in the morning as we were talking to my baby brother. He just turned 25.

I had flashbacks to when he was a kid. I used to make milkshakes for the friends he brought home. He used to climb into the bed with me when he was little.

Now he's in the army, stationed in Germany. I saw a picture of him wearing my dad's old brown bomber jacket. Dad always said one day it would be my brother's.

"So how are you?" My brother asked me meaningfully.

"I know you've been trying to get ahold of me for a couple weeks," I replied. "I've appreciated your texts. I just don't feel like talking about anything just now. I love you though." I smiled, looking at his face that looks just like my dad's. "Happy birthday baby bro."

My family gets frustrated with me and my lack of communication about my personal life sometimes. I've realized it's because if I talk too much about what I want to do, I talk myself right out of it.

Better to act. Better for it all to be done. I'd explain later.

I slipped and had to catch myself. Though, I was surprised at how easily my body worked through this new challenge. I had been working out consistently, and due to this I hadn't really needed to stop and catch my breath. So I just kept watching my feet, finding a rhythm.

Up ahead there was a fellow skier coming my way. Oh Lord.

I slowed down and made to move to the side, easier said than done with meter long sticks stuck to the bottom of your feet.

"Hey, thanks." They said. "Have a good ski."

I thought about how I always make the first move for getting out of the way. How I always step aside and let others around or through or past. How I always hold open the door.

How I don't know how to be any other way.

I moved to get back on the path, but caught one of my skis beneath me. I tumbled into a three foot snowbank, with my skis sticking out.

"Ow." How the hell was I going to get up?

I moved like a baby fawn. First step, straighten out the skis. Second step, try to get up from the side.

I finally stood up, but realized my head felt cold. I looked behind me and there was my hat, covered in powder.

"Ugh," I exclaimed. I hadn't mastered moving backwards in skis.

I ended up doing some sort of weird kinda backbend and using a ski pole to lure the black hat to me.

Brushing off the cap, I looked around.

The landscape stretched before me, the snow looked like frosting on trees, like a down comforter on the ground ready to swallow me up and rock me to sleep.

The mountains in Alaska don't look real. They sit in the background like Mount Olympus. Hermés could be in that wispy cloud atop Mt. Denali, carrying messages to and from the other gods. Zeus could choose his throne in any of these peaks.

I stared in silence at the peaks and blanket white landscape. All I could hear was the soft wind channeling through the mountains.

My mind transports me to the quiet I feel when I'm out on the bay with my kayak. No one's around. You can scream and no one will hear you, or judge you, or ask you what's wrong.

Nothing, I just needed to scream.

But the illusion is broken as another skier comes down the path. I step to move to the side again, only to laugh as I look up. She had moved to the side, too.

"Please, come on." She said with a smile.

I glide past her. "Have a good ski."

It's nice and awkward to find people like me.

I move in silence for a while, thinking of the conversation with my brother earlier.

"I'm really happy you're doing music again." My brother had said. "How's that going?"

"Fantastic actually." And I catch my dad smiling at me. "We had a really big gig on Halloween. We're gaining momentum."

At one of my recent gigs a few of my friends, including Sierra and Lauren, surprised me. It was a Halloween 80s bash, so I was dressed as

Freddie Mercury at Live Aid, complete with mustache. A friend from high school, Tyler, whom I hadn't seen in a decade ended up coming to see me, too. I saw him enter as I was singing and my heart filled with happiness. During my first break I walked purposefully to their table.

"Oh. My. God."

"Sing to me, Sandi!" He said by way of greeting.

I touched his face and just looked at him fondly for a few seconds, letting the moment sit.

"And just like that it's like no time has passed." Tyler said, grabbing my hand.

"I know."

Our friends at the table smiled at us.

"Now, I want you to guess my most prevalent memory of you."

I thought for a moment. "It has to be the bomb ass lake party."

"Yes! But what happened?"

"You gave me my first 30 Seconds to Mars CD."

He burst out laughing. "Oh my God I did! But that's not it."

"What is it then?" I couldn't come up with the answer.

"You sang for me, a cappella, the song you would do for the talent show."

I closed my eyes, "Oh my God. Straylight Run. Yes. Sing Like You Think No One's Listening…. no… that's not what it was called. It's called Existentialism on Prom Night!"

"Yes!!!"

Lauren asked, "Wait, you sang at the talent show?"

We then reminisced over our high school days. I looked at my friends, all queer, wonderful people.

I had a memory of when President Obama was elected in 2008 and so many of my friends came out of the closet. They felt safe, they felt like the world might accept them, that it was changing.

I thought about how happy I was to be surrounded by people who wanted to see me do what I love.

"I have to go," I finally said. "Duty calls."

I touched Tyler's face again.

He just said, "Sing to me, love."

"I'll get you some wine." Lauren said.

My heart swelled like a symphony as I, again, took the stage and sang like I thought no one's listening.

Or like everyone was listening.

Like everyone should hear.

I noticed the sun setting behind the mountains, the pastel colors filling the sky.

I texted my dad, asking him if I should turn back. Then I looked down at my skis again.

I realized I had been looking down at my feet for a long time in my life. I had been so busy trying to watch my step and keep moving forward that I had forgotten to look up as often as I should have.

I look up, and I have amazing friends.

I look up, and I have an amazing career.

I look up, and I have a family who loves me.

I look up, and I love the view.

I look up, and there is beauty everywhere.

It's when I look down to concentrate that sometimes I forget where I am.

Who I am.

I smile as I turn back, seeing all the views I've already seen, but with a new perspective.

Because this time, I know I've already done the hard stuff. I've proven what I'm capable of.

Now? Now it's just doing it all again.

With style. With finesse.

"Sing to me, Sandi."

And I glide back the way I came.

Chapter 2

Toast

I take one last look out to the Resurrection Bay and mountains beyond in Seward, Alaska. The clouds are heavy with impending snow, the bay slowly getting angrier by the minute. An otter plays in the water, flipping in circles one after the other.

I set Toast on a rock in front of the water. Toast is a small stuffed rhinoceros my children gave me to take care of before I left home.

I snap a photo and message the picture to my children with the caption, "Toast in Seward, Alaska."

I pick up the stuffed animal and look towards the beaten up grey Ford truck my father left me in order to get back to Anchorage. I thought I broke it the first day. The windshield wipers don't work when the brakes are applied. The passenger side window wouldn't roll up until I called my dad for instructions. The parking brake light is always on, and I'm pretty sure no one knows exactly how much gas is in the truck at any given moment.

But it has four wheel drive—and I'll need it.

I begin the trek home and note the roads are slick with ice. Large snow covered Christmas trees line the roads, ice fog covers the mountains in the distance.

My boyfriend calls.

"Hey sweetie!"

"Hey hey. Whatcha up to?"

"Just leaving Seward."

"Get a lot of inspiration for your book?"

"I think so." I pause. "I miss you."

"I miss you, too. I just got you and then you have to go off to Alaska for a month."

I smile.

"That's alright though." He continued. "I can't believe my girlfriend is writing a book in Alaska! I got a pretty damn cool girlfriend."

"Let's hope she stays in one piece on the way back to Anchorage."

"Uh oh. Is the weather bad?"

"It's pretty icy. Dad says to watch out for fishtailing."

"How's that truck?"

I pat the steering wheel. "Exactly the kind of truck my father would own." I explained the quirks.

"And he's taking you to an isolated cabin after this?" He laughed. "Do you understand why I'm a bit concerned?"

"You're referring to the man who dropped me off on an island when I was fourteen."

I hear him sigh through the phone. "I just really like having a girlfriend. I'd like her to come back to me alive."

"I'm going to do my best. Hey, guess what?"

Silence.

"Hello?"

I look down at my phone and see the call dropped. I have no cell service.

"Welp." I say to myself. I look at Toast in the passenger seat. "I guess it's just you and me."

I think of my daughter handing Toast to me. "He'll protect you in Alaska."

"Yeah." My son said. "Write the book and make me rich."

My kids were a bit peeved with me for not bringing them with me this time. They had so much fun on my last trip. We went to a reindeer farm and the North Pole, sledded, made snow cream and even climbed to an ice cave.

But this time, I knew I couldn't take them.

"Come with me." I said to my boyfriend.

He shook his head. "I can't."

"Yes you can!"

"No Sandi." He smiled and pulled me close. "If I go, you won't write your book."

"Ugh. But we'd have so much fun."

"I'll go in the summer sometime." He kissed me. "But when you come back." He ran his hands down to my waist. "You're all mine."

A green sign appears to my right.

"Avalanche Area. 5 miles. Don't stop."

"Well that's comforting." I say under my breath, gripping the steering wheel a bit tighter.

I ride in silence for a while, taking in the views around me. Everything is so different here. Instead of ocean waves, there are mountain peaks. In place of palm trees, black spruces. No alligators in Alaska but there are…

"Moose!"

I catch a glimpse of one off to the side of the road. I don't dare stop to get a closer look.

Everywhere I turn, there's something new. Something I haven't seen before.

I grab my phone and swipe through to my music. I put on Badfish by Sublime, my boyfriend's favorite band.

I listen to the Reggae band for a while, allowing the funny dichotomy of the music versus the winter scene racing past my windows to set in.

Then I decide it's time to switch it up. My bandmate and I wrote an album and it's set to drop in two months.

I click on the first song in the album and begin listening. My voice booms through the speakers, the sound crackling a bit out of the old stereo.

"Hey, Toast." I say, glancing towards the passenger seat. "My music's being played in Alaska."

Toast doesn't respond.

But I think he likes it.

I'm an artist

"Sounds to me like you're an artist." My therapist said.

I cringed.

"Why did you just do that?"

"Do what?"

She laughed. "You made a face."

"Oh," I smiled softly. "I hate that word."

"Why is that?"

"I guess I just always thought it sounded so flaky."

"You *always* thought that?"

There was a long pause.

"Hm." She said. "Let's explore that a bit."

"Okay."

"It's just that you're a singer, songwriter, pianist, writer, marketer..." She ticked off the list with her fingers.

I said nothing.

"Sure sounds like an artist to me."

The truth was, there was a lot of baggage that came with that word.

Public school for me was a nightmare. It's nobody's fault and I'm thankful to live in a country that provides free public education.

I have a new piano student who is about 10 years old. As we were working on her first lesson, I asked her what her favorite subject in school was.

"I really like science."

"Oh yeah? You'd probably get along with my husband then. He has a Physics degree. What's your second favorite subject?"

She had to really think about this. "I would say reading class, but they don't let you read in there. They just give you a bunch of worksheets."

It was like I was staring into the face of my younger self.

"Once," I began. "I was reading a book in reading class and my teacher had to take it away because I was off task."

My student looked at me in the eyes for the first time in our 30-minute lesson. "But you were reading! Isn't that on task?"

I remember crying after my first week of 8th grade because there was so much homework.

"If this is affecting you like this now," my mom said. "High school is going to be tough."

I didn't cry because I was lazy.

I cried because I had just spent eight hours in a place that told me what to do all the time. Where doodling in the margins was frowned upon, where writing poetry instead of doing the science lesson was considered rebellion, where singing was confined to Mondays, Wednesdays and Fridays when I had choir.

I begged my parents not to make me take advanced classes in high school. Not because I wasn't ambitious, but because if I took advanced classes I was allowed fewer electives in my schedule.

Electives like theater, art, band and choir.

If I had things my way, I would have taken all of them.

I wanted to be all of them.

But then I was sat down in front of the guidance counselor.

She took one look at my grades and standardized test scores and asked my father, "Why isn't she signed up for the MAPPS advanced program?"

And that was the end of my dream of coasting through high school. I was allowed one elective.

I chose choir.

I studied my choral music like some study math or science. I was placed in the Advanced Ensemble, Show Choir and recommended for a solo at state.

As a Freshman, this meant I was above par.

Exceptional.

I also joined an after-school theater program called ITS, the International Thespian Society. I became part of a band that practiced out of my garage. I wrote songs and mixed them myself, uploading them to Myspace music. I became the music leader for a club called FCS, the Fellowship of Christian Students.

I wrote poetry and essays and stories in my school notebooks.

The problem was, I ignored my regular core classes. I refused to do homework, as I believed that school already took up so much of my day. Why should I give it more of my time?

Time that could be used for creativity.

Eventually, it came back around to bite me in the butt. I was grounded for a whole summer because I failed College Algebra.

Twice.

With a score of a 36 F to show for my effort, which translated to none at all.

This led to a roundtable meeting with both my parents and all of my teachers. All of them trying to figure out what was going on in my head. Why someone with so much potential refused to try in school.

My Geometry teacher, Mrs. M, felt bad for me.

"Well, I don't know what my opinion is worth, but Sandi is very kind to me. I think she's great. Very polite."

I had a C in her class.

I started dating my husband my Junior year and the stakes were high. I was on my third round of trying to pass College Algebra. If I didn't, I would be grounded for the entire summer.

Again.

But I had a new teacher this time, his name was Mr. W. and I liked him. He was a straight-forward, no-nonsense kind of teacher who left me the hell alone.

Which is why it surprised me when he called me up to the front of his classroom one day.

"You're showing exceptional results in my class, Miss Klüg."

"Thank you, sir."

"You've gotten high As on the first three tests. Two of those were a 100%."

"Yes sir."

Then he looked at me suspiciously. "But you only have an 80% in my class."

"Yes sir."

"Why is that Miss Klüg?"

I sighed, gearing myself up for a lecture. "Because I don't do the homework, sir."

He stared at me. "You've taken this class once before, haven't you?"

"Twice before," I corrected him. "Sir."

He squinted and looked at me with an evaluating look. "Why have you failed twice?"

It took years and perspective to realize he wasn't judging me, but genuinely curious.

I loosed a deep breath. "I refuse to do homework, sir. I think it's a waste of my time."

Hey. No one can accuse me of not being honest.

And stubborn. I'm that, too.

He rolled his eyes. "You can sit down now."

Later on that year came the defining moment. If I didn't manage exactly a 78% on my final exam in College Algebra, I was going to be grounded for another whole summer.

After the bell rang on the last day of school, my husband and I ran to Mr. W's class. My husband stood outside the door, waiting on the results.

"Miss Klüg, what can I do for you?"

"I was wondering if you had the exams graded yet, sir."

A questioning look marked his face. "This is the first time you've ever cared to ask me for your grade. Why?"

"Because if I don't get exactly a 78% on my final, sir, I will get a D and be grounded for the whole summer... again."

He laughed. "Exactly a 78%, huh? You did the math?"

"Yes sir."

Still laughing, he flipped through his pile of scantrons until he found my name.

"Miss Klüg."

My whole body tensed. I could feel my future husband's anxiety through the door.

"What was the grade you said you needed again?"

"A 78%."

"78%." He repeated, shaking his head. He looked at me, back at the scantron, then at me again. "You got a 78%."

I whooped with glee, thanked Mr. W and ran out of the classroom to give my then-boyfriend the amazing news.

It wasn't until I was in my mid-twenties that I looked back on this moment in my life with dawning understanding.

I'm 95% sure Mr. W helped me finally break free of College Algebra.

God bless that man.

Today, I do math all the time.

I do math to calculate the ROI on Facebook ads. I do math to calculate my client's invoices. I do math to draw up my taxes.

And I'm good at it.

It took years after high school, and dropping out of community college, to figure myself out. I had been conditioned to believe that my brand of genius was lazy, unmarketable, unworthy...

... that if I went down the creative path my soul longed for, I'd be a starving artist.

So instead of just hating the phrase "starving artist" I hated the word "artist."

But sitting there with my therapist, looking back on my life, I finally started to embrace it.

I have a total of six streams of income coming into my household right now, because of my art.

A few years ago, I hit an income goal of 30k made in one year through my business. It wasn't a million dollars...

But I got to wake up every day...

...and PLAY. Just... play.

And make a living doing it.

It's only gone up from there.

"I guess, yeah, I am an artist." I finally replied to my therapist. "It's just that the word feels icky to me. That word carries baggage to me. It's synonymous with lazy, incompetent, childish, impractical, unorganized and so many other awful words. Words I used to describe myself with."

"What would it feel like to embrace that word again?" She asked.

I thought for a while before replying with a small smile. "I don't know."

There's no outrunning who you are, because there is no other way to be.

They asked me in school, "What color will you choose?"

"What job do you want?"

"Who do you want to be?"

"What are your goals and your dreams?"

"But, no. Not those."

Yet, I had no choice. It's in my makeup, it's how I live, move and breathe in the world.

My heart and soul whispered, "All of them. I want to be everything."

Asking me to choose one thing to do with the rest of my life is like asking a painter to choose one color.

I just can't do it.

There is so much to DO in the world. So much to BE.

There is just SO MUCH COLOR!

So I paint with my life a wondrous masterpiece, pushing the boundaries of what it means to be successful, what it means to make an income.

There are a million ways not to starve.

I get to wake up every single day of my life and PLAY.

It's work, yes. So much work.

I've never had to be more organized than I am right now.

But freedom. The freedom. To paint the life I always wanted. To move through this life gloriously untamed.

An artist.

I'm an ARTIST.

Damn it.

And not the starving kind.

Chapter 3

Paradise Haven

Smooshed cranberries look like blood on the snow beneath birch and white spruce trees.

All is quiet on the Albert's loop in the Chugach mountains of Eagle River, Alaska.

Besides the sprinkle of dropped cranberries lining the trail, the world around me is in greyscale. Moose tracks are left embedded in the snow, the only sign of any life out here.

"No need to worry about bears." My father said before leaving me in a cabin called *Paradise Haven*. "They're hibernating."

It's a fact about the animal kingdom I knew, but it was still a comfort to hear it after the story I heard that morning. A bear earlier in the year had destroyed the siding on all the Yurts, looking for food. The poor animal had to be tracked down and euthanized.

"Right." I said.

My father, bonus mom and their labradoodle ("Boo Bear") had spent a night with me in the rustic cabin. We cross country skied a mile or so before arriving to the wooden house in the forest, my father towing a sled full of supplies behind him.

"I think you'll find some inspiration here."

Truthfully, it would have been impossible not to.

Plush pillows of snow covered every inch of the ground, the only flat terrain being the trails winding through the expansive forest that seemed to go on forever.

The white witch of Narnia peeks through the trees, silently beckoning me deeper into her kingdom.

Back home in Florida, the wildlife is always chattering. And if the birds aren't singing some song, the wind is shifting through the trees, clinking the leaves together like wind chimes.

But all is quiet in this forest. Even the snow falls softly, as if some force understands the need to tiptoe as not to wake what slumbers in the winter.

I finish my hike down Albert's loop and make my way back to my cabin, beating the snow off my boots before entering.

It's still warm inside, the small stove in the corner alighted with an orange glow.

I walk to the wood pile and feed the flames a couple logs before looking around to my new home for a couple days.

There are wooden bunks set into the far side of the wall, a table, two fold up chairs and a bench. Supplies and food litters the table, an Italian coffee pot still sits upon the small propane stove.

I take a deep breath. The smell of burning wood fills my nose.

No cell service out here, of course. I heard my boyfriend pause slightly over the phone when I let him know I'd be unreachable for a few days.

"Your dad is taking you to an isolated cabin in the middle of the woods… in Alaska… in winter… alone."

"You did say you wanted a girlfriend who was strong and independent, right?"

He groaned.

"It's just for a few days."

"Again. I just really want my girlfriend to come back to me in one piece."

"At least I'm not boring?" I teased.

"No one would ever say that about you, Sandi MarLisa."

Tingles ran up my spine. I really, really liked the way he said my name.

I think of his voice now, as I put the kettle on the stove to heat water for my dinner. Noodles in a cup.

I open a pack of beef jerky as the water heats, the sound of the ripping package echoed by a crack from a log in the fire.

Toast sits on the table next to the small Tupperware container of coffee grounds. Firelight dances in his glassy eyes.

"I guess it's just you and me." I say.

Silence answers me.

Sandi MarLisa

"I'm changing my fucking name."

"Okay." The godfather said warily.

I opened up my laptop and pulled up Facebook and Instagram, going straight for the user names.

"From now on." I said, hot tears threatening to spill over. "From now on, my name is Sandi MarLisa. No man's name will ever be on my shit ever, ever again."

MarLisa was the middle name my mother gave me. Now, it felt more like a middle finger.

It's a combination of her name, Lisa, and my Mema's name, Margaret.

To say my name is to utter the name of three generations of women.

I made a post for social media. "I decided to use a stage name and pen name. From now on, I am Sandi MarLisa."

I submitted the post and closed my laptop.

"How's the set list coming along?" I directed the question to the godfather.

"It's going." He answered, his tone still bracing.

"I'm so angry."

"I know."

I wanted to be alone, but there was nowhere to go in my house.

"I'm going kayaking." I said, making my way towards the master bedroom to don my swimsuit.

"It's too cold for that, isn't it?"

"Yes."

The godfather said nothing else as I closed the bathroom door and got dressed. I put on a water resistant jacket and pants atop my swimsuit, exiting the bathroom and aiming towards the front door without a word.

My blue kayak was under the carport, my paddle right beside it.

I clipped the key to my truck onto the zipper of my jacket and tugged the string attached to the end of the kayak, pulling it towards the car. I threw the kayak into the back with a shove, tossing the paddle next to it.

The park I liked to kayak at was only a few blocks away. Once I arrived, it took a total of three minutes to be in the bay.

It was a bit of a strong current, but I didn't care. All the better.

I paddled my way to the middle of the inlet, until the Hathaway bridge was visible.

The Hathaway was the bridge that connected the town side of Panama City with the beach side. I liked to look at it, reminding me that the sea connected everything. The sea was often the only thing that made sense to me.

I could be myself out on the water. The first song I ever wrote was when I was paddling alone in a boat on a lake at ten years old.

I remember thinking, "I'm alone. No one can hear me out here."

I tested it. Singing and looking towards the shore to see if my family turned their heads.

They didn't.

So I sang louder. I sang and sang and sang until a song that didn't exist before came barreling out of me.

I had no song that day looking at the Hathaway.

Only rage. Only pure, unadulterated, seething loathing.

But I let it out, screaming into the wind that made the waves buck against my kayak.

I didn't care that I had a show that night. I didn't care that the sound coming out of me ripped through my vocal cords.

Then I offered up a prayer of white hot anger. Yelling into the wind as if it would carry my words up to God.

Maybe he would listen to me if I screamed loud enough.

"I feel like I am a good person." I said hoarsely. "I'm not a saint. I'm not perfect. But I'm a good fucking person who loves her people pretty damn well." I bared my teeth, my blood and the wind roaring through my ears. "I loved that man."

And I broke then. I cried and cried, wept until I couldn't breathe. Until I was hyperventilating with the grief, until my nose ran and my neck was drenched in saltwater; from the frigid bay spraying me in the face or my tears, I didn't know.

Didn't care.

"I. can't. do. this. alone." Every sob echoing a word.

I thought I had one person. One fucking person in the world that had my back and I had theirs, no matter what.

But that person was gone, taken by his own mind. How the hell, how the *fuck*, was I supposed to fight for someone who was at war within themselves?

I had to let him go. I had to release him.

If I was honest with myself, he was gone anyway. He'd been gone a long time.

"I just want one person." I whispered. "I just want one person."

And it became a chant. Over and over again I repeated my heart's greatest desire.

I reached over the side of the boat and scooped some water into my hands, splashing my face. I tasted salt on my lips.

I was reminded of the salt covenant I had taken with my husband at our wedding. It was a Hebrew tradition. The husband and wife each took a vial of salt and poured their share into one container. If one of them wanted to break the covenant of marriage, they had to separate their salt from the other.

An utter impossibility.

Just like this grief. Just like this pain.

I never pictured a life without my husband. Never. Never ever.

It was always us against the world. Us against everyone and everything.

One fucking person.

The sun began to set on the horizon and I knew I had to go. It was time to get ready for Papa Joe's, an outdoor music venue with food trucks, overlooking the same bay I was now floating in.

Tonight, I would announce myself as Sandi MarLisa for the first time.

I splashed more water on my face before lifting up a final prayer to a God who had long stopped answering me.

"I want him to be okay. I know I can't go with him any further. But I want him to be okay. Give him back his mind. His beautiful, beautiful mind." I heaved a sob, but no more tears would come. They were spent. "But is it too much to ask for me to be okay, too? I want to be loved as fiercely as I love. Please. Just one fucking person."

I put my paddle back in the water and made to return to shore. It would be more difficult coming in than it was going out, the current pulling me to the left and back out to sea.

I embraced the challenge. I wanted—needed—to get every last drop of poison out of me. I leeched it from my muscles. Setting my eyes in determination.

I had two children to love and raise. I had gigs to perform. I had new projects to complete.

I would stay busy. I would work myself into the ground before I gave up.

With each pull of the paddle, I settled myself into my new journey.

There was no map. No guidebook.

I never wanted this. Any of it.

And I certainly didn't want to do it alone.

But I was here. This was my lot in life.

I knew I would do it. I knew I'd keep getting up.

I always did.

I pulled and pulled, the shoreline inching closer.

"Sandi MarLisa." I whispered to myself.

No man's name finished it. No man's name was a bookend to my own.

Not my father's. Not my husband's.

"Sandi MarLisa."

A prayer. A promise.

A war cry.

A declaration to make my life my own.

Sandi MarLisa was an artist. A musician. A writer. A mother. A fierce lover and friend.

Sandi MarLisa didn't take shit from anybody.

The sun set behind me, the color of the bay turned pink, purple and orange in response to the end of the day.

Sandi MarLisa. She had the power of three women behind her.

She was an echo of every tear shed by the women who came before her.

My mother had a stillborn before me. She was in a horrible car wreck while pregnant with me.

She called me her rainbow baby.

I am the embodiment of prayers and wishes, hopes and dreams.

Dressing for my gig in silence, I briefly took a look at my phone and saw I had matched with someone on a dating app.

He had responded to a prompt I had posted.

My ideal date from home is when you cook for me, then we play Scrabble and I beat you because I'm a writer.

Or be super upset that you got destroyed by a non writer!

The audacity of this guy.

I typed out my response as I brushed my teeth.

I'd be upset by the possibility but we both know there isn't one.

I spit into the sink as the phone dinged with his response.

Hmmm. I feel like comparing me to most of the guys that you would talk to on a dating app, may be an advantage for me. ;)

I smiled a little, running to the closet to grab my high heels.

My phone dinged again. I slipped the shoes onto my feet as I read the message.

I may not be a writer but believe it or not, I do read for fun.

Sold.

I clicked on his name and read his profile. Ex-navy, skateboarder, a year younger than me at 28, tattoos, black hair and tan skin. He had responded to a prompt saying, "At the end of the day, sea turtles are better than most people."

"Okay, Sk8er Boi." I thought to myself before typing out my response.

Not comparing. I'm just really sure of my Scrabble playing abilities. What do you like to read?

His responses came more quickly.

We talked about Neil Gaiman and Kurt Vonnegut. He shared books he read on his last deployment.

This is by far the most intelligent conversation I've had on this dating app… or any other dating app for that matter…

Glad to know I stand out in some way.

I grabbed my car keys and called out a goodbye over my shoulder to the godfather before heading towards the car. My sister had my children for a church event. Once inside the car, I looked down at my phone for Sk8er Boi's response.

It's refreshing. Trust me there isn't anything on your dating profile that doesn't stand out to me.

I smiled.

I'm even better in person. ;)

His response came before I could press the start button on my car.

I hope to be lucky enough to have the opportunity to find out for myself. But I really don't doubt you.

I paused for a moment, mulling over what I wanted to say. I looked at his location, he lived in the next town over. Destin, Florida.

He had plenty of time. I made my decision.

I'm headed out to a gig. You seem like not a serial killer so I'm giving you my number. 850-555-5555.

I'm horrible at notifications. And sometimes I take forever between texts. I'm just busy, nothing personal. If I'm not interested in talking with you anymore I'll tell you, I won't ghost you.

Have a good evening, Sk8er Boi.

My text notifications lit up immediately.

Hey. It's Sk8er Boi.

I laughed.

Hey.

What kinda music do you play?

Tonight it's 80s Synth Pop.

That's so rad.

I really had to go. I threw the car in reverse and quickly backed out of my driveway and drove through the quiet streets of Lynn Haven.

No music blasted through the speakers of my car on my way to the show.

I arrived, throwing open my door to the cold. My high heels hitting the gravel.

I checked my phone as I slammed the door.

I want to come see a show sometime.

And in that moment, I just didn't care. I didn't care about scaring him off. I didn't care about making meeting up his idea. I didn't care about seeming too pushy or desperate. Or about the fact that I had only exchanged a few messages with this stranger.

I didn't care about anything. So I sent my response without thinking twice.

Well, come on then.

I began walking, phone in hand.

People lined the sidewalk as I approached the pavilion where my bandmate waited for me. 80s synth pop blared through the speakers.

I greeted my bandmate who could tell something was off. But I silently grabbed the microphone and looked toward the crowd. My phone vibrated in my leather pants.

What's the address?

I gave it to him.

The playlist music shut off, my bandmate began the opening riff to my first song.

Okay. Yeah. You're way too rad to not come see whether or not it holds up in person.

I grinned and typed…

See you l8er, Sk8er Boi.

I threw my phone down on the speaker beside me, focusing my attention on the crowd.

"Hello everyone." I greeted the crowd with a smile. "We're Denuvo, your favorite 80s duo, and we'll be serenading you until 9pm tonight. That's my bandmate over there on the keys."

I paused to let them clap. A cold wind blew, ruffling my hair.

"And I'm Sandi MarLisa."

Back to basics

My mom says I started reading when I was four years old. I can't remember if the first great love of my life was singing or reading books that took me someplace else.

There's not much difference between the two to me. Because reading has a pace, and in music we call it a tempo. It's this pulse in life you can only really discover through art. The sound of a world unseen.

I loved reading. I read books like Babysitters Club or Nancy Drew, but also Jane Eyre, Moby Dick, Treasure Island and that one time I tried to read Les Miserables.

We had this program in my school called the Accelerated Reading program, or A.R. for short. Every student had to get a certain number of A.R. points yearly by reading an A.R. book and taking a test.

I wasn't very good at these tests. They always asked about dates and names, when those weren't the details I focused on. Especially when I read books like Jane Eyre. The subject matter was way over my head, but I liked to read them anyway.

There was this one girl, I'll call her Mary, who always got more A.R. points than me.

I couldn't understand how she read so fast, or how she managed to scrape all the points out of the tests. You see, if a book was worth 5 points and you got an 80% on the test, you only got 3 points.

So I tried to read like her. I tried to go fast and focus on the details of the story, but I could never resist the pull to get lost. I always missed the trees and chose, instead, the forest.

But one day, I had enough. It was the end of term, and Mary had 50 points more than me.

So I came up with a plan only a 7th grader bent on revenge can concoct.

I decided to read Les Miserables. It was worth 150 A.R. points.

"Even if I only got an 80% on the test," I said. "I'd still beat her."

So I checked out the book from the school library and when I got home I set to work on it.

Little did I know how much of the book is written in French.

I couldn't follow along, and before I reached page 10 I broke down in tears.

I think that's when it all started. That was the moment when I knew there would always be a Mary.

When I auditioned for a play called, "Christmas With the 3 Bears," I decided to go out for the lead role. Little bear.

I didn't get the part and got visibly upset, so the Director pulled me aside.

"Listen. You're really funny. That's why I gave you the part of the Dopey Deer. You're really going to pull that off."

Dopey Deer had a total of maybe three lines. Mary had won again.

In high school, Mary managed to get a score of 6 on her standardized writing test.

I got a 4. An average grade.

When I reviewed the score with my teacher, she said it was because I didn't follow the five-paragraph structure we had spent our entire adolescence learning.

"You don't state what you're going to talk about in the beginning paragraph. And your following paragraphs aren't organized by topic. Plus, your conclusion doesn't restate what you've stated previously. It's a really good paper though. Great imagery. This is just what they score on."

"But why would anyone reveal what they're going to talk about in the beginning paragraph?" I thought. "None of the books I read actually do that. What mystery is there to that? And why would I repeat what I already said? They read it. They know what I said."

I spent my entire high school career in Choir. I was in every ensemble imaginable and competed as a soloist every chance I got. I was also in every talent show and in any band I could possibly manage.

But in my senior year, I didn't get the choral scholarship awarded at the end of the year to one male and female student.

A fellow student whom I barely knew turned around to me during the award ceremony. "I thought it would be you." He said.

I thought it would be me, too.

So I wrote an email to my director complaining and she handed me my butt in return.

"Mary deserved that scholarship, Sandi. It's unfair for you to try and make it about you."

Not my proudest, most mature moment. The shame was written on my face, but I still felt like I deserved that scholarship.

She sighed. "You need to realize, Sandi, that you ARE music. That voice of yours will take you anywhere you want to go with it. You auditioned to sing at your graduation and I heard you got the solo. Is that true?"

"Yes." I answered.

"That's your opportunity to shine. So shine."

And I did shine.

But I was still jealous of Mary.

Mary was everywhere. She was the one who always bested me, always reminding me that I was never enough, never the best.

I went to school for business. I cried to and from the college.

I have a distinct memory of the day I stopped going to classes. I drove right past the college, rode over the bridge that took me straight to the beach. I parked, grabbed a towel from my trunk and walked to a beach access point tourists didn't frequent.

Then I took off my shirt and pants, stood fully in my bra and underwear and waded into the water.

I've never lost my flair for the dramatic. So as I stared into the horizon, hot anger boiled up inside me.

I screamed. I yelled. I pitched a fit. I let the Gulf of Mexico catch my tears and the wind carry my scream.

I hated myself. I hated life. I hated Mary and everybody who thought she was better than me.

Only the best could be artists.

And I was never, ever, ever going to be the best.

I don't know. That day I let it all go. I subconsciously decided that I didn't care what the world thought I deserved anymore. If there wasn't a place for failed artists like me, fine. I'd make a life where I could do what I loved if it was the last thing I'd ever do.

I quit college.

I got a little less bitter over time. Every time life sent something my way that sucked, I'd laugh.

In my mind, I had already been through the worst. What's worse than burying a dream? What's worse than accepting that you'll never be good enough?

I made a business out of my failures. I used all my talent and frustration with the world and turned it into a marketable product my clients would pay for.

Then I decided to write a book no one would read.

"Who cares?" I said. "It's something for me to do."

Then I auditioned for the lead in a play for a public theater.

"Who cares if I get it? Just something to do."

Then I voraciously read books like I did before I found out about A.R. points.

"Who cares if I get the material? Or if there's a point to what I read? I just like the story."

Then I started writing songs no one would hear. Singing loudly in my home and banging on the piano, like I did before I knew about scholarships.

"Who cares if anyone ever hears it? The acoustics in my living room are fantastic."

I forget when I stopped being angry with the world. Maybe when I stopped looking to be accepted by it, or searching for someone to say, "Hey. You're the best."

Or maybe it was at the bar after my ten year high school reunion. A boy that went to all the same schools as me, grade school and up, stopped by my table.

"When I found out you were planning the reunion, the weirdest memory I have about you came up."

"Oh yeah?" I smiled.

"Yeah. Our whole class went to go see your play. You were this funny deer. I remember you leaping across the stage in your costume and I laughed so hard. I just remember thinking, 'Man. She's good and really funny.' Anyway, the things you remember. Yeah?"

Or maybe it was when I was stopped in a restaurant by our waitress.

"You're a Klüg daughter, right?"

"Yeah." I smiled.

"Do you still sing? You had the most beautiful voice. I still remember it."

Or maybe it was when "Mary" pulled me aside.

"Congrats on your book! I remember when you won that writing contest in school. You used to make up all these stories. And you were always singing. You sang a song you wrote once at 5th grade graduation. You were never afraid of sharing or performing. I always thought that was so cool."

Or maybe I stopped being so angry that day in the Gulf of Mexico when I completely gave up on being "the best."

I'm really not sure.

But now, sitting here, typing out this non-standard, non-five-paragraph-essay that, no, I didn't outline …

I tell you this from the absolute bottomless chasm of my soul …

Give up.

Give up on being the best.

Instead, learn to be.

Baptize yourself in the ocean of your failure and understand that at the end of the day …

you're standing in the middle of the freaking sea.

You are alive … and it's worth dancing, reading, writing, painting and singing about.

I just didn't want to hate myself

I remember a day vividly.

I was 18 years old.

I looked at myself in the mirror and finally accepted it.

That I hated myself.

That acceptance started a long process, finding out where the hatred came from. Sitting with that hatred and learning how to love it.

Using that hatred as a starting point.

It changed my whole life. What was holding me back was the fact that I couldn't admit that I hated myself.

I didn't move immediately from hatred to love. I moved from hatred to acceptance.

"I accept that I hate myself."

Lots of tears and angry crying followed me for years. But every day got better, the more I sat with myself.

Lately though, a decade later, I've been angry. About a lot of things. I'm well acquainted with my anger at this stage of my life.

It burns like coal, internalizes heat and produces energy that burns long and slow.

My therapist said something the other day. "You're kinda like Bruce Banner. He controls the Hulk because he's 'always angry.'"

And that struck me.

Because that's what it feels like sometimes. There's this weight on my chest, like an anchor that might crush me at any moment. It's enough to turn me into a monster.

But I've learned to accept the rage as a part of who I am. When I feel it rise in me, I write. I create. I sing.

Obsessively.

"Art is how you cope." My therapist said. "It's almost like a compulsion for you. Own that."

So when life becomes too much I pour myself into my work. It's what controls the scary green monster.

I'm always angry.

But my feelings don't own me. I own my feelings.

By accepting them. By allowing them. By recognizing them and giving them names... without shame or fear of judgement.

By letting the anger burn long and hot, I keep it in check. By raging through my art, by picking up a pen or using my voice, I quell the emptiness, the darkness, the nightmares.

I conquer my anger by making something beautiful out of it.

I conquer my anger by feeling it, accepting it.

By making it mean something.

Making it mean something.

Something.

I've felt the monster want to explode out of my skin, felt the heat rise in my cheeks, felt the rage just beneath the surface.

It rattled my cage.

Let me out. Let me out. Let me out.

"I'm leaving. I'm going to take a long trip."

"But why?"

"Because it's either this or drinking," I wanted to say. "Because it's either this or I explode and tear down every good thing I ever built for myself."

"Can't you just..."

NO! This kind of burning requires ice.

Alaska.

For years I didn't think snowflakes were real. I think a friend in middle school convinced me of it. That's what I get for getting my snow facts from a Floridian middle schooler.

But one day, I was in Arkansas and a soft snow began to fall. I looked on my black coat and saw it.

The most perfect snowflake. Actually, thousands of them.

"They're real!" I said to my friend.

"Um, yes?" She was from Idaho.

I laid in the snow for hours after that, letting every distinctly different, perfect snowflake swirl around me. A dragon cooling off her scales.

Yesterday, my kids experienced their first snowfall. They stuck out their tongues just like they do in the movies. They made snow angels and sledded down steep hills.

I thought of how quiet the snow is as it falls. So unlike the rage boiling inside of me.

Did the people around me witness a mysterious cloud of steam rising from my general vicinity?

Because how can people not FEEL this when I walk into a room? How do they not recoil when I get too close?

Coals. Burning coals.

Maybe they're just cold.

But me? I'm burning. I've been burning for a long time. I've been burning and stoking this fire.

I was born of the flame and I won't settle for smoke.

Smoke. Like false promises. Like empty words. Like the hope of fire, the signs of fire, just to come away disappointed.

I looked my daughter in the eyes and saw her then. I saw how she looks to me for how she carries herself through the world. I saw how she models her demeanor from mine.

She even burns like I do. God help her.

God help us all.

She reminded me of that mirror I looked into all those years ago.

Instead, I saw hope.

Hope.

There are decisions you'll have to make in this life.

Decisions that will require every fiber of life experience you've acquired.

Decisions that leave you with a heavy heart and soul... but peace. There's that, too.

Decisions that will be about sacrificing yourself for the people you love...

Or...

Being able to look at yourself in the mirror, and not hate the reflection.

Day, after day, after day, after day.

Sometimes, it comes down to that.

You didn't ask for it. You didn't want it.

You wish the decision would fall to someone else.

But, it didn't. The decision fell to you.

So you sit with it. You struggle with it. You wrestle with what you want and what you know to be right.

You burn.

You burn and you burn and you burn.

You burn and you have to find ice to keep it under control. You burn and you know there is a responsibility that comes with that burning.

You burn and you know you never wanted to hurt anybody.

You burn, and you realize sometimes that's just inevitable.

Because you? You're fire. You're flame. You're coals and hot metal and wood and pine straw.

Darling, you're kindling.

You're a living pyre.

So you make your choices, for good or for ill.

You OWN them. Because they're yours.

Peace. God. I need that. I need peace.

Peace like snowfall. Peace like ice crystals on a frosted window. Peace like evergreen trees blanketed in white. Peace like swirling snow smoke on the pavement.

And I don't know how it's all going to turn out. I don't know if I made the right choices. I don't know anything except...

One thing. Just the one. Today, I looked in the mirror.

And I didn't hate myself.

Chapter 4

Sk8er Boi

"So..." My sister began, eyebrows peaking over her glasses. "Where were you last night?"

I had gotten home late, Sk8er Boi dropping me off at home. We went out after my gig and he tried to return me to my car at Papa Joe's at around 3am. But the gates were closed, blocking my car in until the gates opened later that morning.

I really, really hoped he wasn't actually a serial killer. I was 99% confident.

My sister's new boyfriend, Mr. Airforce, was seated on the couch along with the godfather. I made breakfast for everyone and they paused their eating, awaiting my response.

I didn't know how my sister knew I was out late. I was back well before anyone woke up.

She must have read my thoughts, smirking. "Your car isn't here, Sandi."

Oh yeah.

"I had a date." I said simply.

My sister rolled her eyes. "Yes, I guessed that. With who?"

I took a sip of my coffee before answering. "A gentleman caller."

Mr. Airforce and the godfather snorted.

"Sandi…" Kelli said exasperatedly.

"It was just a date. Nothing serious."

As if to spite me, my phone buzzed. It was Sk8er Boi.

I couldn't stop my grin from betraying me.

"Just a date, huh?"

"Yep." I said, reading the text.

Got your car yet?

Not yet. I will soon.

I had an amazing time with you last night. The radness definitely holds up in person.

My smile reached my ears.

I didn't recognize him immediately when he walked across the lawn of *Papa Joe's*. I didn't have my glasses on and I'm nearsighted.

He came in the last hour of my show and the crowd had dissipated by then, the cold driving them away. He grabbed a beer and sat down at one of the fire pits.

I made eye contact and smiled, offering a small wave.

He smiled back at me.

I performed the rest of my set, trying not to look at him too much. But I paid close attention to his movements. When he looked at me, when he went to get another beer, when he got excited after he saw a dog and petted it, making conversation with the owner.

During the last ten minutes of my set he sat closer at a table, staring at me.

When I finished the last song, I finally made eye contact with him. I held up a finger to signal that I just needed a minute.

He winked at me.

Something in my stomach clenched.

I grabbed the tip jar and organized the bills, counting as I did so. I tried to act as if I didn't feel his eyes on me.

I halved the money and walked over to my bandmate—clutching the band sign with our social media info on it—who was in conversation with other musicians who stopped by to watch us. I got sucked into the conversation while handing over the tips.

After a few minutes I stole a glance at Sk8er Boi, offering an apologetic, I'm-trying-to-hurry-but-they-won't-stop-talking face.

He raised his eyebrows and smiled. My stomach did that thing again.

He was exactly my type, I noticed. I wouldn't let myself think he was attractive.

Yet.

Not until he opened his mouth and either confirmed or denied his intelligence.

I found an opening to dismiss myself from the conversation without seeming rude and walked over to Sk8er Boi.

"Hey." I said.

"Hey." He responded. "You're an amazing singer."

"Thank you."

"Would you like to grab a drink with me?"

I nodded in response.

We walked toward the parking lot. I adjusted my shirt which was slightly off the shoulder and looked up at the sky.

He watched me.

"So, if you don't mind me asking, what's your ethnicity?" Sk8er Boi asked.

"Ummmm. A little bit of everything."

"You look a lot like me." He said, stroking his black beard. "Even your hair is wild like mine."

I smiled slightly, taking a hand and smoothing my mane. "Yeah. It's a struggle sometimes."

"Tell me about it." He said as we reached the parking lot. "Do you want to take my car?"

I paused. I really didn't feel like dying that night.

"Promise you're not a serial killer?"

He grinned in response.

"Okay. Let me just put a few things in my car first."

We reached my car and I threw the band sign in the passenger seat and grabbed my red lipstick out of the cup holder. I reapplied it without looking and threw it into the car without seeing where it landed.

He had already walked to his car, which was parked just across from mine, waiting with the passenger door open.

It was a black mustang convertible. The mustang symbol shone in a bright white light on the concrete.

"Fancy." I offered.

"Have to impress you somehow."

I climbed in the car.

It was clean. A bottle of water sat in the cup holder.

"That's my favorite kind of water." I said.

He looked at me from the corner of his eye. Amused. "Yeah?"

"Yep."

"So where to?"

"There's a bar right up the road called *No Name's*. It's probably our best bet."

"There's a bar called *No Name*?"

I shrugged.

"Sounds good to me." Sk8er Boi shifted the Mustang into reverse. "I'll let you tell me where to go."

It was less than a five minute drive to the bar. We chatted, Sk8er Boi doing most of the talking.

"So, what's been your experience in the online dating world?" He asked.

"A bunch of emotionally unavailable men."

"You met your fair share of douchebags, huh?"

"You could say that."

"What do you mean by emotionally unavailable though?" He stopped at a red light.

"Not dating to find a committed relationship, essentially."

"I see. Well, I'm still finalizing my divorce. So if anything were to progress into anything… it would be after that." The car started moving again.

I looked at him, assessing. "I'm finalizing my divorce, too. I understand." I looked up and pointed, seeing the turn coming. "Okay, so you have to turn here in the parking lot of these yellow condos."

A confused look graced his face. "But… those are condos."

"Yep." I said simply.

He turned and we reached a small gravel road leading toward the bay. No streetlights lined the path.

"You know, you keep talking about me being a serial killer. But are you sure you're not leading me to an isolated place to kill *me*?"

I laughed. "The parking lot is right there."

No Name's sits on the water, a large deck on the side facing the bay. Sk8er Boi parked, walking over to my side of the car to let me out.

"I've never been here." He said.

"It's a spot for locals. Usually there's music."

We walked up to the front door, the security guard asking to see our licenses. He gave us wristbands and we headed inside.

"Let me buy you a drink." Sk8er Boi said.

"Gin and tonic." I said to the bartender.

"Lime?"

"Please."

"Gin and tonic." Sk8er Boi repeated.

"What?"

"Nothing. Just a little surprised I guess." He told the bartender his order, handing him his card. "I'll start a tab."

"The bartenders at the *Salty Hobo* say they always know it's me because of my drink order."

"I've heard of that place."

"Yeah." I leaned in, conspiratorial. "When I asked them why, they said, 'Sandi. No one orders gin and tonic at the *Hobo*.'"

He laughed as the bartender handed us our drinks.

"You want to sit inside or outside?" I asked.

"I've never been here. I'm following you."

I led him outside to the deck and walked over toward the pavilion. A country duo played, loud and rowdy.

We found a picnic table and sat down.

"So, you have kids?"

I took a sip of my drink. "Yes."

"How many?"

"Two. My son and daughter."

"How old are they?"

"8 and 6."

His eyebrows lifted in surprise.

"Let's just say I started young." My attention wavered. I spotted a food truck. "Oh my god, yes. I'll be right back."

I grabbed my wallet and left without another word, walking to the food truck and ordering nachos.

"They said they'd bring it to me." I plopped back down next to Sk8er Boi on the bench. "Thank God for them. I'm starving."

He had that amused expression on his face again. "I guess you are just getting off work, huh?"

"Yep!"

He leaned back against the table. "Being a musician you must have all kinds of stories."

"You could say that." My food was brought out. "Thank you!"

"And you're a single mom. That's crazy to me."

"Why?" I said a bit defensively. Then perked up. "Want some?" I offered my nachos.

He studied me and slowly took a chip. "I've dated a lot of single moms. They're boring. I get bored easily."

"Wow. That's incredibly rude." I said, not stopping my attack on the chips.

"It's true though."

"I disagree. Single moms are rockstars. Maybe they seem boring to you because their kids come first and they have a lot of responsibilities."

"I try to avoid responsibilities as much as possible." He said, munching on a chip. "You're a single mom though. You're not boring."

"I just happen to have a job that people consider cool." I crunched on a chip before winking at him. "But I assure you, my job is the only thing about me that isn't incredibly boring."

"I don't believe you for a second."

I smiled, looking off towards the band.

"You wanna go inside so we can talk?" Sk8er Boi motioned towards the bar inside. "I can't hear you well out here."

"Okay." I said, grabbing my chips.

At the table inside I asked him about his work. He worked security for an aerospace company, a job he took after getting out of the Navy.

"So what happened with you and your ex?" He asked.

I paused. I hated that question. Hated it because of people's reactions. Hated it because people didn't understand. Hated it because of the judgement.

"I respect the hell out of him. But…" I gripped my hands in my lap. "He has a lot of mental health issues and I just couldn't be with him anymore."

He frowned, studying me. "That's sad."

"It is what it is." I swirled my drink.

"How'd you know that was my mantra?" He said, perking up.

"It's a good one." I put my hands on the table. "I'm actually supposed to be in France right now."

"I knew you had good stories!"

I explained to him about my ex being accepted into a school in France to pursue his PhD in Physics. I was supposed to join him as soon as France opened its borders. The pandemic was the only reason I hadn't already moved.

"Damn." Sk8er Boi said. "That's really… sad."

"Eh, honestly it worked out for the best." I took a deep breath. "I mean, I definitely wanted to be writing in coffee houses, eating baguettes everyday and drinking champagne like water… but… you know. I really like my job. I'm happy I didn't have to stop."

"My ex is just a bitch. Pretty sure she was fucking the neighbor." He took a sip of his beer. "And she took my dogs."

"I don't like the word 'bitch.'" I said. "But it sucks that she took your dogs. My friend, the godfather, was heartbroken about his ex because she kept the dog. We're actually starting a duo act. Our first show is in a couple weeks."

"Well that's exciting! More 80s?"

I almost spit out my drink. "No. No, the 80s stuff pays the bills. Our plan is to start the duo, doing mostly early 2000s pop punk covers and then transitioning to a four piece band before next season. I want to play bigger bars." I took a breath, looking out the window. "And do originals."

"I honestly thought you just really liked 80s music."

I half smiled, turning my attention back to him. I studied his face.

I did think he was extremely attractive, actually.

"Well." I put out my hands in a dramatic sweep. "I am an entertainer, Sk8er Boi." I put my elbows on the table and leaned in, the gin had fostered confidence in me. "And I'm really, really good at what I do."

His eyes flickered and he leaned in, too.

The conversation deepened. I found myself playfully touching his arm and sharing about my recent trip to Alaska.

"I even cross country skied!"

"Really? I love to ski."

I pulled out my phone to pull up a picture. "I guess being from Stockton, California you were close to some skiing?" I found the photo and passed my phone to him.

He looked at the picture and chuffed before handing the phone back to me. "Yeah. People forget California is a very big state. I played hockey in school. It's a big sport there. And yeah, I skied a lot."

"I found skiing to be a lot like skating."

His eyes snapped to mine. "You skate?"

"I got some new skates for Christmas! I can't stop very well, but I really like it."

He grabbed his phone. "Isn't there a place around here?"

I laughed. "I mean, there's this place on the beach—"

"*Rockit Lanes*?" He showed me his phone, the address already pulled up.

"That's the one!"

He looked at my hands, folded on the table in front of him, then jerked his chin towards the door. "Let's go."

"Wha—" I started. "Now?"

"Yeah." He said, already standing. "Let's go."

Sk8er Boi closed out our tab and we left the bar.

Somewhere over the Hathaway bridge, he put his hand on my thigh.

The lights on the beach seemed to zoom past, Sk8er Boi's thumb moved in slow circles. I started giggling.

Giggling.

"Sublime?" I asked.

He squeezed my thigh. "Yep. Kinda my favorite band."

We arrived in the parking lot of *Rockit Lanes*, an arcade, bowling alley and skating rink combo.

"I used to have school field trips here."

"So you haven't left Bay County, huh?"

"No, I've left." I thought about living in Jacksonville with my ex. We were incredibly broke, trying to get him through school. But I simply smirked. "I just showed you pictures of Alaska."

He rolled his eyes softly before they met mine, his hand moving from my thigh to my face. He gently pulled me in.

And he kissed me.

I liked it. I liked it a lot.

We made out a few times between the car and the door of *Rockit Lanes*. He purchased the rental skates—him rollerblades, me quads—and we stepped into the rink.

He took off. I was left slowly getting my balance, trying to adjust to the rental skates.

He made a trip around the rink and back before I had taken three strides.

"So this is why you were so ecstatic about skating!"

He passed me on my right, saying into my ear. "I told you." He made a quick spin, skating backwards. "I played hockey!"

"Show off!" I yelled.

And then I fell. Hard.

Sk8er Boi was hovering over me in an instant, looking at me with that amused expression that I thought might actually freeze on his face. "I thought you said you liked to skate?" He offered me his hand.

"I also said I can't stop." I took his hand and let him haul me up.

He surveyed me, lingering on my leather pants before meeting my eyes. Still holding my hand, he started skating backwards again, taking me with him.

He pulled me into himself, putting an arm around my waist. "Come on. I won't let you fall."

I tried to fall. Over and over again. But Sk8er Boi was true to his word.

He didn't skate.

He danced. All around me.

He'd let me go a few times to zoom around the rink. Everyone stopped and stared.

It was truly a sight to see. I could tell he was in his element, his facial expression changing to one of concentration.

He took my hand and led me to the side bench, sitting me on his lap and kissing me deeply.

I didn't, couldn't, think about anything else. I liked the way his body felt against mine.

He pulled away. "Wanna get a drink and play some arcade games?"

"Okay!"

I bought that round of drinks and we filled up a game card with points. We wandered around, laughing, talking, and making out every thirty seconds.

"This seems a little juvenile, doesn't it?" He asked.

"What?"

"Not being able to keep our hands off each other. Making out like teenagers."

"Whatever it is." I grabbed the front of his shirt. "I like it!"

Eventually we came to an air hockey table.

"You said you play hockey." I said.

He gave me a lazy half smile. "Sandi, I will beat you. I will beat you so bad it will be embarrassing."

I rolled my eyes. "My pride is already ruined after skating and busting my ass. I don't care. I just want to play!"

So we did.

And he beat my ass, as promised, in about three minutes.

"Ugh!" I slid my goal handle at him.

He laughed. It was breathy and deep, his eyes lighting up. "I told you."

"Whatevvvverrrr."

His eyes narrowed slightly and he—I don't have a better word for this— swaggered over to me. He played with the belt loops on my leather pants and pulled me close, kissing that spot right beneath my ear. "I wanna go to the beach and make out with you."

My breath hitched, heat filling my veins. "Yeah, okay." I breathed.

I probably giggled again.

Probably.

And I definitely forgot entirely all of the rules for what was appropriate first date behavior on the beach that night.

Chapter 5

He's back

I burst into the master bedroom without knocking. The godfather sat with a guitar in his hand.

"What's wrong?"

"He's here."

"What?"

I started pacing. Hands on my hips, deeply breathing. In through my nose, out through my mouth. "He's here."

"Who is here, Sandi?'

I stopped, looking the godfather in the eyes. "My ex."

"No."

"Yes."

"Where?"

"He's ten minutes away, on his way here."

"He didn't tell you he's in town?"

"No."

The last time I saw him was Christmas. My ex had flown home, quitting school in France, insistent that he be in the States to be around the children.

I told him to stay in France. He had completed some groundbreaking work over there that I didn't understand, but he let me read the emails from the professors he worked with.

"What you have accomplished in three months is nothing short of extraordinary."

I wasn't surprised, of course. I knew he was brilliant. It was one of the traits that attracted me most to him. And if his brilliance could have saved our marriage, we would have been the happiest couple alive.

But that's not how it works.

I continued pacing. "I can't." I stopped and put my hands on my knees. "I don't know if I can do this."

"You don't have to see him, Sandi. You don't owe him anything."

I straightened up and tried to calm my breathing, "I have to see him. He says it's about the kids. He honestly sounded well over the phone. I could hear that it was him talking."

Because sometimes it wasn't. Sometimes it wasn't him talking.

"Plus." I added, mainly to myself. "He isn't a pariah. He's the father of my children and our situation is complicated."

"It will be okay." The godfather didn't get up to comfort me, but I could feel his empathy. Our first show together was in a couple weeks.

"Maybe things have gotten better since Christmas." He continued.

I had invited my ex to stay at the house for the holiday, but neither of us could handle it. The godfather would sit in whatever room we were in, watching both of us carefully.

At one point I burst out into the carport panicking. My chest tight, my breathing heavy.

The godfather found me and lit up a joint, handing it to me.

"I can't stay here." I said, tears rolling down my cheeks.

"He's…" the godfather struggled to find the words. "He just hasn't accepted that you're really gone. I'd say something, but I have a feeling it'd make it worse."

I took a long drag and coughed out the smoke.

"That'll help." The godfather took the joint from me. He eyed me warily. "Go stay with someone and I will make sure he's okay. And the kids, of course."

"I don't want to put that pressure on you."

"I'm putting the pressure on myself."

I thought about it, the tears on my cheeks turning cold from the breeze. "Sierra offered for me to stay with her and Lauren."

"That's an amazing idea."

"You're sure about this?"

"Yes."

"Okay… okay. You're a good friend." I hugged him. "This isn't fair to you either. I know you love him like I do." I pulled away and put my hand on his cheek. "You make me feel like I can breathe."

I turned up at Sierra's house a little past 10pm that night, after my show. She lived with her parents. Her and Lauren had tried to move back to San Diego, but the pandemic changed their plans.

Her mom greeted me at the door with a cocktail. "Hey sweetie, come on in."

Sierra sat with her iPad, drawing out a tattoo. It was a beautiful leg sleeve, a sea turtle the main focus of the piece.

"Oh Sandi." She said, standing and giving me a hug. "You're going through a lot, girl."

"So are you." I whispered back.

Her father had cancer, the prognosis gave him two years. If Sierra wasn't tattooing or working on her shop, she was with her father.

Lauren walked into the room with a bottle in her hand. "Shots!"

We stood around the table and took shots of peanut butter whiskey with Sierra's mom before Lauren snuck us out the front door, waving a joint in front of us. We walked down the dark street, the streetlights still weren't fixed from the hurricane.

"Let's walk through the graveyard!" Lauren said.

Sierra's parents lived in the same house I remembered from my childhood. It was right down the street from a graveyard and it was a staple memory to walk through it and hang out at night.

We walked and talked, passing the joint around, holding cocktails in our hands.

The past few months, I had really focused on rekindling friendships. Sierra and I met regularly for coffee, the godfather and I were starting a duo, Michael and I stayed laughing over texts and Greg and Michelle popped into my shows frequently, hyping me up.

My best friend, Jessica, moved to Asheville, North Carolina after the hurricane with my godson. The godfather, the kids and I stayed with her for a week, hiking mountains and hanging out, laughing and watching terrible movies.

It was a new season of life. It was different. Fun. Something I hadn't really had too much of before.

We finished our walk, silently entering the front door and zooming to Sierra's bedroom before her mom noticed we were high.

Lauren handed me some clothes to change into and I flopped on my bed for the night, an oversized bean bag. We watched anime until we fell asleep, Sierra and Lauren curled up on the bed.

I wished I could run away to Sierra's when my ex texted me that he was in the driveway.

I walked outside to find him in the driver's seat, nervously drumming his thumbs on the steering wheel. I opened the passenger door and slid into the seat.

"Hey." I offered a small smile.

"Hey." He smiled back.

He looked good. His eyes were clear, his skin not so yellow. His hair was fixed and he wore business attire.

"You're all dressed up." I said, buckling the seat belt.

"That's kinda what I wanted to talk to you about." He put the car in reverse. "Bailey Bridge?"

I swallowed. The Bailey Bridge held many memories for us, including our first kiss.

"Okay." I agreed.

It's a short drive to the bridge, less than a few minutes. We parked by the bay and stared out into the water as we had done many times before.

Our daughter's fifth birthday party was there. Our kids learned to swim there. My ex and I wandered countless nights under the oak trees, walking the bridge to reach Southport.

We often joked that we might have met even earlier than we did. Southport Elementary and Lynn Haven Elementary held an event after the Twin Towers fell on September 11th. They called it Wings Across the Bridge. Both 5th grade classes of the elementary schools walked to the bridge and participated in the event. It was supposed to represent the spirit of unity felt all across the country. I was a part of the choir for Lynn Haven and sang a solo for all the teachers, parents and students. My ex went to Southport.

He said he remembered the choir singing and the event. We probably walked right past each other that day.

Our partnership always felt written in the stars. I never once questioned whether or not we should be together. I knew it was meant to be.

And then, the day came when it was over.

Over. Over. Over.

His presence beside me felt familiar, welcoming.

I wanted to hug him. I wanted to tell him it was all a mistake, that I never wanted any of this. That we could try again.

But I had tried for years, made the effort so many times before.

It was time to try something new.

"So," he began. "You're probably wondering why I'm in town."

"Mhm."

"The truth is, I had a few job interviews."

I sat up straighter. "Okay?"

"I don't want to stay in Jacksonville. I know I could keep living with Granny, and she would love having me. But…" He turned in his chair and looked at me intently. "The kids need their dad."

"Don't."

"Don't what?"

"Don't talk to me like I haven't been the one saying, 'The kids need their dad' for years."

"That's not what I meant, Sandi. Could you not be so defensive? I'm trying to tell you something."

"If I'm defensive it's because you made me that way."

He hung his head, dropping his eyes. "Let's not dwell on the past."

I whirled on him. "I'm not bringing up the oh-so-distant-bygone-past." I seethed. "I'm bringing up. Two. Months. Ago."

"Okay, okay." He put up his hands in surrender. "Listen, I know why you had to do what you did. Okay? I've been back in therapy. I've been back with my psychiatrist. I understand why you had to…" He swallowed hard. "… leave me."

My eyes softened. "I hate all of this."

"I know." He made a move to reach out his hand, but thought better of it. "I know." He grabbed his other hand, massaging his palm. "Listen. I never would have respected you if you stayed with me. I…" He took a sharp intake of breath. "You're a rare woman, Sandi."

"Please don't."

"No, I have to say it. And I promise I'll move on from it and get to what I want to talk to you about." He gripped the steering wheel, looking out towards the bay. "I need you to know I'm getting better. I've been seeing a life and nutrition coach, too. I am working my ass off. I've dropped like thirty pounds."

"I've noticed." I said. "You look healthy."

"And not for you." He gripped the wheel harder. "That didn't sound right. But stay with me. It's not for you, it's for me. I want to live, Sandi. I want to live for *me*." He put his hand on his chest in emphasis. "There's things I want to do. Things I want to accomplish. And I want to be here. I want to be here for the kids. I thought about what you said about Judah. About passing on the burden to him if I died."

I looked out the window.

"And you're right. You're right. You were always right. I…" He stammered, putting his hand to his mouth. "I was awful to you. Some of it was the illness, but a lot of it was me being stubborn. And you didn't deserve it. But you…" He looked at me again. "Sandi, you saved my life. Not just once."

My mind went to that horrible night, the iPhone still open to a FaceTime call in France. The godfather holding me, gripping me tightly, trying to keep me standing up.

"Did I kill him? Did I kill him?"

"Sandi, you can't think like that."

"Is it my fault? I can't do this! I don't know how to do this!"

The nightmares that drove me out of bed, the rising panic in my chest.

"PTSD." My therapist said. "It's a normal reaction."

I really did love him. I still loved him. Would always, always love him. Would always be grateful for his existence in my life and his continued presence in the world.

And I would always feel the pain. The pain of looking at him and wondering what could have been if it weren't for a fucking category five hurricane, a pandemic and a handful of mental illnesses the American healthcare system didn't want to fund treatment for.

But there would always be another hurricane or another pandemic.

Another huge obstacle out of our control.

And one of us had to be okay. We had two children and they needed *somebody* to be okay.

My ex physically couldn't be. He couldn't.

I was starting to wither away into a shell of a human. I finally went on depression medication and it took the edge off, but...

I couldn't work. I couldn't do *my* work. The creativity leaked out of me, driving away everything that made me, *me*.

My hair fell out from stress.

I couldn't stop gaining weight.

My face broke out in acne.

It became harder and harder to get out of bed.

"You don't have to feel ashamed." My therapist tried to soothe me over our Skype call. "There's a stigma surrounding divorcing a mentally ill spouse. But this is not your fault, Sandi. You are doing the best you can with a terrible situation. In my book, you are an amazing person. If that counts for anything."

I tried to believe her. I tried to believe the godfather. I tried to believe my friends.

But I knew, I knew I'd never forgive myself for leaving him.

"Sandi." My ex relaxed, looking at me.

I sniffed, looking at him finally. "I've always only ever wanted you to be happy. I'm glad you're finding your way."

We sat in silence for a while, soaking in each other's familiar presence.

"Your interviews?" I began.

"Right." My ex turned to face me. "I had a few, but one is for a private school in Walton County. It's a Montessori school."

I perked up. "Grade levels?"

"K-12."

I grew excited. "So Judah and Lorelai—"

"Yes."

"Oh my God. That's fantastic!"

"I also got offered a coding job, it's a lot of money."

I hesitated. "I don't have any say in your life, of course. But I really think you'd get bored quickly with that."

He smiled. "I thought you'd say that. I'm definitely leaning towards the school."

"That's amazing. Really."

"Either way, I'll be moving back. I'd like to move to a rotation schedule with the kids."

"Done. We'll work out the details when you're here officially."

The conversation lulled.

"So what about your work in France?"

"Actually, I've started up my own company."

We chatted for a while, the sun slowly beginning to sink towards the horizon.

"I'll get you back home. I got to drive back to Jacksonville tonight."

I wanted to offer for him to stay the night, but I couldn't. I let him drive me back home and I resisted the urge to hug him as I exited the car. He rolled down his window to speak with me.

"You want to come in and see the kids before you go?"

"No, I don't want to get them all excited just for me to leave."

"Okay."

"Thanks for meeting with me today."

"Of course."

An awkward silence fell, full of the weightiness of what we wished we could say to one another. All the things left unsaid.

"Drive safe, okay?"

"I will…"

I turned towards the house.

"Sandi?"

"Yes?"

I looked back at the man I knew so well. The man I spent fourteen years battling through life with.

We never had it easy. We always pushed each other to be the best.

Survivors. Fighters.

We made each other strong. We kept each other in the game.

I wished for brighter days ahead for both of us.

"I'll never figure out how to hate you." He smiled.

My lips quirked up at the corners. "If you figure it out, let me know. It'd sure make this a hell of a lot easier."

Find me

I remember the day Death crashed through the roof of the single family house we shared.

He was slippery, cascading down as water that flooded our carpets and smooshed beneath our children's feet.

You must have met him then. Seeing his entrance while our children played and I hid in the closet with a bottle of wine.

I remember when you came through the door.

"Everything is fine! It's fine! Just a bit of water." You flew into the bathroom and came back out with every towel we owned.

"What?!" I followed you into the living room.

But when I looked at the scene, I saw no sign of Death, only water.

You told me he might visit one day.

You must have made a deal with him. You must have told him you were the only one in the house. You must have sold your soul to pay for ours.

I saw no sign of it then. I didn't see your eyes grow cloudy or your mind give over to the darkness.

I just saw your reassuring smile. I leaned into your confidence like a crutch.

"We didn't like this carpet anyway." You said. "Tell me what color you want the floors to be."

And through the worst, you held me. When we said goodbye, you told me what a privilege it was to do life with me.

That's the last time I saw you. We went to sleep as the wind howled around us, the pressure sending us into the floor, our children laughing in the safest corner of the house.

It's like you knew. As if you reached through the cosmos and stuck a peg into the stars.

"You can take me. But spare them. This far and no further."

You stroked my hair and backed away without a word.

Then it was over. And you were gone.

I searched for you and couldn't find you. Death left your body, but took your soul.

"It feels like you're far away from me." I'd say, months later. "Like you're in another dimension and I can't reach you."

"I'm here." You'd say.

But I knew better.

Because your soul, your soul fills the entire room. You are a presence in this world that is felt and it's noticed when you're gone.

Your mind, your mind is a puzzle I loved solving. How you overcame, how you survived, how you broke through every wall set to keep you in.

Your love, your love is like water and fire. Never holding me back, always pushing me forward, always telling me to demand more out of life because it's there, right there for the taking.

And your eyes, it is there I discovered your secret.

I saw him. Death.

My breath grew cold.

You made a deal with him, didn't you?

I could see it there, all right there when you looked at me long enough.

"I am lost."

It sounded faint, but like a shout.

As if you were a universe away, screaming across the galaxies at me.

"I am lost. I am here. Find me."

It was then I felt the clock ticking in my heart like a bomb ready to go off.

Death. Death. Death. Death. Death.

"What did you do?" I said through gritted teeth.

But of course, you did what you've always done. Didn't you?

It's like the story you told me about your childhood. You were handed a curse and you carried it with you around your neck.

You were marked with that black spot on the palm of your hand. You knew you were living on borrowed time.

And when Death came through the roof that day because it couldn't get in through the door, you knew he had finally found you.

You looked to us and then back at Death.

"Come on, old friend." You said. Your eyes gleamed with the taunt you gave every challenge you faced, every monster you slew, every dark place you battled through. "You know it's me you want."

So you opened the curse and it took you.

Because of course you did.

Of course you did.

But you forgot, my love. You forgot the most important thing.

That secret between us.

You held Death back long enough for you to find me.

I will not leave you alone.

I will find you. Whatever dark corner you've made your bed in, I'll meet you there and I'll remind you of who you are.

Of your soul that filled the room.

Of your beautiful mind.

Of your love that I miss, like winter hopes for spring.

Death, it can't have you yet.

"I'm here." You said.

I thought you meant you were still here with me, but I knew you weren't.

But now I know, you are "here."

You are somewhere.

But you are lost.

I will find you, my love. I will find you and bring you home.

This time, there will be no black spot. There will be no curse.

There will only be the reward for the soul who has seen Death and lived to tell the tale.

I'll meet you there. In the space where the stars restitch their stories when a human plays out of turn.

We'll keep them stitching, you and me. We'll keep them reweaving the blackness until it turns into the silver thread that adorns our elderly heads.

Remember when we took out the part of our vows that said, "Until death do us part?"

It was our joke. We wondered if anyone would notice.

Death can't do us part.

Because we knew something Death didn't.

You left part of your soul here with me.

It's entwined with mine so imperceptibly, no one knew, no one guessed.

And that part hears its twin. That part feels when it's near and remembers what it felt like, what it sounds like.

How your soul filled up a room.

I lift up the piece you left with me as a beacon, as a lighthouse standing on the rock calling a lost sailor home.

I'll stand here, gazing out at the horizon, knowing we fooled that great hooded spirit. Knowing we turned the tables and cheated him for more time.

I'll raise the torch high, with tears joining the salty abyss below, calling you home.

"Find me."

Chapter 6

Little Village

"I'll grab you another beer," I said to the godfather.

"Thanks."

He was sweating. It was incredible how much he was capable of sweating in February.

I let him handle the equipment, as I was completely pathetic in that arena. He tried to show me how to set up the portable Public Address System, but I froze up. I hated the equipment part of gigging.

"Just go sit down somewhere." He said exasperatedly.

I grabbed a beer from the small bar at Little Village, the owner, Sandy, smiling at me.

"Good luck! I'm excited."

The godfather and I had played an open mic there a few weeks prior.

"All we need to do is kill this open mic." I told the godfather as we walked in. "If we're any good, Sandy will book us our first show. If we get in one venue we can get in anywhere."

We played Drops of Jupiter by Train and a couple other songs. A large gentleman wearing a beanie and black shirt sat with a smaller guy. They lit up as we sang, pointing and commenting on our performance.

Sandy approached us afterwards, beaming. "Let's get you on the books!"

Another gentleman stopped me. "Do you do this for a living?"

"Yes sir, I do."

"Good. I couldn't imagine you doing anything else. Listening to you sing was just like 'Yeah, she should be up there.'"

I breathed in through my nose, slowly, and out through my mouth on the way back with the godfather's beer. I handed it to him.

"Ready?"

He took a long swig of beer and wiped his beard. He had three beers already, trying to calm his nerves. We mostly got alcohol for free when we performed.

"As ready as I'll ever be."

"You'll do great." I looked at him then, knowing how significant this moment was. "You did an amazing job organizing the set list."

The godfather went to the same church I got kicked out of. His parents were still a part of it and he didn't speak to them, nor his sister who used to be my friend. We were in the band together, along with my ex. We all stopped playing music after everything went down. It was too painful for any of us.

It was time to reclaim what was ours.

"Alright. I'll introduce us." I looked at the small crowd.

The Little Village is as unique as the part of town it's located in. St. Andrews is locally known as the artist district in Bay County and Little Village made sure to display the culture; from selling books written by locals, handmade jewelry, hosting local benefits and even the weekly business owners meeting, to featuring local musicians every night of the week, twice a day on weekends.

The crowd in front of me came to check out the new act and it was important the godfather and I gave a great first impression. Word would spread.

We started off with Drops of Jupiter again and we held the crowd's attention throughout the song. The godfather's hands shook slightly, but he didn't miss a beat. Probably due to the fact that his main instrument was drums. He would be the drummer of the four piece band we were planning to form later on after our duo got off the ground.

Movement caught my attention in the middle of a song. Three people walked through the door, a beautiful older woman with white hair, a man with a thick grey beard and a younger man who had on an AC/DC hoodie, the hood pulled over his eyes.

They sat down at the table furthest to the right and became my most engaged members of the crowd, clapping after every song.

I turned my attention mostly to them during my visual sweep around the crowd. It was what my high school choir director taught me to do during a performance.

"You don't have to look them directly in the eye. Just turn your body and head to make them feel as if you see them. Engage the entire room."

During my visual sweeps, I noticed the guy with the hood over his eyes slumped in his chair. I made the assumption that the man and woman beside him were his parents and they kept playfully pushing their son, laughing and pointing at me.

Eventually the younger man couldn't stop smiling, his body becoming animated. He put a hand over his face and laughed.

I wanted to know what was so damn funny.

"Break time." The godfather said, quickly putting down his guitar and power-walking out of the room for another beer.

I set down my microphone and took a sip of water, scanning the room.

I began with the left hand side and introduced myself to each member of the crowd, encouraging them to follow us on our social media pages.

"Where do you play next?"

"This is our second official show actually! We're booking for the season. So if you follow us, we'll post where we're playing next when we get the gigs."

When. Not if.

I slowly made my way around the room, making small talk, trying to seem friendly and not just awkward. I always did prefer singing to speaking.

Eventually I arrived at the table on the far right.

"Hey!" I greeted them. "I'm Sandi. Thank you so much for coming out to the show."

The woman opened her mouth to say something, but the younger man stood up, his hood falling off his head.

He had short brown hair and a chinstrap beard. He looked young, couldn't be any older than nineteen, twenty.

He stuck out his hand and I took it. He put his other hand over mine, giving it a slight shake.

"Hi Sandi. I'm Georgia Boy."

"Nice to meet you, Georgia Boy." I smiled faintly and looked down at his mom. Georgia Boy released my hand, but remained standing.

"I'm Marcia."

I nodded at her.

"And I'm George." The bearded man said. "Hey! Great singing. What a voice!"

"Thank you so much. I really appreciate that."

The godfather came over to the table and I introduced him before he said, "Ready to get started?"

"Yeah."

I turned towards the corner where we were set up overlooking the small lake when George said, "Hey Sandi! Before you go, our son is a musician."

I looked at Georgia Boy, now seated, and he had cut his eyes to his father, silently willing him to shut up.

I chuffed at the expression on his face. So that's why they were pointing and smiling at me.

"Oh yeah?"

"Yeah." George ignored his son. "Any tips for him?"

I focused my attention on Georgia Boy. "What do you play?"

"He plays guitar and—"

"—I sing." Georgia Boy cut in, turning his attention from his father to me. "But I mainly play guitar."

I considered him, allowing my pleasant demeanor to turn into an assessing gaze. Musicians looking for work always asked me how to get into the music scene in Bay County. I didn't mind sharing what I knew, there was plenty of room for everyone.

But most never did anything with my advice, their own fears or lack of ambition keeping them from pursuing my instructions, which I felt were quite simple.

It was frustrating.

I kept giving it out though. That same advice.

"You need three hours of music to start." I began. "Three hour shows are the most typical, but some places require four. You get two fifteen minute breaks, so if you aim for three hours you can probably do four with the breaks. Play an open mic. If you're any good, you'll get a show at that venue. Get into one venue and you can get in anywhere."

Georgia Boy took in my words and nodded.

"For now, anyway." I continued. "Next year it will be harder. Nashville is watching and lots of musicians are moving here to find work."

I didn't let him respond before I turned back to the stage where the godfather was waiting for me, still swigging the beer.

We played our punk set, the crowd getting used to us and cheering. A crowd favorite was Gives You Hell by The All-American Rejects, the table on the far right especially getting into it.

"This song goes out to everybody who's been divorced!"

The crowd laughed and pointed, clapping friends on the back.

Music has a way of making our pain seem less serious.

Song requests were thrown at us, though I didn't know most of them. I was working on expanding my knowledge of typical song requests. If it wasn't 80s synth pop, I knew very little beyond 90s country music.

Growing up in a strict religious household, pop-culture was quite foreign to me. I was allowed to listen to gospel and country music, and whatever I could soak up during car rides with my friends, mainly Mayday Parade. They were a band originating from Tallahassee, Florida.

The godfather added a capo to the neck of his guitar and began playing Jaime All Over by Mayday Parade. One of the godfather's and my favorites.

I thought of my beach escapades with Sk8er Boi as I sang it. We were supposed to go to a hockey game on Valentine's Day in Pensacola.

You tricked me. Sk8er Boi texted me a few days after setting up the date.

Tricked you?! I would never trick you.

"There's a Pensacola Ice Flyers hockey game on the 14th. Wanna go?" Very clever.

I smiled, but I feigned ignorance.

You said you liked hockey.

And you used my love of it to trick me into a Valentine's date.

Are you complaining?

No. I'm just impressed. Are people going to stop you in Pensacola, too?

I laughed. Our last date had been on Super Bowl game day. We had appetizers at Uncle Ernie's in St. Andrews, just down the road from Little Village. Then we hopped over to House of Henry's on Downtown Harrison Avenue to watch the game.

The bartenders knew me and asked when I was playing there again. Sk8er Boi smoothly entered the conversation, making everyone laugh. Then he excused himself to go to the bathroom.

A woman approached me after he was gone. She followed me on social media and had read my first book, *To All Who Wander*.

"I just can't tell you how much your book meant to me."

Sk8er Boi made his way back to the table, looking curiously at the woman.

"Thank you for your support." I said, shaking her hand. "It really means a lot."

She left and Sk8er Boi eyed me with that same amused expression he always conjured up around me.

"'Thank you for your support.'" He mimicked in good humor. "I didn't realize I was dating a local celebrity."

I rolled my eyes. "You should try walking around with my friend Sierra. It's impossible to go anywhere without being stopped by her fans."

"She's the tattoo artist, right?"

"Yep. Her shop is just down the road from here. It's on Harrison, too. Thistle & Thorne will be the bar and Prominent Goat is already open. The tattoo shop."

"I'd like to meet her. I can't wait to meet all your friends."

I considered him, looking into his light brown eyes.

I pictured him meeting my friends, the godfather, my sister.

"Okay." I said. "I'll see what I can do."

Sk8er Boi stood up from his barstool and put his arms around my waist.

"I really like you, Sandi."

My cheeks burned red. He kissed one of them.

"I really want a copy of your book. I'd like to read it."

"Okay. That'll be $20."

He grabbed my chin gently, pulling it toward him. "You're going to make me pay?"

"One should always pay an artist for their work, regardless of relation."

"And what is my relation?"

I didn't answer, my stomach doing flips, and redirected my focus to the game.

Sk8er Boi would periodically turn his attention from yelling at the TV to staring at me that night, kissing me softly, running his hands over my body.

The waitresses and bartenders I knew made eyebrows at me. I winked at them back.

After the game, we went to a store and bought swimsuits, towels and a six pack of beer. We had decided we were breaking into a hot tub at a local resort. The thought might have been alcohol induced.

We made out in the hot tub, the sound of the waves from the Gulf accentuating each kiss.

"Beer?" Sk8er Boi offered a bottle to me.

"No, thank you." I said, leaning into his side. "I don't drink beer."

"She tells me, after we're already here."

I laughed, putting my head on his shoulder. "I'm just content being here."

Sk8er Boi tipped his bottle to one of the condos, the lights in the windows shining. "Do you ever wonder what people are doing behind the windows?"

I thought about it. "No." I leaned my head back and gazed towards the sky. "I prefer to look at the stars."

"So poetic."

"I don't know any other way to be."

Sk8er Boi shifted, seemingly uncomfortable.

"You alright?" I asked.

"Huh? Oh yeah. It's just the piercing."

I burst out laughing.

"I'm glad my pain is funny to you." He said, his smile turning into a wince.

"It was your choice to get a Prince Albert." I replied. "So random."

"It wasn't random." He said, shifting again. "I just make decisions really quickly."

"Well, how's this one turning out for you?"

"We'll find out on the fourteenth, won't we?" He said with a wink. "After I heal."

I tried to keep my breathing even, looking up at the stars again.

Jamie All Over ended. Marcia, George and Georgia Boy stood, grabbing their plates and drink cups. Georgia Boy went to throw away the trash, while Marcia and George came up to the tip jar, throwing some money in as another song began.

"Great music!" They said before departing. George gave a hearty wave while Marcia smiled sweetly.

"Thank you so much." I said into the microphone between song lyrics.

Georgia Boy came up then, his hood back over his head. He took out his wallet, grabbed a few bills and came up to the tip jar.

Before he dropped in the cash, he looked up at me under his hood.

We locked eyes and I paused, the musical interlude going on longer than was necessary.

Georgia Boy didn't smile, didn't do anything but look at me intently, allowing a few seconds to pass.

He finally dropped in the money, nodded at the godfather and turned towards the exit to follow his parents.

I watched him go, his hands in the pockets of his hoodie.

Get out of the way

Ever since Hurricane Michael, when the wind blows my street sounds like a wind tunnel. Where before I heard the tinkling of leaves like wind chimes, I now hear the force of nature when it's channeled through houses lining the street.

"I wonder if they'll cancel," I said to my sister.

"It's pretty bad out there."

"It's an inside gig though."

I had spent all day writing and that night I would get to my other job as a musician. I needed to put the whole getup on. Heels, make up, a leather skirt and sheer black top. I probably wouldn't do my hair tonight as it would be pointless. Just a high ponytail with a silver headband would be sufficient.

I just bought new heels because I wore the others down on the decks everybody around here likes to have for their restaurants and bars. My heels would get caught in the cracks, causing me to do an extra two step as I danced and sang.

My bandmate confirmed we were still a go, so I shifted my mindset from Sandi the writer, to Sandi the performer.

Putting on the gig clothes is like replacing one frame of mind with another. The Sandi wearing her leather skirt and heels is someone who can deal with drunk men parading around the bar making direct eye contact and singing along with every 80s tune. The Sandi in the sheer black top can smile and make a joke, reminding people to tip. I ain't doing this for free.

It's a thing. Like a baptism.

I finish getting ready, running late as usual, and quickly say my goodbyes to the kids.

"Will you be late today mommy?"

"Yes, but I'll kiss you on the head when I get back."

That always seems to comfort them a bit.

God, my kids. I've recognized for a while that I've really made some choices on how to raise them. Free thinkers and spirits. There's no going back from that. It was a choice, whether it's convenient that particular day or not.

They like that I do music again though.

My son says, "Mommy, I love that you sing. You look pretty when you go to gigs. You look happy."

And you know what, son? I am happy.

I lost myself for a while there. I think I raised you guys the way I always knew, though subconsciously, was right for who I am as a person.

But I haven't been that person in a while. Now it's coming out with a vengeance.

I left the house, facing the torrential downpour, happy I just bought some really good waterproof eyeliner. A must for when you're doing shows out in Floridian humidity.

I slam the car door, wiping the drops of rain from my arms and play the hype music.

Social interaction requires hype music, after all.

I focus on the road, watching the rain criss-cross and swirl, making waves dance on the pavement.

The hurricane that destroyed my home sucked. It really did. But I've made my peace with hurricanes again.

They feed my soul. They remind me that life is a lot bigger than my tiny little problems.

Nature always wins.

Forgive me, I've been a bit existential these days. By a bit, I mean a lot.

Asking questions like, "Why am I here?" Or "Am I happy?"

"Are all the decisions I've made in life the result of past trauma?"

You know, the usual.

I've been walking the Bailey Bridge more often these days. So many memories at that place. So many first kisses. So many bike rides. So many times after work I'd go and hang out with my friends.

Five year old Sandi learning to ride her bike. Seven year old Sandi going Sheepshead fishing with her dad. Ten year old Sandi playing at the park. Thirteen year old Sandi going on an all day excursion with her friends, walking down the bridge just talking. Fourteen year old Sandi boarding a boat with her family to watch the 4th of July fireworks. Sixteen year old Sandi making out with a guy in a car, the cops knocking on the windows telling us to go home.

Twenty-nine year old Sandi taking her kids to explore underneath the bridge.

Yeah, it's one of those places to me.

I found myself last night walking back and forth on the bridge after the storm. Eventually I sat on the railing, staring out at the stormy bay.

"Hey! You okay?" A jogger asked me.

I turned my head and almost said, "No." Because I do try to be honest when people ask. Our cultural expectation for everyone to reply "fine" is just so silly to me. If you don't want to know the answer, don't ask.

But then I realized he probably thought I was looking to make a jump to my death.

So I quickly smiled and said, "Yeah, just looking out. Thanks for being worried though."

"No problem."

I pulled up to the bar I was playing at and gave myself one more good look in the mirror.

I have one look, because I'm just not a big makeup girl. Winged eyeliner and red lipstick. It does the job.

I look up to see water gushing over the roof of the old downtown building of House of Henry's. I'll have to be fast.

I hook my car key to my bra (pro tip, by the way) and grab my tablet that has the words to my songs, then make a mad dash towards the door.

It all happened so fast.

I walk quickly to the door and there are three already hammered people blocking my entry. I'm envisioning myself getting soaked from the water cascading off the roof like a fountain and begin to get mad.

But a woman sees me coming and says to her friends, "Get the hell out of her way, she just wants to go to work."

A guy moves, holds open the door for me, and I step right in, barely a drop of water on me considering the circumstances.

I say a quick hello to my bandmate and go to the bathroom to dry off quickly. I made it with four minutes to showtime.

I look at myself in the mirror and register what the woman said.

"Get the hell out of her way, she just wants to go to work."

I stare at my reflection, taking in the dramatic stage makeup, the sheer top, the leather skirt and faux velvet heels.

I did look like a woman about to take the stage.

Work. I'm at work.

I'm a musician at work.

I smiled. If fourteen year old Sandi could see me now.

What would I say to her? Maybe I'd find her at her favorite spot, sitting beneath the bridge on the rocks, writing some depressing song.

Maybe I'd tell her, "Don't believe them when they say your dreams are impractical. You get exactly what you want out of life. You get paid to do what you love, and it pays the bills. You write, you sing, you create... all day. Every day. And one day, a woman at a bar sees you and knows exactly what you're there to do. She tells everyone to get the hell out of the way so you can get to work."

Work. My work. MY work.

I grab some paper towels and quickly dry my clothes, taking deep breaths in, gearing myself up to be seen.

To be seen. God, what a concept. To be seen. To be known. To come out of hiding and step into who you are.

That was always the dream, wasn't it?

I'm living the dream. A life full of all the things I want. And I have kids, who love what I do. I have kids who watch me own who I am, even if that's a shaky practice sometimes. I write, I sing, I dance, I create... and I'm good. People want to pay me for it.

I straighten my back. I hold myself up, because I don't slouch when I perform. No room for that.

I look at myself directly in the eyes. And standing there is an elevated version of myself. Someone who knows how to own a stage, make people comfortable and have a good time.

Just have a good freaking time. Also, what a concept. To enjoy life. To be happy. To step back into who you always were and couldn't run away from.

I worked hard for her. I dedicated a decade of my life to get back to her. I endured a lot of sleepless nights and tear stained pillowcases to be able to see this person again.

She's pretty freaking awesome.

I open the door and take another deep breath.

"Yeah." I think. "Get the hell out of my way. It's time to go to work."

Northern Lights

"How's the forecast?" I direct the question to my bonus mom.

"It will be too cloudy to see them." She answers.

My dad speaks from the other side of the room, across from the fireplace. "You may have to drive to Fairbanks for a couple days to get a good view."

"That's if I finish this damn book in time."

"How's it coming?"

"Eh."

Truthfully, I had accomplished quite a lot.

Well. I've written half the amount of words that are in _The Sorcerer's Stone_. I texted my boyfriend.

Are these just random facts you keep in your brain?

Yes. Just for these occasions.

I missed him. I was ready to be back home in his arms, creating more memories.

It's not too late for you to join me, you know.

You know this isn't my journey.

I had invited him to come along, but he was insistent that he stay behind.

"You won't get any work done, you know that." He said when I asked him.

"But we'd have so much fun!"

It was probably for the best. I'm having trouble focusing as is.

I didn't have any plans for this trip beyond getting away from home and having time to focus, but my dad and bonus mom kept me busy. My only wish is to see the Northern Lights. We tried so hard to catch them on the last trip, even driving up to Fairbanks which is about eight hours away from Anchorage. But the phenomenon remained elusive.

My parents have plenty of food in the fridge for me. They both love to cook. Listening to them bicker in the kitchen has become my nightly routine.

I heat up a bratwurst and scoop some homemade potato salad onto my plate, grabbing a locally made hard seltzer from the basement.

I gaze out the window to the snow covered mountains beyond, willing inspiration to come my way.

This next part hurts a little bit to write about and I'm not looking forward to it.

Maybe the pain will avoid me just like the freaking Aurora Borealis.

Chapter 7

Lie'brary

I slammed the front door of my home and yelled.

"Ahhhhhhhhhhhh!"

"That seems unnecessary." The godfather drawled from the master, which was right by the front door.

"I hate this!" I continued my rampage, walking towards the kitchen. I grabbed a glass out of the cabinet and walked over to the fridge to fill it with water. "I hate it! I hate it! I hate it!"

The godfather left the master and entered the living room, taking a seat on the couch. He rubbed his eyes and pinched the bridge of his nose. "What are we hating today exactly?"

"I hate dating. I hate it! And I don't want to take any man kayaking with me! They need to stop asking! That's *my* thing."

"Sandi. I'm really gonna need more context."

I took a sip of water as I walked into the living room, pacing.

"I want a love story!"

"A love story." The godfather repeated.

"Yes. A love story, godfather. A love story." I continued my pacing.

"Is this about Sk8er Boi?"

"Ugh. I don't know." I made an overly dramatic sweep of my hands, slamming the glass of water on my electric fireplace.

"I thought your last date went really well?"

"It did." I paused. "It really, really did."

"So... what's the problem?"

"He says he can't see me for three weeks. Not before I take him to the MMA fight in March."

"I thought we weren't doing that until May?"

"We aren't." I sighed, putting my hands on my hips as I walked. The godfather and I landed a big show to perform at an MMA fight called

93

Beatdown on the Beach. Twelve hundred people would be in attendance. "But I got tickets to check out the event ahead of time and I invited him to go with me… as like a Valentine's gift."

"Didn't he just get a new puppy?"

"Yes." I waved my hand dismissively. "And he says he's got to train it and can't leave the house for long periods of time."

"Well, Sandi. That's true. Puppies are like babies. They need a lot of work."

I grunted.

"It's a sign he's a good dog owner which is a good thing."

I stomped dramatically.

"Now that's pathetic."

I looked towards the ceiling. "I saw a psychic."

The godfather let the silence ring.

"I'm sorry. Can you repeat that?"

"I. Saw. A. Psychic."

The godfather burst out laughing.

"She said I wouldn't be single much longer, that by summer I'd be with someone. He has dark hair, he's cute, younger than me. When I first met him he was unavailable at the time. Butterflies are significant—WHY ARE YOU STILL LAUGHING?"

"I'm crying real tears." The godfather had his head between his knees, then sat up quickly looking up at me. He took one look at my face and started laughing even harder.

"This is who I've become, godfather! This is who I am now! Dating is making me lose my mind!"

"Thank you so much for telling me this." The godfather wiped tears from his eyes. "God, this is great."

"Sk8er Boi fits the description!"

"Sandi, I fit that description. A million people fit that description. It is so incredibly vague. You know this! People used to call you a prophet!"

I had almost managed to forget about that.

"You had to bring that up." I said, my head drooping.

The godfather and I had very little secrets from one another. We'd known each other fourteen years, my children's names were tattooed on his arm beneath an image of a lion and a butterfly. I'd given him advice about women since his first love interest, texting back and forth trying to dissect what was happening.

I first met him when he accompanied my ex to a choir performance. He was maybe fourteen. As part of my choir uniform I had to wear fake hair to cover my bun in order to make it look more poofy.

The godfather's first words to me were, "Why do you have a rat on your head?"

And so, the saga began.

To many people I was this person to aspire to, an author and musician (and to the charismatic pentecostal church we were a part of, a prophet) who spent her life at the front; being seen.

To the godfather I was just me. Just weird, awkward Sandi who had doubts and fears and had no idea what she was doing half the time.

A third of the time.

Most of the time.

I started laughing with him, allowing what I had done to sink in.

"Sandi," The godfather said, finally catching his breath. "Your problem is that you put way too much emphasis on romantic relationships."

"Says the guy who's been cooped up in his room because of his ex."

"Well, I'm meeting with someone tonight."

I straightened. "Who? Jacqueline? Peach cobbler girl from the dating app?"

"Yep."

"I thought she was blonde."

"She is."

"We don't do blondes."

"Well, I'm just seeing where it goes." He narrowed his eyes at me. "Just like you should be doing. Not everything has to be so serious."

"But I want serious!" I threw my hands up. "I want passion and love and romance! I want to build something with somebody. I want my one fucking person. And I want a love story! A real one! At least me and my ex had a cool story and we built something together even if the rest of it was tragic. I want to feel alive with them. I—" I pinched my fingers together, bringing them in front of my chest. "I want something… exquisite."

The godfather offered a half smile. "Well, Sandi. Exquisite takes time."

"Ugh! That's all anybody says." I put up a talking hand. "'Just be patient. Just be patient.'" I mocked, rolling my eyes.

"Well. I've got to start getting ready." The godfather said, standing up. "Don't you have a show to get ready for?"

"Yes. Taproom."

"Welp, I'll see you there. That's where we're hanging out."

It was cold that night. The Taproom was located in St. Andrews and had outdoor gas fire pits and heaters strategically placed around the outdoor area. Boss Man, the owner, whistled when I walked in.

"Sandi. Always fabulous."

"Hello, Boss Man." I said, grinning at him.

"Wine?"

"Please."

I stepped onto the stage and greeted my bandmate. He was dressed to the nines in an 80s suit, rubbing his hands together against the cold.

I wore a long sleeve black sequin dress with a V neck, black tights and my regular black heels. My hair actually wanted to cooperate that day due to the lack of humidity, a different look than the mane that usually sat atop my head. My usual face of black eyeliner and red lipstick was sure to stay on that night instead of melting into a puddle by the end of the show.

Boss Man brought me my wine, cabernet, and I set it down on the floor of the concrete stage. I pulled out my phone and scrolled social media. A friend request on Facebook was my first notification.

I clicked accept as I always did. Being an entertainer meant constantly expanding my social media pages. I clicked on the profile, curious to see who my new "friend" was.

It was Georgia Boy.

I had some time before the start of the show so I explored the page, beginning with his information section. I went to his birthday first. It was listed as January 17, 1969.

I rolled my eyes. He definitely wasn't older than twenty then if he thought 19"69" was funny.

I continued scrolling.

He was married.

I swiped over to Instagram, curious. Sure enough, Georgia Boy had followed me on that platform, too.

He didn't have much on that platform, I easily scrolled to the bottom. I spotted a picture of him and his wife, she was pretty. She looked really young, too.

I followed him back.

My first set began, starting with I Ran by Flock of Seagulls, the godfather and Jacqueline coming in about halfway through. They brought another musician I knew with them, Jacob, his dog sitting beside him next to the fire. A couple women accompanied him.

I chatted with them around the fire on my break, the night growing even colder.

"What are you doing after this, Sandi?"

"Oh, I don't know. My sister has my kids tonight and they're in bed. I can stay out for a bit."

"Wanna go to the Hobo?"

"Sure. That sounds fine. I probably won't drink much though."

The conversation wove in and out. I began tuning it out, trying to gather energy for my next set. I checked my phone again. I had a message on Instagram.

Georgia Boy's name popped up.

You should come down to the Lie'brary after your show! I'm playing with a friend!

I hadn't heard of that venue, so I pulled it up in my GPS. It was in St. Andrews, a quick walk from the Taproom.

"Actually guys. I think I'll head to the Lie'brary after this. There's some musicians playing there tonight that I haven't heard yet."

"Where's the Lie'brary? I haven't heard of that place."

"It must be new. But it's right down the road. Pretty much caddy corner to us."

They all agreed to come after the show.

A couple hours later, I was counting out the tips and making small talk with Boss Man. The godfather and I would be playing at the Taproom with our duo act soon.

I finished off my remaining wine and exited the bar, deciding to walk to the Lie'brary rather than drive.

I hurried down the sidewalk, the frigid air driving me forward. I soon entered the bar and was greeted with warmth.

Bookcases filled with old leather bound volumes lined the walls behind the bar. A piano sat in the corner.

I heard music coming from the back, past a long hallway. I walked towards the sound, my heels clicking on the hardwood floors.

The band was immediately to my right upon entering, Georgia Boy held an acoustic guitar next to a larger man who looked familiar. He also played an acoustic.

"Oh!" The larger man said in the microphone. "Sandi MarLisa just walked in everybody!"

The small crowd sitting at the tables cheered. I ducked my head and took a seat by the wall.

"Where were you playing tonight, Sandi?"

I smiled. "The Taproom."

"Oh, that's a great spot everyone if you haven't checked it out." The crowd murmured in agreement. "Hey Sandi. Since you're here, you want to come up and do a song with us?"

"Uhhhh…"

The people at the tables started cheering, beckoning me to go up.

My eyes flickered to Georgia Boy who gazed at me. He spoke into the microphone. "You know, Beanie, I did just learn Gives You Hell."

"Ohhh shit."

I grinned. I did love that song.

"Okay yeah." I said, standing and smoothing my dress. "Why not?"

Everyone clapped and I took the stage. Beanie lowered the mic stand and moved to the side, leaving me to stand beside Georgia Boy.

I looked at him. "Ready?"

He started playing in response.

The crowd clapped as we moved through the song. I put on a smile and danced a little, looking at Georgia Boy every so often.

He wore a red ball cap turned backwards and red sneakers. He was showier with the guitar than I was used to, moving it around as he played.

He had energy, like he couldn't stand to keep in one place.

The godfather and Jacqueline walked in, along with Jacob and the two women. I looked at the godfather, but he wouldn't meet my eyes. Beanie seemed to know who they all were and greeted them.

We finished the song to cheers and I gave a slight bow to Georgia Boy.

"That was fun. Thank you."

"Absolutely! You were great"

He high-fived me.

"Hey. There's some people I want you to meet."

I walked Georgia Boy over to my table of friends. "You've met the godfather. But Jacqueline and Jacob are in a duo together, they're musicians. Jacqueline, Jacob… this is Georgia Boy. He's also a musician."

Georgia Boy shook their hands and then glanced at me.

I turned to take my seat back by the wall as Beanie and Georgia Boy began to play another song.

"You were great!" A woman turned in her seat to speak with me. "Your voice is amazing!"

"Well, thank you!"

"What are you? You're so exotic looking! Especially in that dress!"

"Ummmm…"

"Oh my God." Beanie had suddenly stopped playing. "It's Mason St. Germain from Sons of Saints everybody!"

I turned to look, and sure enough, the lead singer from one of the biggest bands in town walked in with his guitar player.

He waved. "Hey Beanie."

"Mason! Will you come do Fat Bottomed Girls?"

"I'm just here to see you, man! I had a gig over at House of Bourbon and we're on break."

"Please! Get on up here!"

So Mason relented and took the stage, his guitar player borrowing Beanie's instrument.

The place erupted when they began the song by Queen, the energy electric.

I looked around smiling. It was a rare night. We musicians lived for energy like this and there were many of us in the room.

"Well. There's no following that." Beanie said into the mic after they had finished. "We're taking a break."

The godfather, Jacqueline, Jacob and their crew said their goodbyes and left. I stood to follow them out.

"You're not leaving are you?" Georgia Boy stopped me as I moved towards the door.

"Yeah, Sandi." Beanie said, wandering over after Mason and the guitar player left. "Come outside and talk for a minute."

So I followed them out to the small patio in the back.

"Thanks for singing one with us, Sandi!" Beanie said. "How was Taproom?"

"It was good! Great crowd, especially for the weather. I made pretty decent tips."

"Was this with your 80s thing?"

"80s thing?" Georgia Boy cut in.

"Yeah, she's in an 80s synth pop duo, man."

"Interesting." Georgia Boy's eyes flickered to me. "So you're in more projects than the one with the godfather?"

"Just those two." I smiled.

"I'll have to come see your 80s stuff sometime."

We talked for a while, Beanie leading the conversation. I dove into what I thought about the growing music industry in Bay County, how the hurricane shaped the growth in the entertainment industry.

Georgia Boy didn't say much, he just listened.

"Sandi." Beanie said. "Come do a few more with us. Do Drops of Jupiter. I loved that one when you did it at Little Village."

"That's where I know you from!"

"I don't know that one," said Georgia Boy.

"Yeah. It's your show, Beanie." I laughed. "I don't want to take up your time."

"No, don't worry. I don't get jealous." Georgia Boy said. "You both do it. I'll watch."

So we all went inside and I once again took the stage. Georgia Boy leaned up against the wall, watching Beanie and I perform the song.

I'd catch his eye every so often, his lips curled up in a lazy half smile.

"Come on, Georgia Boy." Beanie called over as he insisted I sing another song his friend didn't know. "You can pick this one up easily."

"Nah." Georgia Boy said, looking at me. "I don't get jealous." He said again. "You guys go ahead. I'm enjoying this."

I sang No Scrubs by TLC, taking my liberty with singing runs and hitting high notes as the crowd cheered me on. Georgia Boy kept leaning against the wall with his arms crossed over his acoustic guitar, smiling that half smile.

The show ended and the crowd slowly dispersed, talking as they stood around in small circles.

"Thanks for coming to my show." Georgia Boy said, wrapping a cable.

"You were quick to get a show!" I said.

"Yeah." Georgia Boy set down the wrapped cord and picked up another. "I just met Beanie and we kinda went for it."

"Well you sounded great. I'm looking forward to hearing more."

"And I'll come see your 80s—"

"IF YOU'RE NOT WITH THE BAND, GET THE FUCK OUT!" A bartender came out from around the corner, gesturing with his hands towards the exit.

"Bye." I squeaked to Georgia Boy. "Bye Beanie!"

"Bye Sandi!"

I hurried quickly out the door and stepped into the even colder night, my phone buzzing in my hand as I ran as fast as I could in heels towards the car.

I swung open the door and sat down in the driver's seat, shivering. I pressed the start button and heated the seat warmers, then rubbed my hands together before checking my phone.

Bonnie. The text simply said. A picture of an Australian Shepherd puppy was attached.

Awwwww

How was your show?

Good. Lots of tips. Then I went to see some friends play and they pulled me up on stage. That was fun. How's your night?

I waited a few minutes for a response, but none came. I put the car in drive and headed home.

Arriving in my driveway, I noted the godfather's car was still gone. I opened the front door and immediately took off my heels, tip-toeing to the kids' room.

My niece and daughter shared a bunk, sprawled out over the sheets asleep. My son was on the top bunk with headphones over his ears, his tablet screen the only light in the room.

I stood on tip-toes and gently took off his headphones, removing the tablet from his weak grip. I set them on the side table before returning to the bunk, caressing my son's head with one swoop.

I kissed my niece, then my daughter before quietly exiting the room.

The house was quiet, as it was only at night. I showered quickly and put on an oversized t-shirt, grabbing my book and turning on the lamp next to the couch. I checked my phone one last time.

It was good! Wanna come over tomorrow?

My heart soared and I immediately wondered how I could work out childcare for a few hours. But even the fact that he asked me sent me reeling.

I'll see what I can do!

With that happy thought, I snuggled into the couch and began to read.

I must have fallen asleep. My next memory is hearing the lamp switch off beside me. I peered through half open eyelids, but only heard the master bedroom door close.

I felt for my book, but it was nowhere to be found. I sat up and patted the couch around me, my eyes adjusting to the dark.

Then I saw it, sitting neatly on the ottoman across the room with my bookmark peeking out of the top.

I smiled toward the master bedroom before curling back on the couch and falling into a deep sleep.

Chapter 8

Keep going on

"Yes, but how are YOU doing?" My therapist asked me.

Long pause.

"Really take your time." She said.

So I did.

And then.

"I'm not feeling anything. I'm not dealing with it. I'm not processing anything. It's like after the hurricane. I just did what I had to do to survive and keep things going. I know eventually I'll have to deal with it, but right now I just don't have time. I have to survive. I have to make sure the house keeps running. I have to make sure the kids are taken care of and supported. I don't have a choice. I'm working on it though and I know I'll have to set time aside to deal with it soon. I knew I needed to go to therapy. And I knew to reach out for help so I don't crash."

She smiled. "It's good that you recognize that."

"It's amazing to me how humans can survive. It never feels the way people think. It's not courage. It's not strength. It's not anything but our natural instinct to be able to keep going on. It's fascinating and wonderful to me."

I shift in my chair, thinking.

"I think the trick is to know that eventually you have to step out of that survival mode and live intentionally. One day you wake up, and the moment to deal with it has arrived. That's the tricky part for a lot of people. But I look forward to that day and as soon as I can manage, I'll step into it."

Don't run

I walk Boo Bear, my parents' dog, through the snow covered sidewalks. A small church is on my right, homes and mountains on my left.

The cold wind hits my face. The day is clear and sunny in Alaska, though the Northern Lights still remain elusive.

I let Boo Bear pull me, gripping the leash tighter in my hand.

My bandmate and I were featured on a local podcast, Salty Field Recordings hosted by Ashley Feller, a local musician herself. The premiere just aired and I watched it on my computer while Face-timing my bandmate, responding to comments from viewers.

I'm doing it. I'm really doing it.

I'm in Alaska writing my next book and I took a month off to do it, gratefully collecting donations from my readers. I have a successful music career back home waiting for me, a release party for my new album scheduled, my bandmate texting me newly booked dates for the coming season.

"Mike Thompson wants us on his radio show Radio Cosmos Live. He specifically wants us to do the call while you're in Alaska and I'm in Florida. We talked for like forty five minutes."

I chuckled. "Okay. Set it up."

"Come on Boo Bear." I say, gently tugging on the leash. "Time to go back."

Boo Bear leads the way, pausing to pee on a random snow mound. I look towards the mountains, waiting, and sigh.

So many emotions have swelled in my heart during this time away. I'm accepting all the things I did while I was surviving, just trying to make it through each day and find joy somewhere along the way.

Most of it was good, beautiful even.

But some of it…

Boo Bear finishes and we continue on the path, my parents' townhouse coming into view.

There's no outrunning who you are.

It's time I stop trying.

Monday Night Little Fest

"What is this event again?" I asked the godfather.

He was sitting on his drum throne, guitar in hand. We were practicing new songs to add to our set list.

"It's called Monday Night Little Fest. Jacqueline told me about it and introduced me to Kirk, the host. He gave us a slot. It's a lot of musicians filling a three hour show at the Taproom. You know, like a mini festival. It's every Monday night."

"And we're not getting paid for it?"

"Usually Kirk finds a big donor and each act splits the money. We also get tips. Plus, the sets are only like half an hour." He drummed the body of his guitar. "Free beer." He added as an afterthought.

"Okay." I blew some hair out of my face. "Well, it's good exposure anyway. We debut at the Taproom soon." I looked at the godfather, who was studying a chord chart on his phone. "Great work."

"Yep."

The children burst out of the bedroom, I had both my nieces and my children for the day. Schools were closed for a Covid-19 outbreak. My sister and I had exchanged childcare so I could meet Sk8er Boi at his home in Destin the day before and go to the Little Fest that night.

"That's that outside energy!" I called after them.

"Yeah." The godfather agreed. "We're trying to practice in here."

"Sorry mom." My son said.

I smiled. "Come here, Judah."

Lorelai and my older niece ran in circles around the kitchen table, giggling. My younger niece toddled after them.

Judah came and sat on my lap. I ruffled his hair before saying, "Take Triniti and Lorelai outside to the backyard, and keep an eye on Sophia." My backyard was fenced in and I was in the habit of shooing the children outside on nice days to play. It was a sunny February day. "I'll make lunch after we practice."

"Got it."

I kissed my eldest on the cheek, giving his butt a pat as he ran towards the sliding glass door yelling, "Come on! Outside! Mom's got band practice."

"Ugh!" Triniti groaned. "Aunt Sandi!"

"Mom!" Lorelai echoed.

"Ousside! Ousside!" Little Sophia squealed.

I pointed towards the backyard. "Go. Now."

Their complaints were muted once the sliding door closed.

The godfather was frowning at his phone.

"What?" I inquired.

"Huh?" He looked up, still smiling. "Oh nothing. Jacqueline got a new kitten from the Little Village pet adoption day."

I stood, walking over to where he was seated and looked at the Instagram story. The caption mentioned a name I recognized.

"Georgia Boy bought it for her?" I asked.

"Yep." The godfather confirmed, swiftly putting away his phone. "Ready?"

"Yeah." I groaned.

"All musicians have to practice, Sandi." He chided.

"Sure. But I hate it."

My mind drifted during practice to my last show at Papa Joe's with Denuvo. Georgia Boy walked in during the last fifteen minutes of my first set.

He sat at the closest picnic table, turning so he could face his body towards me, leaning back and propping his elbows on the table.

He wore another baseball cap turned backwards and watched me perform with that lazy smile, clapping after every song.

When it was time for my break I sauntered over to him, my heels clicking on the concrete, and sat down beside him, my back facing the stage.

"Well that was really cool." Georgia Boy said, gesturing towards my bandmate's synthesizers. "Interesting sound."

I took a sip of the water I brought with me and set it on the table. "Yeah. That was my first impression when my bandmate first auditioned me."

"You auditioned?"

"Oh yeah." I confirmed, taking another sip of water. "My bandmate does everything very professionally." I chuckled, a memory surfacing. "He actually found me on Facebook and sent me a message."

"Really?"

"Mhm." I looked at the ceiling, gathering my thoughts. "He saw some video of me and messaged me, asking if I'd be interested in a musical project. I agreed to look into it and he gave me the address to come audition." I started laughing. "I pull up to his house and realized, 'Oh my God, Sandi. You're walking into a strange man's house who you met on the internet. He's the guy your parents warned you about.'"

Georgia Boy laughed.

"But no, it was cool." I said, smiling down at the table. "The synth pop sound is incredibly unique, especially what my bandmate does with it. It's a big sound for a duo, so we can do the bigger venues acoustic acts can't. Most people around here only do country and I'm not so into that."

"Mhm."

"Once he told me his process about getting gigs, shared with me that he had toured in England with his band for 17 years and showed me just how organized he was… I was sold. I could tell he knew what he was talking about. Plus, I figured there was a market for the 80s stuff, just because it's so different than people are used to around here. Even if I don't understand the sound or it's not my preference."

Georgia Boy looked at me, willing me to continue.

"So, here I am." I finished, gesturing vaguely.

"Here you are." Georgia Boy repeated.

I sat quietly, gazing off towards the people in the field beyond the covered pavilion we sat under. The sun was setting.

"I really liked Tainted Love." Georgia Boy said.

I turned my attention back to him, but still averted my eyes from his. "Yeah? That's a fun one to sing."

"So what happened to you?"

My face screwed up in a look of confusion. "What do you mean?"

"What happened to you to make you sing that song like that?"

I shrugged, indicating I didn't know what response he was looking for.

"When I saw you at Little Village the first time," he continued. "I thought, 'Damn, that girl can sing. But she's holding back.'" He smiled. "For some reason."

My eyebrows furrowed. I drummed my fingers on the table in front of me, agitated.

"I ain't never heard a voice like yours." Georgia Boy turned, facing the table now. His hands clasped in his lap. "Why would you hold something like that back?"

I smirked, looking at him.

I wanted to say something to put his assumptive attitude in place. I wanted to say that I was one of the only women who sang professionally at all in the town; much less put on sparkly dresses and dance around with energy on the stage, rocking some of the biggest bars. I wanted to tell him I had been kicked out of church, in part, for that voice he said I was holding back; losing my entire community in a single day while I was newly pregnant with my daughter.

I wanted to say I had to find childcare for every single show I performed in as a single mother, or bring my children with me, even though I nearly doubled the amount of shows many of my musician peers performed weekly.

I wanted to say it didn't matter how late my gig ran, I still had to be up at 6am in the morning to get my kids to school. I wanted to say my children cried in the evening because I wouldn't be there to kiss them goodnight. I wanted to say I was judged for standing on that stage, my chosen profession and work uniform not a perceived desirable one for a mother of two children.

I wanted to say I had been groped while performing, whispered obscenities in my ear while I was dancing. I wanted to scream at him that I was constantly sexualized, by crowd members, fellow musicians and business owners alike, frequently spoken down to and otherwise pushed into a box I refused to fit into.

But I didn't.

Because I chose it all. I chose it all every damn day and took the criticisms mostly in silence, my thick skin having long been seasoned by hardship in innate regularity.

What happened to me?

What happened to *me*?

I happened to *it.*

So I kept the smirk on my face and swung my legs around the bench, grabbing my water and staring at the sun setting over the bay. I noticed my bandmate standing by his synths, waiting expectantly.

I turned to Georgia Boy and said, "My bandmate is summoning me." I took a sip of water, staring at him over the rim. "Thanks for coming to the show for a bit." I said, smiling sweetly.

"Of course." Georgia Boy said. "Just making my rounds. I'm gonna head out of here soon though and see some more friends play."

"Have fun." I said simply, and rose to take my position.

I was late. Late late late late late.

Actually, my sister was late getting home from work. Bless her soul for always being there to help with the kids though.

I passed Sophia to her when she entered the threshold as I scurried out the door.

No 80s getup that night for the Little Fest. I got to dress like myself when the godfather and I performed.

I pulled up to the Taproom at ten minutes past six, snagging a lucky parking spot in the closest lot.

I wore my black converse, so I easily jogged to the outside gates entering the Taproom courtyard.

I heard a familiar voice singing a punchy tune. "Love is overrated! Love is overrated!"

I turned my head towards the stage to see Georgia Boy singing his heart out, belting out the song.

I rolled my eyes at the lyrics.

I scanned the patio and found the godfather sitting with Jacqueline and Jacob. I walked up to the group.

"Hey! Sorry I'm late."

"It's fine." The godfather sighed. "You just missed some of Chinstrap's set."

"Chinstrap?" I asked, looking at Jacqueline for an explanation.

But it was Jacob who laughed, petting his dog. "Georgia Boy."

"Oh." I said, taking a seat facing the stage. "Right. Cause he has a Chinstrap." I sat up straighter. "Hey. That's mean."

"What's mean is him wearing that thing on his face."

"I seem to recall you making some questionable choices with your facial hair over the years." I said sardonically.

"That was because I was being ironic."

"Well maybe he's being ironic."

"Sandi." He laughed. "No he isn't. There's no defense for that thing."

I rolled my eyes. I had a feeling I'd do it many more times that night.

"You just get one free drink tonight, Sandi." Jacqueline said smiling.

"Oh okay! Thank you. I'm not drinking tonight."

"Well give your free drink to me." The godfather said.

"Okay. What do you want?"

Georgia Boy's voice cut over the conversation. "Thank you! That was an original song of mine called, Love is Overrated. I wrote that after getting divorced—"

My attention snapped at that.

"—and I wrote this on a trip I took across the United States. Just had to get away. Here's another original called Agave Blood and then I think—" He scanned the crowd, finding the godfather and me. "There they are. Yeah. I think the godfather and Sandi MarLisa are up next. So stick around."

He began the opening riff to the song. I stood to walk to the bar and get a drink.

I waved to my friend Bartender behind the bar.

"Hey girl!"

"Hey! Can I get a beer?"

"You're playing tonight, right?"

"Yep!"

"Okay so this one is on the house then, but just the one since there's so many of you tonight." She paused. "Wait, Sandi you don't drink beer."

I laughed. "You're right. I'm giving the godfather my freebie."

"Haha. I'll allow it."

I specified the type of beer he wanted and she poured skillfully from the tap before handing it to me.

I turned back towards where my friends were seated, Georgia Boy had just finished his last song.

"Ready?" I said, handing over the beer.

"Yep." The godfather squeezed Jacqueline's thigh before standing, grabbing his acoustic.

It was a plug and play show, the host providing the PA system. A good crowd formed, sitting around the fires, laughing and drinking.

"You want to try Atlantis?" The godfather asked.

"Ummm." I looked at the crowd. "Let's try Masquerade first."

"Okay." I said, addressing the crowd. "We'd like to thank our host, Kirk, for inviting us." I paused for applause. "And of course, Boss Man, the owner of this glorious Taproom. We've got Bartender behind the bar. Be sure to tip your bartenders, folks!"

Everyone cheered.

"Now, this one's an original. I wrote this when I was about fourteen. It made me Mosley High School famous." I nodded at the godfather, signaling to begin.

I sang the chorus, allowing my voice to swell. "... I know I can be a condescending natural disaster..."

I looked out at the crowd and noticed Georgia Boy had wandered over to where his parents sat closest to the stage around a fire.

I sang the song I had sung a thousand times before. Applause met the last chord the godfather strummed on his guitar.

"Atlantis, Sandi." The godfather said firmly.

"Ugh." I relented. "Okay."

He picked out a beautiful cadence on the strings. The song was slow, so slow a regular strum would sound strange.

"...You're sailing away in this relationship we made. You will find Atlantis before you ever reach the shores of my forgiveness..."

The crowd continued to talk, conversation swelling as the song continued.

The godfather picked the last few notes on the guitar and the song was done.

I left the godfather to unplug and hopped off the stage, aiming to warm myself by the fire.

"Hey!" Georgia Boy's dad said from where he was seated. "Sandi, right?"

My palms faced the fire he sat by. "That's right!"

I couldn't for the life of me remember his name. I was really bad at names. I was horrendous at memorizing song lyrics, too. Even my own songs were hard to pin down.

"I really liked those originals. That Masquerade song. You really wrote that when you were fourteen?"

"Well thank you. And yes I did."

"Pretty heavy stuff."

I said nothing.

"Hey girl." Georgia Boy nudged me, holding a beer.

"Hey." I rubbed my hands together.

"So I was right."

"Right about what?" I rotated until my back was facing the fire.

"You've been hurt before."

I froze, remembering what he had said about being recently divorced. My song Atlantis was about my divorce, pretty obviously so.

But this was not about to be a bonding experience.

"Everyone's been hurt before." I said, turning back to face the fire. "No one's special."

"No one's special." He repeated.

I looked over to the godfather, praying for him to come rescue me.

"I didn't know you wrote songs." Georgia Boy continued.

"Mhm."

"I write songs, too. I saw you came in late, but I shared some of my originals also."

"I heard them." I said. "Love is Overrated."

It took everything in me not to openly and unabashedly roll my eyes.

"Yeah! I took a trip across the country after my divorce. Stayed in Nashville for a while. You'd love the songwriters circle there."

I doubted it. We had a lot of Nashville artists living in Panama City, many of whom were my friends and I had nothing against them personally. But many of the places on the beach would only hire so-called Nashville artists. It was a running joke that you could take a weekend trip, play one show in Nashville, and come back touting the title, "Nashville Artist."

I refused.

"I've actually got a song I started there that I'd love for you to add a verse to. It's called Hurricane."

"Interesting."

"You wanna beer?"

"What?" I said, not understanding the question after being lost in my head.

"A beer? Here I'll get you one."

"Wait—"

"Hey Dad. You want another beer?"

His dad wasn't listening, chatting up a woman next to him on the couch.

Georgia Boy's mom elbowed him, pointing to her son and saying, "George."

Right. George. George George George. Like my dad's name.

"A beer?" Georgia Boy said again.

"I really—" I started.

"I'll be right back." He said, patting me on the shoulder.

I heaved a sigh, frantically looking around for the godfather.

Him and Jacqueline were talking to other musicians. My propensity for social interaction was quickly waning, but I thought it would be polite to stay for the whole show.

I walked over to them, making conversation. Georgia Boy found me and handed me the beer.

"Thank you." I said, taking a polite sip.

The godfather eyed me, staring at the beer in my hand.

I glared back. He had left me unsupervised.

Georgia Boy stood holding the other two beers in his hand. "Great job, godfather! Really enjoyed your set."

The godfather broke eye contact with me and lifted his lips in an easy smile. "Thanks man."

I always admired his ability to be a chameleon when the situation called for it. If I felt awkward, I looked it.

My lips were in a tight line, my legs bouncing. The godfather went back to his conversation with Jacqueline.

"So I saw on Facebook that you kayak." Georgia Boy said, smiling.

"O-oh." I stammered. "Yeah. Yeah I go all the time."

"Where do you like to put in at on the beach?"

"I don't kayak on the beach." I acted like I took a sip of the beer, keeping my lips closed. "I put in near my house in Lynn Haven at the bay. I can't lift the kayak to my rack on top of my SUV so I throw it in my trunk and ride down the road holding it on a string that's attached to the end."

He laughed, shaking his head. "A bay girl, huh?"

I gave a short nod, looking into the fire.

"I like to kayak, too." He said, trying to catch my eye. "We should go together sometime."

"Sure." I said, idly swirling my glass, still looking into the fire.

"Well." Georgia Boy turned. "I need to bring this beer to my dad."

"Right." I said, remembering my manners. "Thanks for the beer. That was sweet."

"Of course." He answered, calling over his shoulder as he walked towards his parents. "Gotta take care of my friends."

"Beer, Sandi?" The godfather said when Georgia Boy was out of earshot, holding back a laugh.

"Oh shut up and take it." I shoved the beer into his hand, letting some of it spill on his jeans.

He took a sip. "That's disgusting."

"What now?" I said, exasperatedly.

"Chinstrap's horrible taste doesn't just end with his facial hair."

Chapter 9

Beautiful

"Write about something beautiful," my heart whispers.

"Now?" I whisper back.

"Especially now," it chimes in response.

So I think hard. I think long and hard about the beautiful things I've witnessed in my life.

A few years ago I bought the only kayak I could afford, an inflatable one. It had a car adapter to blow it up and I left my house at 5 a.m. to start my adventure.

I pushed out into the familiar bay down the street from my home, the sunrise gently peeking over another beautiful summer's day in Florida.

The water glowed in the morning light, pink, purple and orange hues danced along the surface.

I like being out on the water. There's something about being right smack dab in the middle of something that is so much bigger than you are. There's no one around, everything is quiet.

Except for the soft splash I heard in the distance like someone had blown air into a bottle.

I know that sound. All you have to do is hear it once and you'll know it for the rest of your life.

"Dolphins," I said softly. I looked around and saw what my eyes were searching for.

A group of birds circling in the distance. I knew I had found my target point.

I began paddling farther out into the bay, my eyes straining to see the treasure my heart longed for.

A gleam, a shimmer, a tail smacking the water, then silence.

Then another. Then another. Then another.

A pod of 5 or 6 dolphins were feeding beneath the circling birds.

I paddled harder, but they sensed me, the pod slowly drifting away from an unknown intruder.

I took my paddle and lightly smacked the water.

"Come on," I said. "Please come see me."

The pod sent a scout. One lone dolphin weaved through the waves to come check out who was spying on them.

Friend or foe?

The dolphin exhaled through its blowhole mere feet from my kayak, as if it were asking me a silent question.

"Should we be worried about you?"

And that feeling I've always sensed around dolphins flooded my heart.

Fear. Intelligence. Wonder. Mysticism. Intrigue. Truth.

I thought of my bedroom when I was a teenager. I collected dolphin figurines and begged my parents to let me paint my room a specific blue. To decide which exact hue of blue I wanted for my walls, I looked at a picture of the Gulf of Mexico by my home.

There are four distinct blues you see as you look out into the horizon.

The first is more of a light sea foam green, the second is more like a turquoise, the third is a riviera blue and the fourth is a deep, deep blue.

I knew exactly the color I wanted. Riviera.

So my dad, reluctantly, helped me paint the walls that exact color. My mom bought me a dolphin bedspread.

But it never was exactly right. There is no capturing the beauty of the Gulf in a single color.

As a kid, I always thought I had a weird connection with dolphins. My favorite book was called "Island of the Blue Dolphins."

Their eyes look like portals to other worlds, like they know the answers to the questions you only ask in your dreams.

So I watched the dolphin who circled my small boat with a mix of fear and wonder.

"What sort of things have you seen, my old friend?" I asked of it. "What's going on down there?"

But the scout flipped its tail and rejoined the fishing party.

I watched them, following them around for an hour, drinking in the sunlight spilling over the clouds, breathing in the salt air that smelled exactly like home.

I watched the birds dive deep for their own share of the fish, the water reflecting the sunlight on their wings.

Then I felt it. The wind shifted suddenly as summer storms in Florida do.

I sighed. "Time to head back."

I paddled towards the shore, knowing it was probably too late, the wind gusting through my hair, drying the salt into the strands like shampoo.

The waves began to rock the boat, the nose of my kayak pushing through the crests.

And then the sky opened up and I knew it was all over. I had lost the race.

Nature, like always, had won.

There was no warm-up, just buckets and buckets of rain pouring from the sky, cold droplets that chilled your bones and dripped into your eyes.

I shivered and breathed in humidity. The fog curled over the water like smoke and the shore could barely be seen through the curtain of water falling in sheets from the sky.

Then I heard it, music.

Not the music we hear on our radios, but the music found in nature.

If you listen closely enough.

I couldn't put my finger on what it sounded like, the rhythm and sound of rain hitting the water.

Wind chimes? Close.

Coffee dripping into the pot? Maybe.

But no. I finally placed the sound.

Thousands of glass beads dropping on pavement. That's what rain sounds like on the bay.

I smiled because I finally placed that haunting melody, leaned back in my kayak with arms opened wide and drank in the rain.

It soaked me through. And there alone in the middle of the bay with no one to find me, surrounded by all my favorite things...

Rain. Dolphins. Water.

And my voice. Just my voice.

It was then I realized, I wrote my first song out on the water, so many years ago.

It was about September 11th. I was visiting my Aunt in Indiana and she lived on a lake.

I paddled out into the middle and realized that if I sang, if I sang right there in the middle of the lake, no one could hear me.

And I wrote my first tune, as if it was a gift the water gave to me.

"September 11th will be remembered as the day that terror struck our hearts. That fear will never go away, but our courage will grow and grow because of that day."

A child of the Great Recession's first song.

So I sang into the sheets of rain and I could have sworn the dolphins jumped and the sun peeked out of the clouds to hear my song.

It's said, when it rains and the sun is shining, that good luck will find its way to you.

Or, the devil is beating his wife.

Whichever you believe.

But I just sang. A song no one would hear, with words that don't exist, the sound of glass beads on pavement keeping time.

Then I picked up my paddle and continued my slow journey back to shore, the waves seeming to say, "No, stay here with us."

I felt the old wish from when I was young, that I could sprout both wings and a tail. A daughter of the sky, land and sea who sings.

It's why I named my daughter Lorelai. The siren.

But I broke through the waves, the shore getting closer and closer.

When I finally made it, my heart beating wildly, I looked out to where my dolphins still played, beginning to make their way farther and farther out to sea as the afternoon set in.

My skin felt sticky from the salt, my hands cramping from the rowing.

And I tipped back my head and laughed and laughed.

Life. Oh, what a glorious, glorious life.

What a wonderful world it really is.

It's a continuous song and dance, and so, so much bigger than our problems.

Then the thunder rolled, a deep and perilous all-too-familiar sound of warning.

Time to go home.

I've arrived

"Mommy. Your voice is so pretty. I didn't know you could sing!"

My son was 4 years old. He's 8 now. I used to strap him to my chest as I played keyboard and sang.

Now he didn't even know I could sing.

His remark hit me square in the chest. Everything came rushing back in.

Sandi, you don't even listen to music on the radio.

Sandi, you haven't touched your piano in over a year.

Sandi, how the hell do you go from music being your entire life to it just being nothing anymore?

Nothing made any sense. Most memories I have in adolescence are me on a stage.

Most memories I have with my friends are centered around music.

And it wasn't just this that sent me spiraling. It was the fact that I spent most of my days alone writing.

I loved writing, but it's safe. Writing gave me an outlet to the outside world without actually having to ever be in the outside world.

Because I had been hurt. Hurt badly.

I was vexed for years trying to figure out how to get myself back into music again. It no longer brought me any joy.

Just emptiness.

Me and the church have a complicated history, and I've recently cut my ties with all work pertaining to the ministry after a decade in service.

It's been so strange. So foreign. Not to have to worry about people policing what I say or how I behave.

After getting kicked out of church several years ago, music lost all appeal to me for a long while.

Music is so spiritual for me and I couldn't enter that space again. Entering that space meant opening up a well of emotions I wasn't ready to make a connection with or deal with.

I was in therapy for a long time focusing on this specific issue.

One day I dragged out my guitar and played a song I wrote when I was 14 on strings that should have been changed 3 years ago. I posted a video of it on Facebook.

A man messaged me a few hours later and asked if I'd be interested in joining a project.

80s synth pop.

Now, I'm not a child of the 80s, but the music was challenging... and it was the furthest possible thing from church music imaginable.

I tried out and was hired. I've spent the last year dressing up and singing at shows and I now know over forty 80s covers by heart.

I went from singing in church, to singing in bars.

What a change that was.

I began exploring different techniques with my voice. But there was one hurdle that proved difficult to overcome...

Not holding back.

You see, in church I was always told to rein it in, to hold back, to not be a show off. I was overpowering. I was too much.

Then there was the claim for modesty.

The amount of times I was pulled off to the side and told I needed to cover up more... just for wearing a tank top, or a dress that was too flattering.

Yes, playing in bars proved to be a big change.

Slowly I began to realize I wasn't in church anymore. There's no one telling me to hold back.

In fact, they're screaming, "Sing it!"

Or, "Baby, you look like my second wife."

Oh God.

I began exploring my full range and showcasing it. I began putting out the voices that told me to hold back and just go for it.

My confidence I didn't even know I had veiled, started coming back to me. I started remembering things about myself I long kept buried.

Like my intolerance for bullshit.

Like my intolerance for people who try to put me in a corner.

Like my intolerance for laziness in your craft, and my impatience with people who live below their potential.

My life blew up in my face. Music brought back a fire in me that burned away everything that didn't belong there.

I suddenly got more bold with enforcing my boundaries. I suddenly carried myself differently.

I got in an argument with Michael a couple months ago, and he said, "Sandi, I'm getting mad."

This man towers over me at 6 plus feet.

"Good!" I said. "Be fucking mad. Please God feel anything than this apathy you're projecting. It's aggravating."

He came back to me weeks later and said that statement sent him on a path of self discovery.

But it gave me insight into just how much I've been holding back.

He also listened to a cover I was proud of.

"Sandi, you're an incredible vocalist... but you're holding back."

Georgia Boy had told me that same thing.

The truth spoken out loud has a way of creating change you can't stop, even if it hurts to hear it.

I researched keyboards for a week, knowing it's time to bring that into my live shows.

I hit the keys and it transports me back to moments I would get lost in worship as a worship leader, before shame and guilt set in. Before I was rejected. Before I felt like I was too much.

Before I allowed people to bridle me.

And I know it's going to be different. I know once I let go I'm not going to be able to hide anymore.

I know once I really stop holding back, in several aspects of my life, I'll probably lose and confuse people who are used to me being one way.

But I'll tell you one thing.

I'll be damned if my son says, "Mommy, I didn't know you could sing." Ever again to me.

My kids now climb over instruments to get to their room. They're used to mommy being out late because she has a gig.

They're falling asleep on bar couches instead of church pews.

And I know I'm opening myself up to judgment. And I know people will have their opinions of me and how I raise my kids and how I live my life.

Then again... they always did.

I've never been able to do it right. I've never been able to be good enough or spiritual enough or modest enough or contained enough.

But here's what I've realized...

I'm enough.

I.am.enough.

And I fucking love myself. Or at least, I'm learning to.

I love my intensity.

I love my passion.

I love my talent.

I love my zero tolerance for bullshit.

I love my free spirit.

I love my wildness.

I love being an artist.

I'm done living my life based on outcomes.

"Sandi, where is this music thing leading? Where is this going?"

To exactly this.

Me, sitting here at my table, drinking coffee, gearing up to practice for tonight's gig.

Where am I going?

Honey, I've arrived.

The Hathaway

"This is that Beatdown energy!" The godfather said to me over the music.

We were slaying the crowd at Taproom that night. Every song hit, every note soared.

We held the crowd with each song, the godfather skillfully reading the room, selecting music to keep the energy high.

We had both drank considerably that night. My ex and I started childcare rotations and I had every intention of staying out late. I needed a night.

He was doing well. The new job was good for him and I prayed he would be able to continue. I knew his mental health was still shaky, but now he'd have a routine. Plus, he'd have the kids half of the time and I knew he missed them.

Sk8er Boi and I grew more serious, our phone calls and texts increasing throughout the day, the content of the conversations deepening.

"My sister in law is a bestselling author."

"No way!"

He texted me the link for her book.

"Wow!" I said, cradling the phone on my shoulder. "I'll read it."

"Tell me what you think when you're done." The connection went silent for a moment. "I'd really like you to meet her one day."

My heart skipped a beat. I couldn't stop the smile growing on my face.

He hadn't asked me to be exclusive yet, but it felt imminent. He started making comments about the future, asking me about where I saw myself in a few years. Our date for Beatdown on the Beach was a week away and I had a feeling that would be the moment. It would be our eighth official date, with a few hangouts in between at his place.

The last time we hung out we laid on his couch just looking at each other, kissing sweetly and laughing about everything.

He suddenly started feeling sick and feverish. He got up and paced the room, agitated.

"Would you sit down!" I said. "You're making me nervous. And you should be resting!"

He sat down, rubbing his hands on his thighs. I could tell he didn't feel well.

"Listen. I can go home. Let you get some rest." I made to get off the couch.

"No!" He pounced on me, gripping me in his arms. "Stay here with me."

So he took some Tylenol and hit the bong, collapsing into my arms. We watched Star Wars and laughed as his puppy played around us. She had an accident.

"You stay there. I'll get it." I said, beginning to get up.

"Um, absolutely not." He gently pushed me back on the couch and ran to the kitchen to get cleaning supplies. He scolded Bonnie as he got down on his hands and knees, scrubbing the carpet.

He sighed.

"What is it? Do I need to go to the store and get you some meds?"

"No, Sandi." He said.

"Then why are you sighing?"

"I'm better than this!" He said dramatically.

I laughed, sitting up and patting the couch next to me. He finished cleaning and sat down, laying his head on my shoulder.

"I like you just like this." I said, kissing the top of his forehead. "I'm having fun."

"You're having fun?" Sk8er Boi sniffed, coughing slightly. "Even when I'm sick?"

"Even when you're sick."

He watched the movie, not speaking for a long while.

"Well that's nice." He said finally.

When it was time for me to leave, he walked me to the door, holding Bonnie.

"I can't wait for our Beatdown date!" He said.

"Me neither! You sure you don't need anything?" I asked.

"No, I'm fine. I'm just going to take it easy. Is it okay if I stay the night at your house after our date?"

I hesitated. I had the kids that night and my sister had agreed to keep them. He absolutely would not be meeting my kids until we were official, and probably not for a while after that. Plus, there was the whole not-having-a-bed thing.

"I mean, it's just we'll be getting out late and I'll have Bonnie…"

I smiled, giving my head a slight shake. "I'll figure it out."

He kissed me goodbye and I walked down the stairs of his apartment complex to my car.

A bit down the road on my way home, I spotted a 24-hour drugstore. I made the quick decision to stop in.

I scanned the aisles, thinking about what to get. What said, "We're not official but I care about you and want you to be okay?"

Tissue boxes. Tissue boxes said that.

I bought a double pack and headed to the checkout area.

As the cashier scanned the boxes, a thought popped into my head.

"May I borrow a pen?" I asked the cashier.

She handed me one and stared at me as I scribbled a quick note on the box.

"For a man who has everything else. <3 Sandi."

I handed her back the pen and walked back to my car.

Arriving at Sk8er Boi's apartment, I thought about how to give the tissue boxes to him. I didn't want to knock on the door and be weird. I decided to just leave them at the door and send a text when I was back in my car.

I sneakily dropped the boxes on his doorstep, my note facing the door. Then I shot him a text once I was back in the car.

Hey! Look outside your front door.

I drove home, not checking my messages until I parked in my driveway an hour later.

He had responded to my text with a picture of himself, a tissue sticking out of his nose.

Thanks.

I giggled at the picture and swooned at what he had texted next.

You're so sweet. I really like you, Sandi. Text me when you're home safe, okay?

Applause erupted. The godfather and I had absolutely killed our first set.

I turned to look at him and I couldn't stop my grin at what I saw.

The godfather was smiling, a real smile. Not the chameleon one he offered the world for other people's benefit, but a smile that reminded me of the sun peeking out of the clouds after rain.

Happy. He was really, really happy.

I hadn't seen him look like that in a long time.

He met my eyes and let his smile shine. Openly. Unashamedly.

I wanted to cry tears of joy.

I leaped off the stage. Our friends who had come to see us surrounded me.

"We're going to the Hobo after this!"

"I'm sooooo down!" I answered.

"Hey Sandi! Great job!" Georgia Boy cut through the crowd, beer in hand.

I smiled at him. "Thanks! How's your foot?"

He winced a little. "Still hurts, but it'll heal." He tipped his glass at me. "Hey. I really liked kayaking with you the other day. We should do it again sometime."

I still couldn't figure out how the kayaking trip happened. It was hard to say no to Georgia Boy's insistence. He was so damn infuriatingly enthusiastic and for some reason, I really didn't want to crush him.

"You're kayaking with who?" The godfather asked as I zipped up my water resistant jacket.

I sighed. "Georgia Boy."

"Chinstrap? But you said—"

"Yeah I know." I interrupted. "I have trouble turning people down sometimes, okay? And anyways, it's not a date."

He burst out laughing.

"What?" I put a bite on the end of the -t, throwing my hands up in the air.

"I'm impressed by how oblivious you can be sometimes."

"He's a youngin'. He probably just wants to butter me up so I'll throw him some overflow gigs."

The godfather let out a groan. "Sandi, the guy doesn't stop buying you beer."

"I don't know why you're complaining, I hand them all to you."

"Ugh." He grimaced. "I wish you'd at least tell him to buy something good."

I glanced at my phone. "I'm late."

"Where are you meeting him at?" The godfather asked, turning his attention back to the video game he was playing.

"The usual spot."

He gave me an amused look. "Sandi, that's literally two minutes up the road."

"I know! And I'm late!" I said, slipping on my flip flops and aiming for the door.

"Enjoy your date with Chinstrap!" The godfather called after me.

"It's not a date!" I said as I slammed the door behind me.

"Was it a date?" I thought to myself, holding the string of my kayak while slowly riding down the road. I hit a bump and wound the rope tighter around my hand.

I pulled into the parking lot to find Georgia Boy sitting in the back of his truck, playing a guitar I hadn't seen before.

Did he ever put that thing down?

I parked next to him. The anthem Could Have Been Me by The Struts abruptly ended as I cut the ignition and tumbled out of the vehicle.

"Sorry I'm late!"

He met me at my door, still holding his guitar. I glanced at it.

Someone had painted a sunset beach scene on it, birds flying in the sun's rays. Georgia Boy's name was painted on the top near the knobs.

But Georgia Boy wasn't looking at me. His eyes stared at the back of my SUV, his mouth agape in slight wonder.

"You weren't kidding."

"What?" I said, following his line of sight.

"You…" He pointed the neck of the guitar towards my kayak in the back. "You actually hold that thing by a string while you're driving."

"Oh." I said, walking towards the back to grab my kayak. "Yeah. I live just right down the road."

He followed me and stood at the back of my car, rubbing the back of his head. "Sandi, that's so dangerous."

I pushed the button to lift the trunk. "It's really fine."

"I've got some ties in my truck. You gotta let me show you how to secure it. It won't take long."

I was growing agitated so I changed the subject. "You ready to go?"

"Yeah!" He said, perking up. "Let me put this in my truck and I'll get your kayak for you."

He opened the back door of his truck and put the guitar up. I grabbed the end of my kayak and gave a quick pull, letting the bottom of the boat hit the dirt with a bang. I moved to grab the rope so I could begin pulling it into the water like I always did.

"Sandi wait." Georgia Boy said, moving quickly to assist me.

"It's really okay." I said as Georgia Boy bent over to pick up the kayak. "I do this all the time."

He wordlessly shouldered the boat, moving to put it in the water. I sighed, turning to grab my paddle and a bottle of water before closing the trunk. I slid my flip flops off my feet and shuffled them under the car.

Georgia Boy was already walking back, his face screwed up in concentration, saying nothing. I tied up my hair and hooked my car key to the string on my swimsuit and walked down to the boat, carefully avoiding the large rocks in the water that lined the shore. I took the paddle in one hand and steadied the boat with the other, sitting down, and waited.

His kayak was red. Because of course it was. Red shoes. Red hats. Red boat.

He gingerly stepped into the boat, making me wonder if he had ever gotten into a kayak before in his life.

I looked out towards the bay. It was a perfect day. The bay was calm with hardly any wind.

I started paddling out, calling over my shoulder to Georgia Boy. "I figured I'd show you the Hathaway!"

"The bridge?" He asked, paddling after me.

"You live on the beach, right?" I asked, aiming for a concrete dock slightly to the left that marked the halfway point. The current was calmer going that way instead of cutting straight across open water.

"How'd you know?"

I smiled. "Lucky guess."

"Well yeah. I have a condo out there."

We paddled in silence for a while. It was warm for February, a promise of spring lingered in the air. I breathed in the smell of salt and watched a bird dive for a fish.

"Sandi..."

I stopped paddling and turned to look at Georgia Boy.

"I don't want to look." He stuck out his foot.

Blood was trickling out of a long cut on the sole of his foot.

"Oh, Georgia Boy." I said, trying to hold back a small laugh.

"Don't say anything else." He said, closing his eyes and sticking his hurt foot back into the boat. He closed his eyes and took a deep breath. "I just won't think about it."

"How'd you cut it?"

"On those rocks when I put your kayak in. I sliced my foot right open as soon as I stepped in. Why are there so many sharp rocks everywhere?"

I started paddling again. "I'm sorry, I didn't think about mentioning it. The rocks are there because they help protect the shoreline. They usually build a bit of a seawall. They're scattered right now because of the Hurricane."

"Oh, Hurricane Michael?"

"Yep."

"That was a bad one. The beach didn't get too much."

"Mhm."

He noted the tension on my face. "Were you affected by it?"

I wanted to laugh bitterly.

Affected? Try my life was completely turned upside down. Try I lost my home, my lover, my friends, my hair, my sanity—my hope—my entire town because of it.

But I just gave the answer I always offered to people who couldn't possibly understand. "I did better than most."

He pulled his kayak next to mine, looking down at his foot as he paddled. "I really hope I don't attract sharks."

I couldn't contain it, I laughed then.

"What's so funny?"

"You really aren't from around here, are you?" I said. We reached the dock. "I like to go under, not around." I turned my head toward him and wiggled my eyebrows. "Duck."

I didn't wait for him to heed my instructions before lying back on my kayak, the bottom of the bridge overhead. The sound was slightly muted here, the only sound the waves lapping on the barnacle covered posts.

After we passed under, Georgia Boy continued the conversation. "Nope. I'm from the good ol' United States of Georgia."

Oh boy.

"But I lived in Texas for nine years." He finished.

"You poor thing."

"Hey! Don't let anyone from Texas hear you say that!"

I chuckled softly, rolling my eyes. "Everything may be bigger in Texas, but everything's crazier in Florida. I'd like to see them try and say something."

"A Florida girl, huh?"

"Through and through." I gazed towards our destination. "We're halfway there." I stopped paddling, looking to the left before letting my eyes flicker towards Georgia Boy. "I'd like to show you something first. Let's paddle closer to shore."

When we reached the shore, an idea popped in my head. I let Georgia Boy catch up to me and turned my kayak to point towards his. I grabbed the bottle of water I had brought with me and took a sip, then unzipped my jacket and shrugged it off.

I wasn't wearing a revealing swimsuit. It was more sporty, my high waisted bottoms acting as shorts and my top only exposing a piece of my midriff, covering my chest completely.

But Georgia Boy, almost imperceptibly if I wasn't specifically looking for it, let his gaze sweep over my body before turning his head towards the shore, dropping one hand from the paddle and rubbing the back of his head.

A date, then.

My lips quirked up at the corners.

Oh my sweet summer child.

I motioned with my paddle. "So up here, you'll see clearly where the storm stopped."

"What do you mean?"

"You'll see."

We easily paddled down the shoreline, our kayaks cutting through the water like diamonds on glass. When we reached the spot, I beckoned for Georgia Boy to join me. After he pulled up beside me, I set my paddle down by my side pointing towards the trees.

"What am I looking at?"

"Do you see the line?"

Georgia Boy squinted. "The trees are leaning."

133

"Mhm." I said in confirmation.

On the left hand side, the trees that were left standing tilted. Vines began reclaiming the fallen ones, the underbrush thick and wild. The right hand side looked untouched, magnolias blooming, their fragrance reaching me across the water. Pine trees stood tall and dogwoods swayed in the gentle breeze. Large oaks cast a shadow over the bay.

On the left, destruction. On the right, beauty. The beauty I fell in love with as a child.

Home.

"Wow." Georgia Boy began. "The difference is so… distinct."

I gave a slight nod. "I like to come here and remind myself."

He waited, but I didn't offer more. "Remind yourself of what?"

I stared at the magnolias and thought of the tree in the backyard of my home. I had always hoped it would bloom again, but it had been two and a half years since the Hurricane, and the magnolia tree hadn't bloomed once. A branch had fallen off it earlier that month, proving my hopes ill founded.

The godfather offered to cut it down for firewood. I hadn't let him yet.

Not yet.

I shook my head to clear the memories, remembering Georgia Boy had asked me a question. "I like to remind myself that life is completely random sometimes. Why did the storm stop here?" I threw out my hand towards the boundary line in the trees.

Death and life. Life and death.

"I had neighbors who left for the storm in the middle of the night and their house was completely destroyed. It's an empty lot now." I lightly touched the water with my fingers. "Then I have neighbors who left in the night who ended up riding out the storm as their friends' house blew apart around them." I looked in the direction of the Hathaway, still not visible yet. "Random. Completely random."

Georgia Boy said nothing, but continued to look towards the trees.

"Townside. Beachside." I continued. "The townside was destroyed while the beachside was left virtually untouched." I turned my focus back on the trees. "One tree stands while the one next to it leans." I picked up my paddle from my side and placed it in my lap. "Sometimes life chooses for you." I smiled, putting one side of the paddle in the water. "It's terrifying and strangely comforting to know some things are just out of your control."

Georgia Boy followed my lead and started paddling, too, continuing our trek toward the Hathaway. "Did you ride out the storm?"

"Yes." I said simply.

"Do you regret it?"

I thought about it like I had so many times before. "No. I did the best I could with the information I had at the time. It… exploded so quickly. Hindsight is always 20/20." The storm hit land at 162 miles per hour, only one of four storms in history to ever hit the United States mainland at a category 5. Mexico Beach got the worst of it, followed by Lynn Haven and Callaway. My paddle slapped the water rhythmically. "My writing exploded after the hurricane. Some good can come out of even the worst situations."

"Your writing?"

"Yes. I wrote a book. Two actually, but the first one sucked." I perked up. "Hey. There it is." I said, pointing.

The Hathaway was finally visible in the distance, the bridge that connected townside to beachside peeked out of a light fog.

"Hey! You really can see it from here. I'm surprised. It seems so far away. It took me a good half hour to get over here. I'd never been to Lynn Haven."

I looked at Georgia Boy and smiled. "Water connects everything." I considered before offering voluntarily, "When I was a kid, I used to call it the half-a-way bridge. Because it was half the way to the beach. I think I was like sixteen before I knew any different."

Georgia Boy laughed, paddling a bit further than me, taking a moment to stare out at the bridge. The bay melted into the Gulf of Mexico not too far from where we floated, brackish water turning from brown to a beautiful deep blue.

He turned his kayak to face me, the waves slapping our boats the only sound.

"Thank you for showing me, Sandi."

I said nothing, but offered a small smile before turning my boat back towards the way we came.

After we had loaded the kayaks back up, Georgia boy limping to push mine into the trunk, we faced each other. I put my jacket back on, slipped on my flip flops and unclipped my car key.

"Well, that was fun." Georgia Boy said.

We didn't hug goodbye.

"Yeah. It was fun." I said to Georgia Boy, exiting the memory and gazing towards the doors leading to the inside bar of the Taproom. The godfather had just walked through them. "Hey, listen. I need to talk to the godfather. Thanks for coming out!"

I half jogged towards the door without waiting for Georgia Boy's response. I looked around for the godfather but didn't see him.

Thinking he must be in the bathroom, I pulled out my phone to look for a text from Sk8er Boi. I had texted him at the house long before I left for my gig with exciting news.

Hey! Good news! You can stay over Beatdown date night!

My sister agreed to get all the kids out of the house. She happened to be babysitting for a friend that night and the kids would all have a big sleepover. The godfather was staying with Jacqueline so I could have the bed.

My plan was to introduce Sk8er Boi to everyone that night after Beatdown, meeting my friends at a local bar. My sister would come over alone in the morning to meet him.

No text from Sk8er Boi though. I frowned slightly. It wasn't usual for him to not get back with me for so long.

I checked the time stamp on my text. I sent the message three hours ago.

The godfather emerged from the bathroom and I ran to him, throwing my hands around his neck.

"I love you." I said.

"I love you, too, Sandi." He squeezed me back.

"Forever?"

"Forever."

We pulled away and I cupped his face in my hands.

"Listen. We go and do the Beatdown on the Beach gig exactly like this. This is the sound." The godfather continued. "Now come on, break's over."

I nodded, patting his right cheek before frowning slightly. "Hey. What does it mean when a guy doesn't text you for hours when he usually texts you back within fifteen minutes."

"That he has a life." The godfather answered as I let my hands drop. "Or that he's—"

"With another girl, yeah."

"It *is* Friday night." He said. We started walking back towards the stage. "You're not exclusive."

"I know." I said sadly.

"Have you been seeing anyone else?"

"No." I said. "I haven't wanted to."

"Except Chinstrap." He said.

I looked over and found Georgia Boy in the crowd. "It was barely a date."

"Does he know that?"

"We didn't even hug. Plus, he's too young for me."

"How old is he anyway?"

"I'm not actually sure. At least 21 if he's drinking." I said, stepping up onto the platform. "But definitely off limits for me. Plus…" I looked for him in the crowd again. "He's too…"

"I know what you mean."

"He's nice and I don't want to hurt his feelings." I paused. "I could probably sleep with him and he wouldn't be so interested anymore."

"How is that logical?" The godfather fitted the guitar strap around his shoulder, moving to turn the PA system back on. "Or are you that terrible in—"

I smacked his arm.

"It's what happens." I said. "Men are interested until they sleep with you and then they lose interest." I was still looking at Georgia Boy, considering. "It might be fun."

"So you're going to sleep with Chinstrap?"

"Yeah." I said finally. "Why not? Like you said—oh thank you!" Bartender had brought me a sour. "I'm not exclusive with Sk8er Boi."

"I wonder about you sometimes." The godfather said, strumming an open E chord.

My phone buzzed then, it was Sk8er Boi.

His text offered no explanation for why it took hours to respond. I frowned at the message, putting my phone in my pocket.

I had made my decision.

I downed the sour and asked Bartender for another one over the mic.

My next most lucid memory is of Georgia Boy gripping my thighs. We were sitting on a bench outside the Salty Hobo.

Actually, lying. We were lying on the bench. A soft rain beginning to fall.

Next thing I know, I'm opening my eyes to a beautiful beach scene. A large window covered the entire wall and the sun had just peeked over the horizon of the Gulf of Mexico.

I sat up slightly on my side and looked around the room without turning over. Clothes were strewn all over the floor, the bed was in the middle of the room at an angle.

And it was cold. The window was open and I could hear the waves of the Gulf crashing on the sand.

I felt someone next to me and silently rolled over to see Georgia Boy's sleeping face, his hand resting on my hip.

Chapter 10

A crown of silver

"I'm losing my hair."

"What?"

"I'm losing my hair!" I cry.

I woke up that morning and it was just gone. A small patch of hair right at the front of my scalp just disappeared.

So I did what every person shouldn't do.

I googled it.

The word "Alopecia" popped up on the screen.

"Please see a dermatologist," was the recommendation.

I did. This morning.

"Alopecia." They repeated. "It's temporary. Have you been stressed?"

I smiled and felt like crying.

Living and feel like dying.

Have I been stressed?

Hilarious. Absolutely hilarious.

They don't talk about losing your hair after Hurricanes. They talk about insurance and the triple rent. They talk about property values and community togetherness.

But not about your hair. Your glorious hair that has always been a great joy in your life.

Ash brown and lovely, it cascades down your back. It's starting to be speckled with grey, two kids and your late 20s will do it to you.

But still, it's your crown. Just with some silver.

And it fell off.

My hair. My beautiful hair.

One more thing the hurricane wants to take from me.

It wasn't enough to drive me from my house? It wasn't enough to take my roof? You have to take what grows at the top of my head, too?

They give me a shot right in the middle of the perfectly hairless circle. They remove three moles, too. Might as well while I'm there.

"Just finished a conference where they said Allegra has been successfully used to treat this. Take one every day. It's not serious. You'll get your hair back in no time."

It's not serious.

My scalp burns and goes numb, I replace my headband.

Just temporary, like recovery after a storm.

"This doesn't define me." I repeat to myself over and over and over on my drive home. "You're alive. You're okay. It's just hair. It grows back."

"It's just stuff," comes the familiar echo. "You can get more stuff."

Will my hair fall out more if I cry about this? I can hold my whole life together after disaster, but I can't stress about it?

Your body will betray you no matter how well you handle it.

"You're so strong."

Am I though? My hair is falling out.

Another friend moving away, another is looking for a new job elsewhere. I hear a story about another person who cracked because businesses don't pay PTO for trying to piece your life back together.

A loved one is being put on more medication, because it's probably better to be over medicated and a zombie than dead because you can't.take.it.anymore.

"Stop being dramatic."

It can be covered with a hairband and some bobby-pins, part it like this and they can't even tell.

Put on a smile and look people in the eye, if you quirk your lips like this they can't even tell.

That you're dying. That you're struggling under the weight of trying to make the summer days fun and exciting for your kids who are more resilient than their mother.

That you're crying. Silent sobs that rack your chest and scream out the words you can't form with your lips.

"It's just stuff. You can get more stuff."

"It's just hair. It will grow back."

"It's just temporary. In two years it will be different."

But between the loss and the new, what do you do?

What's the advice for the in-between? That space between point A and point B?

Time. It's a slow taskmaster.

Have you ever tried to count the breaths you take in a minute?

You stop breathing.

Have you ever tried to count the hairs on your head?

You stop caring.

9 months post disaster and you've given birth to something you've never wanted. It comes out screaming and needing and wanting and demanding.

All the repercussions of carrying something that's too heavy for anybody.

How do you set down an invisible weight?

Reading self-help books didn't keep my hair in.

Therapy didn't keep my hair in.

All the inner strength built up over years didn't keep my body from attacking the wrong cells.

You start to wonder where you went wrong in life to end up here. You think about what you could have done differently, what exactly you did to deserve this.

Still holding on to the measure of control that was never there. Trying to self-improve yourself out of the chances of random terrible life events.

But no. You can't continue down this path. Stress will just make more hair fall out.

"It's just hair. It will grow back."

Your chest heaves and the sobs come. This can't be good for your hair line. This can't be good for your blood pressure.

Stress makes you gain weight, too. Is that why you've been sporting an extra 20lbs?

You pull in your driveway. "Oh look. Another neighbor's sold their house."

You take a breath. Set your shoulders.

Another day, and it really is just hair.

You really will wear headbands, they'll become your staple. And you'll stitch the gap with bobby pins.

Because that's what you do. You take a coverup and make it a fashion trend.

You take pain and make it something beautiful.

You create meaning out of the terrible.

That's who you are. You're an artist and you paint with pain and turn it into something like hope.

You really will be happy again. You may even laugh today, in the next ten minutes when your son shows you a new building he's made in Minecraft.

But for now, you let yourself feel sorry for yourself.

You let out all those emotions no one likes to talk about.

You know you have to feel every hurt and disappointment.

You must feel it so your joy can run as deep as the pain that carved out a chasm.

After all, this is just a chapter in your story, babe.

And you're fixing to turn the page.

The fall

"Well." I breathe. "I live here now."

I fell backward, my skis becoming trapped beneath me under a snowbank.

I didn't see the sharp curve in the trail coming before crashing into a tree. My bonus mom is far ahead and I have been lying here for several minutes.

I've already tried punching the button on my skis with my sticks to release the boots, but the angle is so weird I haven't managed it yet.

"What a metaphor for my life." I sigh at the sky.

142

At least the view is quite something.

I look around under my hood, taking in the frosting capped trees. Alaska was something out of a fairytale.

I blink my eyes to clear the snow flurries from them. It's really coming down today. At this rate, no one will ever find me. I'll just become a part of the snowbank.

"This is how you die." I think to myself.

My mind flashes to another mountain, me complaining and saying that same phrase.

My boyfriend looks at me and smiles before saying something I'll never forget.

Salty Hobo 2

I slammed my front door, breathing hard.

"If things don't work out with Sk8er Boi!" I called through the house. "I'm never dating another athlete. Ever. Again."

"You know!" A voice echoed from the master bedroom. "Most people give a greeting when they first walk in the door!"

I stomped towards the master bedroom door, which was already ajar. I unceremoniously flung it open and found the godfather at his desk, playing video games.

"Also." He drawled, not looking up. "It's not a good idea to change yourself for someone you're dating."

My hands were on my knees, my breathing still labored. "I'm not changing myself. I'm trying to relate to his hobbies."

"He's a runner. You…" He gestured vaguely in my direction. "… are not."

"He asked me to run a 5k with him in May. I'm training. I've been working out consistently for months anyway." I stood, sliding the sweatband off my head.

The godfather said nothing, just shook his head incredulously.

I hopped in the shower. Only a week left before Sk8er Boi and I went to Beatdown.

I hadn't seen him in a couple weeks, he had been busy with work and was now skiing in Colorado for a bachelor party.

I hadn't heard from him for a whole day during his trip, but then I received a mysterious message from an iCloud account.

Guess who lost his phone in the first ski?

My heart fluttered at the message.

No way.

Yep. Anyway. Just wanted to be sure you knew I wasn't dead.

I held the phone to my chest. He cared enough to let me know he lost his phone.

I exited the shower, my hair wet, wearing an oversized t-shirt with leggings.

"Godfather."

"Yeah."

I slid down the front of the dresser we shared. "I'm in trouble."

"Why?"

"I like…" I beat my head against the dresser. "I really, really like Sk8er Boi."

"It's not a bad thing."

"It's not a good thing."

"Why?"

I ducked my head. "Because I want him to ask me to be exclusive."

"Why is that bad?" He clicked a button on his headset. "Guys, I'll be right back." He took his headset off and turned in his chair towards me.

"Because." I started.

"Because…"

I shrugged.

"Listen." He pinched the bridge of his nose. "This is the first guy you've caught feelings for since your ex. Except maybe—"

"Fiddle Guy. Yeah."

"I actually saw him the other day."

"Really? How was—"

The godfather clapped once, regaining my attention. "Here's what you're going to do, Sandi. You listening?"

"Yeah."

"Good. You're gonna go to Beatdown on the Beach, you're gonna chill the fuck out."

"Chill the fuck out." I repeated to myself.

"Exactly. And you're going to have an amazing time and not think about wedding rings."

"I'm not—"

"Thinking too far ahead into the future? That's exactly what you're doing." He used his stern voice on me. "Stop thinking about which retirement plans are best for you and just have a good fucking time with the guy you like."

"We're millennials. We don't get retirement plans."

He ignored me, putting his hands up and making a rainbow motion. "Enjoy yourself."

I closed my eyes and groaned. "I'm just…"

Just scared of what would happen if I suffered another heartbreak so soon. Just intimidated by how much I actually cared for him.

"…I just really like him." I finished lamely.

"You can do that and also…" He made the rainbow motion again. "Chill the fuck out."

"Chill. The. Fuck. Out." I took a deep breath. "Chill the fuck out." I said again.

"You got this." The godfather went back to his game.

I stood up, walking into my living room. The kids were still in school for another half hour. My sister at work.

I had a gig that night and then planned to see Georgia Boy at a late show at the Salty Hobo 2, Salty Hobo's sinister sister. Him and Beanie seemed to be doing well, booking shows at bars I played in often.

Georgia Boy hadn't said much that morning after we hooked up. I was friendly, trying to make conversation.

We rode in the elevator down to the parking lot in silence. He stiffened as I kissed his cheek.

My neck hurt a little. I guess we were a little enthusiastic that night, probably alcohol induced. The bed had moved all the way from the wall to the center of the room.

He drove me back to my car. I had left it at the Taproom. I found myself trying to make small talk, but he didn't help move the conversation along.

Oh, well. Maybe my theory about him getting what he wanted and subsequently chilling out was right.

Back at home, I made myself breakfast before doing my work out, checking my phone when I was done. Georgia Boy had texted me.

Last night was fun! Thanks for being so cool.

He had added an emoji with sunglasses for emphasis.

I stared at my phone, amused.

Cool. *Cool.*

I checked the timestamp, curious.

He had sent the message at exactly 10am, not a minute before or after.

My lips curled into a smile.

I drove to Salty Hobo 2 in silence, gathering my thoughts after my show.

I ended up having to park across the street on the side of the road, the parking lot of Salty Hobo 2 was packed. I touched up my makeup in the car and took two ibuprofen before sprinting across the road.

"Hey baby. You performing tonight?" A patron called after me.

"Not tonight!" I said, swinging open the front door.

It was a smoking bar, hence the ibuprofen. I coughed upon entering, screwing up my nose at the smell. Georgia Boy and Beanie were on the stage. They had a drummer with them that night.

I went to the bar and ordered a gin and tonic.

"Lime, Sandi?"

"Always."

I turned towards the stage, looking for a seat. Georgia Boy's parents waved me over from a table near the stage.

"Hey! Good to see you!" His mom greeted me.

I really needed to get better with names.

George—like my dad's name—asked me where I had played that night. Beanie called from the stage. "Oh! Sandi MarLisa's here!"

I smiled at him and looked at Georgia Boy.

His eyebrows were furrowed, a tight smile on his face.

"What do you think of my son?" George asked.

"I'm sorry?"

"The music!" He yelled over the crowd.

"Oh! Right. He's great!"

I chatted up Georgia Boy's parents until the boys' first break. Beanie and Georgia Boy coming to stand at the table.

"Hey girl." Georgia Boy greeted me.

"Hey, Georgia Boy."

He smiled, but it didn't meet his eyes.

I took him in for a moment. He was clean shaven, except for the chinstrap. He wore his usual uniform, a baseball cap backwards and the infamous red shoes.

"Want another drink?" He pointed to my empty glass.

"Sure." I said, smiling.

"What is it?"

I looked down at my glass and shook the ice. "A gin and tonic."

Georgia Boy leaned in to hear me better over the noise of the bar. "A what?"

"A. Gin. And. Tonic." I enunciated.

He backed up, a confused expression on his face. "What's that? Like gin and water?"

"Um…"

"Girl, you better come with me." He said, motioning towards the bar.

He seemed agitated, his body language stiff, his face taut. He didn't look at me as we walked, but kept his chin up, staring straight ahead.

Reaching the bar, he leaned an elbow on the counter, motioning for the bartender with the other hand.

"A Jack and Coke and…" He made a gesture with his hand, willing me to share my drink order.

"A Gin and tonic." I finished.

"With lime." The bartender said, smiling at me. It wasn't a question this time.

"That's right." I smiled back.

Georgia Boy was looking at me with that same tight expression, his eyes narrowed.

"Great show tonight." I offered. "I like the sound with the drums."

Georgia Boy looked towards the stage. "Yeah. He's Beanie's friend. I think it's going alright."

"It's nice of your parents to come to so many of your shows. They seem really supportive."

Georgia Boy focused his attention back on me. His gaze became assessing. "Nice of you to come by. Papa Joe's tonight?"

"No. Oasis Lounge." I pointed in the general direction. "Just right down the street."

"Right. I'm supposed to play there soon."

"It's a rowdy spot." I squeezed the lime into my drink. "You seem to be doing well. You're getting all kinds of gigs."

He took a sip of his Jack and Coke. "Yeah. The cover stuff is great but what I really want is to do more originals. I've got a song I'm working on —"

"Hurricane." I finished for him.

His eyes widened before he lifted his eyebrows in mock surprise. "Oh, so you listen."

I stood up straighter and raised my eyebrows, mocking his expression. "Yes. You'll find my ears work just fine."

He tipped his head back and laughed then, all tension releasing from his face in an instant. "I'm just not used to it." He said, patting my arm and saying, "Come on girl, let's head back to everyone else."

I grabbed my drink and followed him, winding my way through pool tables and drunk patrons.

I stayed for the remainder of the show, which went well past one in the morning. Between Georgia Boy and his dad, I didn't pay for a single drink for the rest of the night.

After the boys had loaded up, Georgia Boy, Beanie and I went out to the back deck of the bar to get out of the smoke's line of fire.

"Ah! I can breathe!" I said, throwing my hands up in the air.

"Yeah." Georgia Boy said, another Jack and Coke in his hand. "It's rough in there."

"My voice is gone." Beanie added.

"You guys did great though!" I said, taking a seat at one of the outside tables.

We talked for hours about everything. The best venues, what to charge, what musicians and bands to check out.

Soon, the Gin was directing me to signal to Georgia Boy that I'd like a repeat of events from the other night. When I thought Beanie wasn't looking, I'd quickly kiss Georgia Boy's neck, rub his back or make a long sweep up his thigh.

Georgia Boy pretended not to notice, but didn't make a move to stop my advances.

Eventually, Beanie became preoccupied with his phone, looking up some information we were discussing. Georgia Boy turned to me, seemingly amused, and whispered.

"Girl. What are you doing?"

I flashed him my best "come hither" smile.

Georgia Boy sighed, looking up at the sky with a pained expression on his face. "Beanie, I think I'm heading home."

I looked down at my phone. It was three in the morning.

We walked out to the parking lot together, stopping for a few more minutes and talking. Once Beanie left to find his car and was safely out of earshot, Georgia Boy turned to me.

"Where are you parked?"

I wordlessly pointed across the street towards my car.

"Come on." He said, patting my shoulder. "I'll walk you."

I guess we would be taking my car that night.

The parking lot was mostly empty, the bar would close in half an hour. We crossed the dimly lit road until arriving at my driver's side door.

"Well, thanks for coming out to my show and hanging out." Georgia Boy said.

"Of course!" I said. "It was a good time."

His eyes flickered towards the driver's door behind me.

Oh.

Oh.

"R-right." I stammered. I tossed my hair behind my shoulder, trying to recover. "I guess I'll see you around."

"Drive safe, Sandi." Georgia Boy patted my shoulder again and turned to walk towards his truck.

I opened my car door, sitting down and slamming the door. I then put my head on the steering wheel, pounding it a few times before starting up the engine.

I had been dismissed.

I had been royally, incredibly, embarrassingly and unequivocally dismissed.

By Georgia Boy. Georgia Boy who had spent the last month seeking me out at every show of mine he could possibly catch. Georgia Boy who couldn't stop buying me beers.

I must've been really, really bad in bed.

"Jesus tap dancing Christ." I let the phrase fly out of my mouth. It was something my friends and I said in high school.

I drove the half hour it took to get home in complete silence, mulling over what had just happened.

Wow. Had I made a fool out of myself. I thought I was giving advances that were wanted, but as it turned out I was just throwing myself at a guy who was not at all interested in hooking up again.

I thought about my theory. Clearly I was onto something.

Ever want a guy to leave you alone? Show some interest.

Even sexual interest.

Maybe *especially* sexual interest.

"Jesus tap dancing CHRIST." I said again into the darkness.

Chapter 11

The Shepherd

I click my boots into the skis, the cold biting my hands even through my gloves.

"This is a fun run." My bonus mom says, already upright in her skis. "You get to go down a big hill at the end."

My dad is ahead of us on the trail, Boo Bear softly padding through the snow in a trot beside him.

I securely attach my skis and begin to glide.

"It's a lot like roller skating!" My bonus mom calls over her shoulder. "You're lucky you're getting instructions! Your dad told me I had to figure it out for myself."

I laugh, thinking to myself that her last sentence described my entire childhood.

My dad sat me down with my W2 at my computer when I was sixteen. I needed to file my first tax return.

"Numbers. Boxes." He pointed at the W2. "Numbers match the boxes." He pointed at the screen. "Have at it." He gave me a slap on the back before leaving to coach his swim team.

"It's a clear day." My bonus mom continues. "Full moon tonight. We may even see the Northern Lights!"

"That would be so sweet!"

A German Shepherd rounds a corner on the trail, Boo Bear runs to meet him.

They sniff at each other, the owner of the other dog calling around the corner.

Growls suddenly ripple from the dogs. Boo Bear lets out a bark.

"Hey!" My dad yells, aiming to grab Boo Bear.

"Boo Bear!" My bonus mom takes off.

I glide to a halt, watching the scene unfold before me.

The German Shepherd attacks Boo Bear's neck. Boo Bear lets out a yelp.

"This is how you die." The thought flashes through my head as my father falls over, reaching for the dogs.

Relief Skate Shop

"Bonnie! Ugh." Sk8er Boi bended over in the threshold of my house to scoop up the puppy. "No, no." He tapped her nose before looking at me. "Sorry. She's just happy to see you." He raised his eyebrows at me. "And so am I."

I laughed. "It's okay, my sister has a puppy, too." I walked to the kitchen to get cleaning supplies and returned to find Sk8er Boi in my living room watching Bonnie play on the floor.

I moved to clean up the mess by the door, but he grabbed my waist, pulling me in close.

"Hey." He breathed in my ear.

"Hey." My eyes fluttered closed, breathing in his scent.

"I'm excited for our date tonight." His voice was low and mind-melting.

"Mmmm." I groaned softly. "Me too."

Sk8er Boi took the cleaning supplies from me and cleaned up Bonnie's mess. I knelt down and played with the puppy, lightly batting her face.

"She likes you." Sk8er Boi said, entering the living room again. "Bonnie and I have a few things in common it seems."

I looked up at him and smiled before rising to my feet. "I'll show you where to put your stuff."

I walked him to the master bedroom and directed him to put his bag on the desk. The godfather had washed the sheets for me and the whole house would be empty tonight.

Sk8er Boi set down his bag and looked around. His eyes went to my bookcases first, they lined every wall.

"Nietzsche?" He aimed the question in my direction.

"Yep." I bit my lip.

"Wasn't he a terrible person?"

"Eh. I don't think so. He has some interesting ideas worth thinking about."

"And you think about them?"

I used my best theatrical voice, paraphrasing. "'Whoever battles monsters should make sure he does not become a monster himself. And when you gaze into the abyss, the abyss also looks into you.'" I gave a half smile. "I think about a lot of things, Sk8er Boi."

He wiggled his eyebrows at me. "Do you think about me?"

"Right now I'm thinking about brunch." I quipped.

"Well, let's go." He said.

We put some food and water in the laundry room for Bonnie and left out the side door under the carport.

"So where to?" Sk8er Boi asked, turning the steering wheel of his mustang to the left.

"Let's go to the Taproom! It's in St. Andrews. The food truck today has an amazing brunch."

We arrived, ordering our food at the food truck before walking through the gates of the outdoor courtyard.

"Hey Sandi!" Jacob called from his seat.

"Hey! Good to see you." I walked over to pet his dog.

"You playing today?"

"Nah, night off." I looked over to where Sk8er Boi had taken a seat at a table. "Gotta date."

I waved hi to Boss Man and Bartender as I took the chair opposite Sk8er Boi.

"Can't take you anywhere." He smiled.

We got our food, Crab cake Benedict with Hollandaise sauce, and listened to a local musician play while the bar chattered around us.

"Isn't Relief Skate Shop around here?" Sk8er Boi asked.

"It's Downtown Harrison. It's not far."

"Sandi." Sk8er Boi smiled.

"What?"

"Terms like Downtown Harrison, St. Andrews, Lynn Haven don't mean anything to me. It's all Panama City Beach to us non-locals."

I rolled my eyes. "There's so much more to this town than the beach."

We hit Relief Skate Shop. As Sk8er Boi browsed the skateboards displayed on the wall, I looked at the t-shirts on a rack.

"Oh my god no way!" I exclaimed.

"What?" Sk8er Boi walked over to see what I was talking about.

"Dante's Inferno!"

I picked up the paint splattered t-shirt with the Relief logo on the front. On the back was a huge colored picture of a devil with sharp teeth, horns and a pencil mustache. His mouth hung wide open.

"What is it?" Sk8er Boi asked.

"Oh! It's classic. We used to have an amusement park here called Miracle Strip. I have so many memories of going to that park as a kid. The owners sold the property and the park was shut down. We were all so heartbroken about it. My favorite rides were Dante's Inferno and the Abominable Snow Monster." I smiled, staring at the image. "Shipwreck Waterpark was right across the street."

I stopped my rant and suddenly burst into song. "Splashing all day and screaming after dark. Shipwreck Island and Miracle Strip Park!"

Sk8er Boi laughed, shaking his head at me.

I continued beaming at the shirt. "Bartender has Dante tattooed on her arm."

"Wow. So it's a thing."

"It's a thing." I said, putting the t-shirt back.

"Why don't you get it?" Sk8er Boi asked.

I looked at the price tag. "It's thirty dollars."

"And you love it. So get it." He grabbed a t-shirt he wanted for himself and walked over to the register without another word.

I thought about it. I really didn't buy things for myself. I always bought things for the kids and most of my money went to bills or paying off debt from the divorce.

I looked at Sk8er Boi handing the cashier his debit card.

You know what? Yeah. Yeah, I did love this shirt.

I grabbed a size medium and stood next to Sk8er Boi at the register, the cashier handing him his bagged purchase.

She rang me up and handed me a sticker with my receipt.

"Oh my god it's Dante!" I turned my head to grin at Sk8er Boi. "I love stickers! I put them on my keyboard."

He smiled. "Here." He reached into his bag. "Take mine, too."

I squealed in delight.

"Do you have an Abominable Snowman sticker by chance?" I asked the cashier.

She checked the basket of stickers. "Looks like we're out. We'll order more soon."

We left Relief and headed for Sk8er Boi's car.

"What is it?" Sk8er Boi asked.

My hand was on the handle of the mustang but my head had turned towards my friend Sierra's tattoo shop.

I looked at Sk8er Boi and smiled. "You wanna meet Sierra?"

"Sure!"

We stashed our bags in the car before hurrying across the street. When we arrived at Thistle & Thorne, I checked the door. It opened easily.

"Sierra!" I called.

She was on her hands and knees working on the flooring. "Sandi!" She said, looking up at me.

Lauren was fixing something on the wall, grunting.

Sk8er Boi stood a step behind me.

"There's someone I want you to meet." I said, looking back at him.

He looked so handsome. He wore a backwards black baseball cap, black jeans and white shirt that made his tan skin look even darker.

"Sierra, Lauren, this is Sk8er Boi. Sk8er Boi this is Lauren and Sierra."

They greeted each other and started making small talk.

"Hey…" A deep voice came from the back of the shop.

"Oh Michael!" I said, running to give him a hug. "I didn't see you back there."

"Weird. I'm standing right in front of you, Sandi."

"And you're over six foot. Kinda hard to miss!"

"I'm actually leaving." He started walking towards the front door. "Good to meet you, man." He gave Sk8er Boi a nod.

Sierra took Sk8er Boi to the tattoo shop in the back, showing him around. Lauren sat quietly on a vintage sofa eating lunch.

My phone vibrated. It was Michael.

I like that guy. His ego isn't dripping out of him.

I can't tell if you're being sarcastic.

LOL I was around him for like 30 seconds.

How dare you think I'd be an asshole after 30 seconds

Unless he was like going out of his way to be a douche. Which he wasn't.

I chuckled to myself.

Bahahaha. Thanks though. He's pretty great so far. I ship it.

Sk8er Boi and Sierra walked back to the front, Sierra commenting on the artist's work on his arm sleeve.

"Well." I said. "We'll go ahead and head out so we're not in the way. I know you're working." I snapped my fingers. "Oh! Sierra!"

"Hm?" Sierra asked.

"I need to set up my thirtieth birthday tattoo!"

"Oh that's right!"

I set up the date with Sierra before Sk8er Boi and I said our goodbyes, leaving the shop.

"Your friends seem cool." He said on the way back to the car.

"They are." I smiled, looking at him. "You'll meet more of them tonight."

"I can't wait."

We arrived back at my place to change into our clothes for that night. Sk8er Boi rolled up a joint and then discovered a disc golf goal in my backyard, beginning to play.

"Your turn!" He said, handing me the discs.

I groaned. "You know I'm terrible at this. Remember when we played?"

"You got... close."

I huffed, giving him a side eye and handing him the joint.

"But seriously. Why are you so bad if you have a goal in your backyard?"

"It's the godfather's." I said, throwing my first disc.

It went over the back fence.

Sk8er Boi laughed. "I'll go get it."

He ran to the back fence and put his hands on the top, easily pulling himself up and straddling it.

"There's a dog back here!' He yelled at me.

I jogged to the back. "Yeah it's a husky. He's friendly."

Sk8er Boi looked back at me with the joint hanging from his mouth. He indicated for me to come take it from him.

I walked up a few paces, then paused. I put up my hands and shaped my fingers into an L and a 7.

"Yeah." I said, framing his image between my hands. "Exactly like that."

He took another drag and held the joint out to me. I took it before Sk8er Boi disappeared over the fence.

Chapter 12

Waterparks and Snow Tubing

"Mommy! Mommy! Mommy!" Lorelai squeals. "Can we go to the wave pool?"

"But I want to go down the big slide!" Judah points.

I smile tiredly. One of my fans tipped me in Shipwreck Waterpark tickets for the weekend. I worked until 2am the night before and had two shows later that day.

My bandmates and I had just formed the four piece band, practicing weekly. The four of us were invited individually to perform at Play Music on the Porch Day in St. Andrews, an event where local musicians volunteered to stand on street corners and in front of shops, making music all day for pedestrians.

We decided to combine forces and make the summer day a small practice run before our big debut at the Taproom.

But first, mom duties.

"Guys. We have five hours before mommy has to go to work. We have time to do it all.'

"Yay!" The kids giggle as they race off in front of me, their bare feet padding in the puddles.

"Come on Sandi!" My dad calls. The hook on his snow tube drags him up the mountain.

I sigh under my neck warmer and parka.

It's so freaking cold.

My bonus mom steps beside me, holding on to her tube in the wind. The wind gusts are about sixty miles an hour and we are the only people who signed up for the experience.

"So, just hand the handle of your tube to him and he'll hook you to the pulley system. Here, just go after me."

My bonus mom walks up to the attendant and hands him the handle attached to a rubber string on the tube. She sits down in the tube before he hooks her to the pulley and she takes off up the mountain, waving at me with her gloved hand, snow pants and boots peeking over the bottom of the tube.

I walk over to the attendant and imitate my bonus mom.

I exhale quickly as the pulley drags me up, up, up the mountain. A frosted wind blows around me, my hood snapping back from my head.

I had to sign a waiver earlier. The cashier asked my parents while pointing at me, "Is she older than twenty one?"

Everyone laughed.

I took off my hood, smiling. "I'm thirty."

"O-oh." She said, slightly embarrassed.

"It's okay. It happens all the time. I was once carded at Chuck-E-Cheese while I was there for my son's birthday. The door attendant wouldn't let me out until I proved I was an adult. True story."

More laughter.

I'm not laughing now as I reach the peak, another attendant unhooking me from the pulley and helping me up.

"This wind is wild, man." He says to his coworker.

"Yeah! I want to see them go down that thing!"

"Let the record reflect this wasn't my idea." I call over the wind to answering laughs.

I pull my tube behind me like a balloon, it flapping wildly in the air.

It looks as if a snowstorm is roaring around us, but it's only the snow being blown about in the wind.

"Here we go!" My dad shouts. He sits in his tube and scoots to the edge.

There are three lanes. The first two are a straight shot to the bottom, while the third curves in a longer stretch down the side of the mountain.

It reminds me of a water park ride. But instead of concrete barriers with water spurting out of them, the barriers are made of snow and ice.

My dad takes the first lane while my bonus mom goes down the middle. They fly down the slope, twisting and turning all the way down.

It's my turn. I aim for the middle.

I sit in the tube and scoot like my dad did.

Then, I'm flying.

I can't see anything as the wind whips through my hair, the snow swirling around me in a cloud of white.

I hit the side and bounce, my tube spinning with my back facing the bottom.

"Stop! Stop!" My dad cries.

"Put your feet down!" My bonus mom calls.

I put my feet down and the tube slows until I stop completely.

My dad yells over to me. "You were about to keep going down the mountain! No barriers that way!"

"Well, I couldn't see anything!" I say, rolling out of the tube. "And no one told me how to stop!"

We walk towards the pulley, pulling our tubes behind us as they continue flapping in the wind.

I try out each of the lanes, the third being the most fun except for the trek back up. Lane one seems to be the fastest while lane two the most tame.

Our session is close to ending so I stand at the top of the mountain, choosing which lane to make my final ride.

I choose lane two, hopping in my tube and zooming down the slope.

The wind whistles as my hair whirls around my face. I take a gloved hand and pull back my hair like a curtain, looking for the end of the slide.

I reach the bottom and put my feet down, slowing the tube.

All of a sudden, a blast of wind surges around me, pushing my tube further down the incline.

"Stop! Stop!" I hear behind me.

I desperately put my feet down, but I keep going, the inner tube rolling forward and spinning me around.

I feel my tube hit something solid.

I'm launched into oblivion, darkness enveloping my vision.

And I'm flying, flying through the air on a cold Alaskan wind.

My head fills with thoughts. Memories of my life flash like spotlights.

I'm on the stage, singing to a crowd who is screaming back the lyrics to my songs.

I'm wrestling with my children, tickling them and blowing raspberries on their bellies.

I'm at my first book signing, smiling and scribbling my signature onto the inside cover.

I'm in bed with my boyfriend, he laughs softly in my ear. "I love you, Sandi MarLisa."

Between flashing scenes, a phrase reverberates through my head, over and over again.

"This is how you die."

Alice's on the Bayview

Remind me to text you and let you know how fast this ship sank last night. I texted Michael.

The response was nearly immediate. *Did he turn into a douche?*

I turned from making coffee and looked into the living room where Sk8er Boi sat, playing with Bonnie.

Before I could reply, a new text flashed across the screen of my phone.

I've been feeling pent up. Do I need to give Sk8er Boi the Flash?

He texted three side eye emojis.

See what I did there?

It's an entire story, so buckle up.

I put my phone away and brought Sk8er Boi a coffee.

"Thanks!" He said as I sat next to him.

"Mhm." I gripped my sides.

"So…"

"So?"

"Did you really mean what you said last night?"

I didn't respond.

"You really don't want to see me again after today?"

"You didn't exactly give me much choice."

"There's always a choice, Sandi."

I looked away, staring out the window. I gripped my sides tighter.

"What's wrong?"

"I'm going to go take a shower." I said, standing. "I'll be right back."

I walked into the master bathroom and closed the door. I turned on the water and looked down at my phone, texting my sister.

Don't worry about coming over this morning.

Everything okay?

I'll explain later.

I swiped to the conversation with Michael.

Driving back from a date with Sk8er Boi. It went great.

I get undressed.

Guess what flashes across his caller ID on his car GPS?

I grip my sides again, taking a deep breath.

The name "Onna" with a note that says "Tinder."

I step into the shower and let the hot water run over the back of my neck.

I'm hurting. I double over, hands on my stomach.

I step out of the shower after a long while and check my phone. Michael's reply was simple.

WTF

Which is fine. We're not exclusive. I'm a big girl.

"Sandi." Sk8er Boi said, turning down 40oz. to Freedom by Sublime on the stereo.

I looked out the mustang's passenger window, gathering my thoughts.

"Please talk to me."

I sighed. "I don't really know what to say."

"Just… talk to me."

I let my shoulders sag, still looking out the window. "You've made no promises to me, Sk8er Boi. I'm a big girl." I look vaguely in his direction. "Give me a minute and I'll get over it."

We sat in silence.

So we proceed to have the "where is this going talk."

"You know Sandi." Sk8er Boi took a deep breath, gripping the steering wheel tighter. "We've been seeing each other for a while and we haven't really talked about where this is going. I…" He turned slightly in the driver's seat, taking his eyes off the road to let them meet mine for a moment. "I care about you."

I let my eyes connect with his.

His attention went back to the road. "And if we need to have a discussion about where this is going… I'm willing to have that discussion."

I sat up a bit straighter, trying not to seem too excited.

He didn't take the out.

I gave him an out.

And… and he didn't take it.

My heart thundered in my chest. My hope rising.

"Okay." I said, folding my hands in my lap. "We can discuss it."

I talked to him on the first date about being emotionally available. And what does he say in this convo?

"I really care for you, Sandi. But I'm emotionally unavailable for a relationship right now." Sk8er Boi's grip tensed on the wheel. "You came as a surprise to me."

Let me briefly interject.

Go on.

"You came as a surprise."

Coming from someone who has manipulated his fair share of the opposite sex.

Regrettably.

Regrettably.

Nonetheless it happened.

What a shady thing to say.

Like. That's just a way of putting someone down easy.

And if you actually were a surprise, that means you would be able to persuade him into becoming emotionally available.

If not, there's no real surprise and he's just trying to be manipulative.

Okay. Continue.

"I never dreamed I'd find someone like you that fast!" Sk8er Boi ran his hand through his hair. "You're so great. You're *fun*. But if we got into a relationship right now it would be incredibly toxic, Sandi. And I can't do that to you."

Coming out of my reverie, I walked back into the living room and noticed the back sliding glass door was open. Sk8er Boi was outside with Bonnie, throwing discs into the basket.

"Hey." I said.

"Sandi! I made it on the first throw!" Sk8er Boi was beaming. "That means it's going to be a good day. It's a sign." He frowned. "What is it?"

We continue home. I drink a glass of wine.

"S-Sandi?" Sk8er Boi said at the door of my master bedroom.

"What?" I said, leaning over the dresser, drinking wine like a Stepford Wife.

"You... you okay?"

"Yeah." I said, draining the wine and grabbing my coat. "Let's go to the Hobo. You can sit there and look pretty."

Noooooo Sandi

We go to the Salty Hobo to meet the godfather and some other friends.

"You're buying all my drinks tonight." I said to Sk8er Boi. It wasn't a question.

"Okay that's fair."

We find the godfather and I introduce Sk8er Boi to everyone there.

"You want to come with me to get drinks?" Sk8er Boi asked.

"No." I said, as everyone was making conversation amongst themselves. "You can get them."

Sk8er Boi ducked his head and aimed for the bar.

The godfather paused in mid-conversation to stare at me.

I tried to laugh and join in the banter, crossing my legs and bouncing my leg, my chucks and silver anklet knocking the side of the bench.

I wore a simple spaghetti-strap black dress, a fuzzy jacket I borrowed from my sister, a silver headband and my favorite rainbow necklace made of sea glass.

"That jacket is fierce." Jacob said over the noise of the bar.

Sk8er Boi returned with the drinks and handed me my Gin.

"Thanks! It's my sister's."

"Looks like it's yours tonight." Sk8er Boi said, sitting down.

I turned to him. "You don't get to be sarcastic right now."

Sk8er Boi cleared his throat.

I get Gin drunk. And black out.

He drives me home. I am shit faced. Regrettably.

As we do.

The car was silent. Sk8er Boi gripped the steering wheel, occasionally glancing over at me.

"Sandi?"

"I'm angry."

"I can tell."

More silence.

"So this is it, Sk8er Boi."

"What's it?"

"I'm not seeing you after tonight."

"What do you mean?"

"I mean we're done. I'm done. You led me on."

"I didn't mean to lead you on, Sandi."

"Yes the fuck you did. Yes the fuck you did. You talked about the future. You wanted me to meet your sister in law. You led me the fuck on."

"Because I care about you, Sandi."

"No."

"Can't we be friends?"

166

All I know is I wake up the next morning and he tells me what the fuck I did.

So I shall now relay that info to you.

Dude bring it.

I whirled on him. "No, Sk8er Boi we cannot be friends. Friends don't do what you did to me."

"I can't be in a relationship with you right now, Sandi! I just can't. In a few months, who knows? Maybe it will be different."

"No. You either want to be with me or you don't."

"It's not that simple."

"Oh yes the fuck it is!"

I lectured him the entire ride home and gave him a list of "Reasons Why I'm Great."

The listed reasons include:

Ohhhhh nooooo Sandi lololol

"Number one." I held up my hands and counted down on my fingers. "I really like sex. I will fuck you every day. Number two. I am a damn good cook."

YOU DIDN'T

YAS BITCH.

I LOVE IT GO ON.

"I do not chase men, Sk8er Boi!" I turned in the passenger seat to face him. "You still have value and worth but you really fucked up here, my man."

Oh my god that sounds exactly like you.

RIGHT

I'm imagining you beating the shit out of him while screaming out how great you are and how he's a piece of shit.

He says we then proceeded to have the most confusing sex of his entire life.

NO RAGRATS

LMFAO I am loving this!

But it gets better.

"Sandi, what's wrong?" Sk8er Boi held the disc in his hand, Bonnie playing on the ground around him.

"I have a UTI." I said, dead inside. "And I can't find my car keys. I need you to take me to the pharmacy." I didn't meet his eyes. "Please." I added as an afterthought.

Ohhhhh noooo

Oh yes.

He has to drive me to the pharmacy. I can't find the meds on the shelf, I'm in so much pain.

He finds them for me.

THEN

OH AND THEN

We get to the self checkout and I realize, "Oh I don't have my debit card."

Sk8er Boi droops his head slightly. "Oh yeah. You gave me your debit card and license before we went out so you didn't have to carry your wallet around with you. I left them in the cup holder of your car…"

"Just in case you had to make a clean getaway." I said dryly.

He winced.

SO I HAVE TO ASK HIM TO PAY FOR MY UTI MEDICATION.

Did he?

Indeed.

Okay. So here's what I'm taking from this.

He's actually not a terrible guy. He's just a normal dude not thinking past his dick.

Ya'll just aren't aligned as far as what you want.

And apparently, Sandi, you needed to blow off a little steam.

But I still have to say he should've been upfront with not being emotionally available when you gave him the chance to be.

That still bothers me.

He's not a bad guy, you're right. He said, "Can we be friends? You're really fun."

Ouch. I'd rather get fucked over, tbh. But maybe that speaks to my trauma.

He actually took me to brunch trying to convince me.

We sat in the courtyard of Alice's on the Bayview in St. Andrews, french toast, eggs and fruit placed in front of us. We both wore our new t-shirts purchased from Relief.

"Sandi. You gave me a list last night of why you're great." Sk8er Boi leaned in. "Let me give you reasons why I'm great and why you should be friends with me."

I couldn't help but smile, looking off towards the bay.

"Number one. I'd do anything for my friends."

"Sk8er Boi…"

"Number two. I'm really fun to hang out with."

"Please stop." I threw my napkin on the table. "I can't do this. I'm already catching feelings for you and soon I'm going to be over the cliff."

"The cliff."

"Yes, Sk8er Boi. The cliff. The CLIFF. I'm going to fall in love and once that happens it's over for me. There's no reasoning with me. There's no getting me out of it. I'm going to pine for you and hope the entire time we're friends that you'll change your mind. I am not an ignorant woman who doesn't know herself. You…" I looked away. "You led me on. You watched me catch feelings, I didn't hide them from you. You allowed me to take my feelings to this point, knowing you weren't going to do anything with them. It was a dick move."

Honestly though. I'm sad.

Because this specific situation didn't work out?

I caught the feels. Cause I thought we were on the same page. I'm mad at myself mostly. I should have seen it coming. My intuition is usually on point. Why didn't I see this?

Sk8er Boi and I left Alice's and walked back towards the car.

We passed by Oaks by the Bay park. I saw the Sentry Tree standing in the middle of it. When the hurricane happened, many trees left standing were broken in half. The city had recently commissioned a chainsaw artist to carve sculptures out of what was left.

It was my favorite aesthetic. Making beauty out of pain.

"Want to see something cool?" I asked Sk8er Boi

He nodded.

I showed him around the park, pointing out the sculptures. One was an octopus framed by dolphins, another was a mermaid, and one was…

"Sea turtles. This one reminds me of you." I said, pointing. "I know you like them."

He looked at me and sighed, smiling faintly.

"Come on." He said, taking my hand. "There's a skatepark around here."

We found the skatepark and I watched him do a few runs on his board. Then, he walked over to me and helped me stand on the board, taking my hand as I moved.

"I won't let you fall." He said.

"But you did, Sk8er Boi." I thought to myself.

He did let me fall.

Just not physically.

I gripped his hand, letting him lead me, letting him catch me when I lost my balance.

"Sandi." He said as he drove to take me home. "Please give me a chance. Just try to be my friend and see what happens."

I sighed, watching the bay sail by my window on Beach Drive. Thinking.

"Okay Sk8er Boi." I said finally. "I'll try."

This can all be traced back to him misleading you.

You told him what you were looking for. He acted like that was okay with him. That's on him.

You are an extremely intuitive person. Don't let this turn you cynical.

Because I promise you, approaching relationships from a cynical point of view verses a foolish one is a great way to miss out on a lot of great experiences. It might get you hurt more often but you and I both know how much life will hurt you already. Don't add to it by closing yourself off.

You're right. I know you're right.

That being said, it's okay to be sad when something you were excited about doesn't work out. It'll get better, I promise.

I scrambled some eggs in a plastic cup to keep from dirtying a dish and I almost drank them. So, I assure you, you're still doing better than I am.

Thank you Michael.

The black mustang convertible rode out of sight of St. Andrews, taking my hope with it.

Chapter 13

Salty Hobo

Cheers erupted. The godfather stepped out from behind the drums, smiling.

It was Monday Night Little Fest at the Taproom. A full moon loomed over the heads of bar patrons, a full house that night.

I played my keyboard in front of a crowd for the first time in years that night. The godfather played his drum set in public for the first time in a long time as well.

"Great job, friend!" I called to the godfather.

"You too!"

"Sandi!" Lauren and Sierra popped into the courtyard, holding takeout boxes of food.

"Oh my god you made it!" I said, running over to them.

"We heard you in the parking lot, but we missed your set!" Sierra said.

"We got here as fast as we could." Lauren looked me up and down. "You look sexayyyy tonight!"

I was wearing one of my favorite outfits. An open white and black striped long sleeved shirt rolled up to my elbows, a black cropped top and high waisted black shorts with chucks. My silver headband reflected the lights from the stage.

"Hey Sandi." A deep voice said behind me.

I turned around to find Michael standing there. I gave him a hug, squeezing tight.

"Oh my god. You came out for me!"

"Of course I did." He said simply.

Another duo took the stage, a female country singer from Nashville with a big voice and her guitar player.

Her voice was powerful, reverberating through the outside space. My friends and I stood around the fire, laughing and talking, drinking beer and wine.

"Hey girl." I felt someone nudge my shoulder.

It was Georgia Boy, his face shaved completely.

"Hey, Georgia Boy. Great set tonight." I tilted my head to the side. "New look?"

"What? Oh the beard." He stroked his face. "Yeah. I shaved too far and had to start over." He paused, looking at me. "I… I didn't know you played keys."

"Hm?" My thoughts had wandered off. "Oh… yeah. Piano is my main instrument. I've played since I was eight."

"You're…" Georgia Boy cleared his throat. "Well, you're really good."

"Why do you sound so surprised?" I asked, smirking.

"I'm not surprised. I just…" He smiled at me. "I just didn't know. Why haven't I seen you play it before?"

"Because I refuse to be stuck behind a piano." I said immediately. "In previous bands, my bandmates put me on the piano and stuck me in the back."

"Stuck you in the back." He repeated.

"Yep." I met Georgia Boy's eyes. "What is it, Georgia Boy?" I said wryly. "You look confused."

"It's just, you're really good on the keys. That's all. Why would you hide that?"

"Because I won't be stuck in the back." I said again, my agitation rising. He always peppered me with questions. "I've done my time as a backup singer. That time is over."

"Oh." He said, understanding lining his face. "I see."

My face heated and it had nothing to do with the blazing fires around us. Georgia Boy always managed to tap into my anger.

"Try being the only woman in the band your whole life." I sighed. "You learn to fight for yourself. Sometimes that means demanding your place at the front when you've earned it three times over. Regardless of who has a goddamned word to say about it."

Georgia Boy opened his mouth to respond.

"Hey look! It's officer cool as fuck!" The country singer shouted across the bar.

A large cop had walked into the Taproom staring everyone down. He caught the singer's eye.

"Give it up for officer cool as fuck!"

The people of the Taproom gave a thunderous applause.

"Listen officer cool as fuck." The singer continued. "We're gonna be cool as fuck and turn down the volume. So how about you be cool as fuck and let us keep going and not report us?"

The officer rolled his eyes, smiling, and waved to the sound of more cheers before leaving the bar.

I laughed, thinking I could learn a lot from this woman from Nashville.

"That was fucking hilarious." The godfather said, wiping his eyes.

"I love her." Jacqueline agreed.

"Sandi I–" Georgia Boy started.

"Sandi!" Sierra grabbed my arm. "Come over here, I want to show you something."

I left Georgia Boy by the fire and sat down with Sierra, looking at new pictures she had for updates on the shop. Georgia Boy wandered over and sat on a couch opposite of us, watching the musical act.

The country artist finished her set to cheering, the Taproom filling with chatter.

"How are you doing, Sandi?" Sierra asked seriously.

"I'm…"

"What's going on?" Lauren asked.

"You talking about Sk8er Boi?" Michael said, sitting down. "Dude. Fuck that guy."

"FUCK THAT GUY!" The godfather echoed from a fire over. He was several beers deep.

"Hey!" Kirk called from the stage. "All musicians tonight come up here for a photo!"

I left my friends to head towards the stage, taking a big step onto the platform.

"What's going on?" Georgia Boy asked.

"We're taking a group photo." Kirk said, pointing at one of the musicians to move closer.

"Oh! Well, I have one request for that." Georgia Boy walked over to me and smiled. "I want to stand next to Sandi."

The godfather and Jacqueline glanced my way. Jacob and the country singer made eye contact.

"Um. Okay." I said, walking to take my position.

Georgia Boy followed and stood next to me as announced, throwing his arm over my shoulder.

Bartender burst onto the stage, a bar towel hanging out of her back pocket. She put her arms out, smiling wide for the camera.

Once the photo was taken, I rejoined my friends by the fire.

Lauren was dancing around with her arms out. "We getting wild tonight guys? We getting wild?"

Sierra put her head down before sipping her drink.

"Hobo!" The godfather yelled.

"Absolutely not." Michael said, staring down at all of us. "It is a Monday night."

"That means nothing." Lauren said.

"We. Are. Adults." Michael clapped, enunciating each word.

I shook my head, laughing, looking up at the moon above.

A large group of about twenty of us started walking towards the Hobo. Bartender walked with us, her shift over for the night.

"Sandi baby." Lauren said. "What's wrong?"

"She's sad." Sierra said. "Sk8er Boi turned out to be a jerk."

"And she said she'd be friends with him!" The godfather yelled.

"Sandi, no." Michael looked down at me. "We talked about this."

"He just wants to get in your pants!" The godfather cried over the crowd.

"Bruh, exactly." Michael agreed.

"I just." I stared helplessly up at the sky. "I just thought if we could be friends, maybe one day things will change."

"You are pining!" The godfather said.

"Come on girl." Lauren said. "I'll buy you a drink. What do you want?"

"Gin." Michael answered for me.

We get to the Hobo and grab our drinks from the bartender. My friends slowly trickle back outside under the patio, standing in a circle.

"Oh!" I said, a new member joining our group. "Hey Giles!"

"Sandi." He said smiling.

Sierra, Lauren and Michael joined us.

"You know what memory sticks out to me the most about you, Michael?" I said, squeezing my lime into the drink.

"What?" He asked.

Georgia Boy joined the circle, looking at me.

"I got trashed at my very first party on Parrot Bay—"

"Oh my god I remember this. You were so trashed you called it Ferret Fay."

I laughed. "I was lying down in the grass and you stood over me. I was talking nonsense. You turned to Robert and said, 'Dude. Somebody get this girl home.'"

Everyone laughed but Georgia Boy. He just looked at me before asking, "So... did you all go to high school together?"

"Yep!" Lauren answered. "We go way back. Except... Giles. Did you go to Mosley?"

"I don't think—" I began.

"Yes Sandi." Giles said exasperatedly. "You have the habit of ignoring the fact we went to the same school together."

I sighed. "It's just because I knew you mainly from the band we were in together. The Grand—"

"Please." Giles interjected. "Don't complete that sentence."

"The Grand Plan." I finished with a laugh.

I felt Georgia Boy's eyes on my face, unmoving.

"Well. I'm going to find a seat." I left without further adieu.

We pushed several tables together to accommodate the huge group of us. The more people drank, the louder we got.

I looked at the artwork covering the walls done by a local artist. Someone had drawn on the patio with chalk. A skateboarder rolled up and down the sidewalk. A couple girls started making out in a chair, climbing on top of each other. A duo was playing, loud and rowdy.

The full moon glowed over the bay. Not a cloud to be seen.

"SANDI SOMEONE IS SPEAKING TO YOU!" The godfather yelled across the table.

I shook my head, looking for the person who was talking to me. I caught Georgia Boy's eye momentarily and he moved to get out of his chair.

"So what's going on with Sk8er Boi?" Michael repeated.

I broke eye contact with Georgia Boy, who quickly sat back down. "He asked me to be friends and I agreed to see where it goes."

"Tell her, Michael." The godfather said, slamming a hand on the table. Drinks rattled. "Tell her why it's a horrible idea."

"Sandi. Listen to the voice of reason from your male friends."

So I listened and tried to fight the rising lump in my throat.

I was hurt. I liked Sk8er Boi.

Was this just it then? Was it over?

All that time we spent together was just for nothing?

We didn't get to be anything at all?

Sierra read my thoughts and gripped my hand, wordlessly.

The godfather leaned in and said quietly. "Don't look now, but Georgia Boy is after you."

"What?" I said. I looked up to find Georgia Boy still staring at me. He jumped out of his chair.

"I said don't look."

Just then, Giles and another friend walked in front of Georgia Boy's direct line to me. Georgia Boy hung back, sipping his drink.

I continued the conversation with my friends and tried to call Sk8er Boi. He didn't answer. Knowing I'd lose my nerve, I typed up a long message explaining why we couldn't simply be friends, hovering a finger over the send button.

Sierra continued to grip my hand. Lauren brought me another drink. Michael and the godfather stood up, the godfather dropping his pants so he could show off the brilliant thigh tattoos Sierra had just outlined for him. A skeleton sea captain on one thigh and a moon priestess on the other.

People grabbed their phones to take pictures of the godfather with his pants down, flexing his leg muscles and smiling down at the new works of art on his body.

"Only at the Hobo." I said, sipping my drink.

"Hey girl." Georgia Boy had found his way to me.

I slowly set my Gin down on the table.

"Hey." I said warily.

"Can I talk to you?" Georgia Boy asked, motioning for me to follow him to a pavilion overlooking the bay.

I looked down at the unsent text to Sk8er Boi.

I pressed send.

I put the phone in front of Sierra on the table, silently willing her to read.

"Sure, Georgia Boy." I stood, leaving my drink on the table in front of Lauren.

Georgia Boy and I walked in silence towards the pavilion. My own thoughts were with Sk8er Boi. How'd he feel when he got the text. If he'd even care. If I had kid myself the whole time that he actually cared about me at all.

"I fell for a player. A fuck boy." I thought to myself. "How ridiculously typical."

We reached the pavilion and Georgia Boy motioned for me to follow him to the side closest to the water. We leaned over the railing staring out into the Bay.

"Sandi. I've thought about it." He sighed, clasping his hands together over the railing. "And I think we should be friends."

I started. "I'm sorry. What?"

"I think we should just be friends." He said again. Georgia Boy straightened up and turned to face me, looking at my expression intently.

"Bruh." I thought to myself. "I slept with you one singular time."

"Friends." I repeated.

"Yeah. Exactly!"

I turned to face him. "How old are you exactly?" I couldn't hold back the slight amusement I felt.

He made a face, confused by the question. "I'm twenty seven."

Okay, so way older than I actually thought.

I sighed, dipping my head and giving it a slight shake. "I've got plenty of friends, Georgia Boy. I can barely keep up with the ones I have."

"It's just that I think friendship lasts longer. And I think you're really cool." Georgia Boy didn't seem to hear what I was saying at all.

Cool.

Cool. Cool. Cool. Cool. *Cool.*

I looked at him reluctantly and was surprised by what I saw on his face.

"You've really thought about this, haven't you?"

"You have no idea." He hung his head.

I watched him blink his eyes deliberately before looking back out to the bay.

"Ah." I said, understanding dawning on me. "You want to be honorable."

Georgia Boy looked up at me, his brows furrowed. "That's an interesting way to put it, but yeah."

I continued looking at him, considering. "I don't understand why you care so much about being my friend. You don't know me. At all."

"Sandi." He sighed, putting an arm over my shoulder. "Me and you? We're gonna fuck this town up."

I couldn't stop it. I rolled my eyes.

Then, I was agitated.

No, I was angry.

Livid.

So that was it then. He had some outlandish idea that we were going to play music together.

Now I understood. I understood completely.

That's why he wanted to stand next to me for the photo. He wanted to be seen with me.

He wanted people to know we were tight.

Georgia Boy was no fool. He was nice enough, but I saw how fast he made connections in the music scene. I noticed how quickly he got a gig and then another. That wasn't typical.

He was ambitious.

I knew a thing or two about ambitious men.

"So…" My thoughts raced. The pieces were coming together.

He had rejected me at the Salty Hobo 2 that night, maybe to be sure he hadn't fucked up his chances to work with me.

He wanted to be sure his dick hadn't gotten in the way of his ambition.

I was a sought out lead vocalist. Georgia Boy wasn't much of a singer, self-admittedly. He was mostly a guitar player. He had said so himself that first night at Little Village.

My emails and social media inboxes were filled with requests to work with me.

"Sandi! Do you think you could sing this song I wrote?"

"Sandi! Do you think you could play keys for this project I'm working on?"

"Sandi! Ever thought about working with me in a duo?"

"Sandi! What venues do you think I could get into? Do you have any contacts you'd be willing to share?"

But I was holding out, taking no offers. The godfather and I had a plan, and we were making incredible strides.

We were about to play for Beatdown on the Beach in front of twelve hundred people. I booked us that show before we had even done ten gigs together.

I knew what I was capable of musically. I knew what I was building for myself and the godfather, too.

I wanted to build my own band, not step into one that was already established.

Because I didn't want a single person saying shit. No one was going to say anything was handed to me. I would build it all with my own two hands.

I knew it was pride. But pride was all I had. And I didn't apologize for it.

I was biding my time, waiting for the right moment to unveil my master plan.

I worked harder than anyone I knew, finding new venues and taking cancellations when they were offered to me.

And I didn't need another acoustic guitar player. The Love is Overrated guy had no chance at working with me. The godfather was my ride-or-die. Anybody with eyes could see that.

And I could write my own damn songs. I didn't need to write a verse for his song, "Hurricane."

Did he even know what a hurricane was? Did he even know that the weather event he was using as an overused literary device had absolutely destroyed my life?

I thought of the chorus he had shared with me. "On the day love left, there was a hurricane..."

The audacity of this man. The nerve of people who wrote about what they'd absolutely never understand.

I was over it.

Fuck this town up?

No. Fuck you, Georgia Boy. And all men like you. All people like you.

Go use someone else.

But I wasn't a fool. I always could play the little games people spun.

Biding. Biding my time.

So I looked him square in the face, offering a serene smile. "Sure. We can be friends."

Knowing I had no intention of being friends at all.

He beamed, glowed. "Oh Sandi. You just made me so happy!"

Yeah. I'll bet.

I tried not to roll my eyes again.

He kept his arm around me, leading me back to the Salty Hobo. I fought the urge to shake it off and storm away.

"Sandi." He said with that unnerving sense of optimism as we walked, making a rainbow with his hand towards the sky. "We're gonna fuck this town up, girl."

"Cool." I said, looking for my quick escape.

We arrived back at the table, the godfather already crossing his arms and silently laughing at me.

"Georgia Boy caught you, huh?"

"Shut up." I said, picking up my drink and sitting down hard in my chair, splashing some Gin on my shorts. "What? Are you calling him by his actual name now?"

"Can't exactly call him Chinstrap anymore, can I?"

I said nothing, just stared at the artwork on the walls.

"Sandi." The godfather clapped once.

I turned to face him.

"We're not doing this." He said, leaning towards me. "We're not going to fall into despair because a dick head didn't want us."

Tension lined my chest. I felt the tears threatening to spill over.

"What do we want?" The godfather said more gently.

I let my eyes flutter to the side. Michael had tuned into the conversation.

"Sandi." The godfather said. "What do we want?"

"Something exquisite." I whispered.

"What?" The godfather leaned in, cupping his ear. "I'm sorry I couldn't hear you."

"Something exquisite!" I yelled into his ear, causing him to jolt. I laughed a little then.

"That's right." The godfather recovered, grabbing his beer.

"Why does it have to be exquisite?" Michael asked.

"Because that's all I'll accept." I said, staring up at the night sky. The beautiful full moon shone through the clouds.

"So enjoy your night, Sandi." The godfather tipped his beer in the direction of everyone standing in the middle of the courtyard. "We had a great show and all your friends are here."

I looked around, taking it all in. So many people I loved were there.

Even Bartender laughed amongst Sierra and Lauren. And more of my peers filed into the dive bar, musicians getting off their shows at nearby bars and popping in to say hello.

I stood up to go to the bathroom and get another drink from the inside bar. At the door, I plowed straight into Georgia Boy,

"There she is!" He said. "Hey friend!" He held up a hand for a high five.

I lamely met his hand with mine without looking, continuing straight towards the back of the bar for the restroom.

Returning, Lauren stood at the bar holding out another Gin to me. Michael stood beside her, deep in thought.

Upon seeing me, Michael touched my arm. "Sandi, come talk to me for a minute."

Once again, I found myself being led across the street towards the water.

The first words out of Michael's mouth were, "Sandi, do you wanna know why I'm not sexually attracted to you? I've figured it out."

Jesus tap dancing Christ. What the hell was happening tonight?

I looked up at the full moon, squeezing my Gin too hard. I silently petitioned the glowing orb for patience before answering Michael.

"Why, Michael?" I heaved a sigh. "Please enlighten me."

"You remind me of my mother." He said.

Jesus tap dancing Christ.

"Oh yeah?" I said, still staring at the full moon.

"You help guide me. You inspire me. You help everyone through quiet leadership. You never tell people what to do. You just give them space to figure it out, offering support if they need it. I love and admire you so much."

Even though the opening line was odd, I knew Michael was being sweet in his way. I gave him a hug and told him I needed to talk to Sierra about something, she still had my phone.

Sierra took one look at me when I arrived back at the table and stood up, handing me my phone.

"Let's go." She said, taking my hand.

This time I was led to the parking lot. The bar noise soon faded away.

"Has he responded?" Sierra asked.

I looked down at my phone before sticking it in my pocket and shaking my head. No messages lit up the screen.

"Sandi." Sierra said, taking my hands. "I know you're hurting, but I don't think this has anything to do with Sk8er Boi."

I couldn't stop the tears reaching the surface then. I didn't mind being vulnerable with Sierra.

"What do you mean?" I said thickly.

"I mean…" She looked away for a moment before staring meaningfully into my eyes. Her blue eyes shone in the moonlight. "I mean, he reminded me of someone else."

"Who?" I asked, sniffing.

She smiled faintly. "You know who."

I racked my brain, trying to figure it out.

"Your text to him was beautifully done." She said.

I nodded silently.

"What is it?" She asked gently.

"I just…" Words failed me.

Fun. Sk8er Boi told me.

Inspiring. Michael insisted.

Cool. Georgia Boy had said.

What do we want? The godfather asked.

"I just want something exquisite." I said. "And... Sk8er Boi... I don't know. I let myself hope. I let myself for two seconds in his stupid mustang hope that maybe I wasn't going to be alone for the rest of my life. I left my ex truly believing I'd be alone at least for a decade. I have two children. I'm... different. I'm all over the place and with my job... with what I want out of life... how am I supposed to find someone who can come with me? I thought my husband could come with me, Sierra."

Sierra nodded solemnly. Listening.

"I..." I looked back up at the sky, the stars blurry through my tears. "My marriage had been over for a while. For two years we couldn't be intimate. He had stopped talking to me. But we were still working towards something. France." I said, throwing my hands up. "And then everything exploded and I knew... I knew I was hurting him by staying with him."

Tears rolled down Sierra's cheeks, matching my own.

"So I sat down. Praying to God or whatever the hell is out there. And I just knew... I knew I had to leave. I had to kill my marriage to save my husband. But..." I heaved a sob, letting the breath rack my chest. "I didn't want that. He was everything to me. He was *everything*."

I cried and cried. Sierra taking me into her arms.

Pulling away, she grabbed my face in her hands tenderly. "Sandi. I love you. And... that pain you're feeling... it doesn't matter what happens from here on out. You'll heal, you will. It will get easier. But it will always be there like a scar that still hurts sometimes... and you will learn how to carry it without it destroying you. I.." She pointed to her chest. "I understand."

I nodded. I knew she did.

"But..." She smiled faintly. "Think of all that you just said to me. None of this is about Sk8er Boi." She kissed my cheek and pulled me into a hug.

I thought about her words. I let them sink in deep.

And I cried. I cried and cried and cried on my friend's shoulder. And she held me in the dive bar parking lot under a full Florida moon.

I calmed a bit, letting Sierra lead me back towards the table. The godfather stood at the corner of the street, waiting for us.

"I'm taking you home." He said.

"You don't have to do—"

"Your makeup is running." He put a guiding hand on the small of my back and led me back towards the Taproom where our cars were parked.

I wiped my eyes, trying to keep it together.

"You can fall apart in the car." The godfather said without looking at me.

We walked down the side street, a few friends were standing around talking.

"I'm taking Sandi home." The godfather said to Jacqueline, kissing her.

"Oh, Sandi. Don't be upset." Georgia Boy started walking to me.

Michael and Lauren cut him off, both of them trying to soothe me.

"Come on." The godfather took my arm and led me away from the crowd.

I hugged myself as I walked down the street. The godfather saying nothing.

I began weeping, my surroundings becoming unrecognizable.

"We're almost there." The godfather said, gripping my arm more firmly.

My crying became uncontrollable sobs, my chest heaving, my breathing shallow, my vision blurry.

I stumbled and fell to the ground, tears spilling onto the concrete.

"Nope. We're not doing this." The godfather pulled me up under my arms. "Not yet. The car is just a few steps away and you can fall apart in there."

He half dragged me the rest of the way, opening up the passenger side door and helping me inside.

I wept as the godfather drove me home.

"This is what dating is now." The godfather said as he drove. "It sucks."

I couldn't answer. Lights flashed past the windows.

"You can have the bed tonight. Your juices are still marinating from your night with Sk8er Boi anyway."

My laugh at his comment turned into a sob.

"Godfather." I said, my nose running. "I..."

"I know." He said simply.

Part Two

Chapter 14

One Glass of Wine

I have so many memories with you in such a short span of time

More time, that's what I wanted

Not a forever necessarily, but a more than whatever the hell we were

Like that time I told you I was so happy you took me seriously when I corrected you on something

And you said "How else was I supposed to take you? With cream and sugar?"

and it was so fucking corny

And probably a line in hindsight

But I adored it

Now I hate you for it

Because you never even found out I don't take sugar in my tea

Unless it's southern sweet

Maybe that southern hospitality is what had me holding the door to my soul open so freely only for you to leave me open

Wide open

Barren

Hanging in limbo

Waiting for you to step through the threshold

And make yourself at home

Come inside sweetheart,

I'm getting cold,

And you're letting all the heat out

There was a moment when we were laying on your couch where I let myself for a fraction of a second believe that I'd never be cold again

The sunshine through the blinds lit up your eyes in such a way that I saw a future in golden brown pigment

For a moment

A blissful

Regretful

Beautiful

Stupid

Wonderful

Terrible

Incredible

Moment

I know that's weird to say

I've never known how to be any other way than poetic when I meet a soul so exquisite

Was it?

Is it?

I always see the best in people when they show me the worst

I never believe the worst though

I don't

They say love is blind

But I didn't love you yet

So it's fine

Right?

I'm fine

Totally fine

I told you then and there that I thought you were pretty

Then I stopped myself and muttered, "I know that word's not very manly."

And you responded, "No it isn't. But I don't mind it when you say it."

It was so corny.

But I fucking loved it.

Now I covet it.

Now I'm despondent

I told you once I felt safe with you and you asked me how in the world I went from talking about nonsense to that. You demanded I unveil my thought process.

There was no logical path to reveal

I just felt something and I said it. Something real.

I don't think you understood at all what that meant for me

I keep my emotions in check

Until all of a sudden I'm writing damn poems about something that hadn't even really happened yet

I wish I knew why we met

Why the universe saw fit to break my heart wide open spilling out the contents for you to see,

When you hadn't even earned me

But boy you had me until you didn't

Because little did you know I have over a decade of experience shutting shit down quick when it becomes clear the tick tick tick isn't the sound of a clock, or a bomb

But my self respect about to go all the way off

Step back, give me some room to work, because I've become a Queen of throwing up some damn boundaries when people think they're getting away with not giving me what I deserve

Because. fuck. my. feelings.

I mean honestly

I am so tired of my kindness being mistaken for stupidity

I'll take integrity over words that sound pretty

I am so sick of my willingness to be hurt when it comes to love being misinterpreted as a woman who has a proclivity to allow people to walk all over her

Like dirt

I am not naive

I'm not

That's why I'm miserable

Because my heart is visceral

And my brain has it on a leash, pulling me back saying, "Absolutely not, girl. He is playing you like harp strings."

"I know, but hell. He plays so well."

Just let me live in ignorance for a while longer I scream at my head

Why do I always have to see everything so damn clearly

What if I don't want to be responsible?

What if I'm fine with toxicity?

What if I want to let him fool his way into my soul, but then I get to watch him walk away as he leaves?

God, you really are so damn pretty

You tempted me

You almost had me convinced

But no, I can't

It's just that I still believe in love

And if I'm going to love someone

I let them in

All the way in

I give them the power to annihilate me, if they wish, while praying, hoping to God they see and value and understand what I'm trusting them with.

To your credit, you never walked in the door

Instead you said those fateful words, "I'm not ready for commitment."

Well, shit.

God I was livid.

Not at you.

At myself.

Because obviously I must have missed something.

Right?

All those signals?

Your energy tells me one story that doesn't match the one coming out of your lips?

And your hips, goddamn

Is that why they call them mixed?

No, I don't think that's it.

The problem is I felt something.

I've missed you longer than I had you

Isn't that funny?

Isn't that lovely?

Isn't that disgusting?

Isn't that something?

Boy, you had me feeling.

Oh my God I felt something.

I felt something.

It had been so long

I had almost forgotten

these places in my heart I didn't know still existed

Begotten by the pain of your absence you awakened me to the reality that I had shut down my desire for connection

For affection

And absolutely none of this was logical

None of it

I knew you only two months after all

That's what's so wild to me

I am in awe of how you unlocked me

You shocked me sending shivers up my spine

Baby, you made me feel like poetry after one glass of wine

On the tip of my tongue lingers the phantom of all the sweet words I wanted to say to you

But we didn't have the time

More time, that's what I wanted

More opportunities to explore this potential between you and me

I let you go, though

Because I can't chase after what doesn't want to be caught

So now you and me, we're an incomplete thought

A sentence fragment missing a clause

A symphony on pause

A melody without a hook

194

An unfinished chapter of a beautiful book

A story that never got to be told

Darling, won't you come inside, it's…

Wild Root

Snaps filled the old Lynn Haven building. Wild Root Coffee and Apothecary was packed out.

I looked up to see a colorful crowd. People of every hue.

Gauges. Dreads. Head wraps and headbands. Tattoos and piercings of all assortments.

The owner, Eric, was smiling; pleased with the turn out.

When I had asked him if I could host a poetry event at the coffee shop just blocks away from my house, I didn't know what I had expected.

Not this. Not so many people listening quietly to other souls pouring out their hearts.

Greg and Michelle sat on the couch right in front of me beaming. Greg put a hand on his chest.

Taylor, a local artist and barista, sat on the bar top, smiling serenely. Their hair was shaved and a tattoo of roses decorated their head.

Sierra and Lauren were crying in the crowd. Michael looked uncomfortable in the room filled with so many people, his legs shaking. The godfather sat amongst them.

They had come for me. My friends.

I spotted Georgia Boy at a hightop, Beanie sitting beside him.

A man in his late thirties who stood taller than Michael sat on a barstool feet away.

Chase, a fellow musician and poet, sat amongst a crowd of people. He wore suspenders and rings on his hands.

I couldn't have asked for a better turn out. The energy was palpable.

"Thank you." I said as the snaps faded away. "I have just one more before Chase finishes the night for us."

Ghost

It's been 6 years since your mind took you away Sometimes

Then it was part of the time

Half of the time

Most of the time

All the time

I can't remember the last time I had you here within my reach

I make myself crazy stringing timelines together, going over my theories

No, please don't speak words of comfort to me

You don't know what it's like to be me

Trapped in this perpetual state of mourning when I can't bury who I grieve

It's hard to bury the dead,

Try shoveling dirt on the living

Your gravesite is the memories we shared before death became your favorite lover along with her daughter despair

Because there were always second and third parties in our marriage

You wouldn't shut up about Emily Dickinson's stupid carriage

And you were never quite mine

And I'll never quite recover

So I wear black in hopes no one will discover that the color has drained from more than just my clothes

My therapist says that maybe I should host a mock funeral for you, maybe it would be cathartic

What she didn't know is that I had already started.

I've planned your funeral a thousand, thousand times in my head

I have your eulogy crafted so precisely, exactly the way you told me you wanted it

No pretense of a Heaven you'd be sent to, no sweet bye and bye plucked like a coin from a wishing well, but darling we always did know how to make angels sing in hell

All that's left is to dig your grave and say goodbye

So WHY can't I let you go?

Because I live with your ghost

A shell made of human skin

That haunts these halls akin to these promises you said you wouldn't break

Like that vase you threw at me during our first fight

I met the "and" in the phrase you and me that night

I saw the signs then

I waved at them as they passed me by

But God, I loved you

Why?

Because pain is my love language

No that isn't right, that was you

My personal prison is the mirage of our happy times wrapped in the paper thin veil of hope I crafted for our convoluted brand of a love story

But how many of our happy times were happy because I am damn good at dressing up worries and red flags making them look like hope?

And friends and family have the audacity to accuse me of callousness

Of shallowness

As if my love for you drained out of me like water from a leaky bucket or a dripping faucet

Like I could've done more if I had the right sized plug for all the holes in the stories you told me

Well, Sometimes it's easier to appear shallow, so no one can judge my depth.

But darling we were the ocean

And I did all but drown in it

I'm sorry that I didn't

Maybe I should have

Would that have proven my ardency for you?

But I stay quiet

They probably couldn't swim in this current anyway and I've got no plan, no map, no ships for weary sojourners

It's better to be stoic and rage in the way I always did, sweeping debris into the corners of the palaces I can go inside my mind that reality and people can't find

You see you never could believe I loved you

I was a liar either way

If I stayed, you'd never believe the purity of my love

If I left I only confirmed what you always accused me of

You spun contradictions like spider webs and made the blanket of your own misery

Objection

Is hoarding pain like a dragon its trinkets an indicator for true affection?

I killed us to save you,

Must I kill me too?

Was that the promised price of trying so hard to learn how to love you?

Meanwhile, cobwebs decorate these castle walls, the dust settles and this pain lives on

You're still gone

In more ways than one

And all anyone can tell me is "you're so strong."

Peanut

The tall older man stood up quickly after my last poem and walked swiftly towards the door. A couple men followed him.

"Thank you." I said to the crowd. "And now I invite Chase Pospichel to the stage. After this we'll have an open mic. So if there's something you want to share, please let me know."

Chase read beautifully and then Taylor volunteered to read something from their book of poems. The rest of the night flowed seamlessly, with many people sharing their own snippets of writing. People chatted amongst themselves as I began to break down the PA system.

Greg and Michelle gave me long hugs, thanking me for sharing.

"I'm curious." Michael said, when he approached me afterwards. "Did you create this event just so you had a place to share your poems?"

I gave him a wry smile. "Always trying to figure me out."

"I'm onto you." He said before making a quick run for the door.

Sierra and Lauren hugged me.

"That was gorgeous, Sandi." Sierra said, clasping her hands in front of her.

"We want to host events like this up at the shop." Lauren said. "Are you interested?"

199

"Yes yes, a thousand times yes!" I said dramatically.

I looked around the room, but didn't see the godfather.

We gathered those remaining for a group photo, standing in front of the floor-to-ceiling built-in bookcases that lined the wall; the rolling ladder providing the perfect backdrop to our motley crew.

The older, taller gentleman approached me. "Hey Sandi."

"Hey Peanut." I smiled, spotting Georgia Boy closing his tab.

"Your writing was… wow." He said, taking off his ball cap and revealing a bald head. His arms were lined with tattoos he got while in prison. "I had to leave to smoke a cigarette after that last one. It was too real."

I frowned slightly, feeling for him. "I understand. I'm just happy you came. Thanks for accepting my invite."

"Listen, Sandi." He placed his cap back on his head, forward facing. "I'd really like to buy you a drink sometime. I've wanted to buy you a drink since that Halloween Party at the Hobo."

I smiled, thinking back to that night. I had met Chase there as well, though unknowingly. Denuvo had slayed that night and I received several followers on social media the next day.

Chase called me a week later. I had no idea how he had gotten my number.

He invited me to read some poetry at an artist market. While on the phone call with me, he had thought it best to tell me that he was currently naked in the bathtub, smoking a bong.

I remembered Peanut at the party though. He stood next to the stage like a giant, hyping me up.

Men were lewd that night, getting too close to me and trying to whisper things in my ear.

But something about Peanut felt safe and I enjoyed his whoops and hollers during my performance.

"Damn girl!" He said, crossing his arms and bobbing his head. "You are killing it! What you drinking, baby? You ain't buying a single one the rest of the night!"

I looked at him then. Peanut was tall, strong and attractive in an unconventional sort of way. He had a red beard and pale skin, blue eyes.

I knew he had a good job, an electrician. He had gotten out of prison and made a whole new life for himself. I respected him.

He was funny. We had good conversations when we met.

I made my decision.

"Let me know when." I said, looking up at him. "I'd like that."

He got giddy. Shyly shaking his arms and gazing fondly down at me.

"You just made my whole night." He said, taking my hand and bringing it up to kiss it. "I'm gonna get out of here. My son is at the house."

Peanut gave me back my hand and walked out the door.

"Who was that?" A voice said behind me.

It was Georgia Boy.

"Oh. Hey. Thanks for coming!" I said, ignoring his question.

Georgia Boy's eyes still lingered on the door.

"Sandi!" Beanie said, walking up. "Nice event."

"Thank you." I said smiling.

A younger man with long blonde hair and a wide brimmed hat joined the group.

"Johnny!" Georgia Boy said, slapping him on the back.

"Georgia Boy!" Johnny answered.

"Hey Sandi. Have you met Johnny?" Georgia Boy asked.

"No." I said, the pleasant smile still on my face.

"I loved your pieces." Johnny said. "I'd really like to read next time."

"I'd love to have you!"

Johnny and Beanie started talking, Georgia Boy focusing his attention on me.

"So... who was that first one about?"

"Hm?" I said, still scanning the room for the godfather. I guess he had left.

"The first one. 'You make me feel like poetry after one glass of wine.'"

"Oh." I said, meeting his eyes. "Someone you don't know."

"Oh."

"I've got to start packing up." I said to no one in particular. "I need to get back to my kids."

"Here Sandi." Johnny said. "Let me help you."

"Right." Georgia Boy said, breaking his eye contact with me. "Right."

Beanie, Johnny and Georgia Boy helped me load up. I waved goodbye before pulling out of the parking lot and driving the two blocks home.

Arriving, I noticed the godfather's car wasn't in the driveway.

I unlocked the front door and stepped quietly inside.

All was quiet. My sister and the children were asleep.

I opened the children's bedroom door, as was my custom, and kissed them all on the forehead. Even little Sophia was asleep, curled up next to Lorelai.

Closing the door softly, I walked to the master bath to shower and change. After I was finished I checked my phone, the steam from the shower filling the bathroom.

You can have the bed if you want it. I'm staying with Jacqueline.

I walked into the dining room to grab my book, bringing it back into the master and shutting the door. I crawled into the bed, turning on the lamp and staring at the pages of my book without comprehending a single word.

I gave up. I shut the book, turned off the light and set it on the bedside table.

And I cried myself to sleep.

Chapter 15

Earthquake

I awoke to the ground rumbling. It felt like a train was headed right toward me.

I sat up straight in the bed, looking around. The walls seemed to shake and sway.

"This is how you die." The familiar thought scrolled through my head.

Then, the feeling of shaking was gone.

I snatched the covers off myself and ran to the den outside my bedroom door in my parent's house in Alaska.

They had set up a tent for the kids to sleep in.

I unzipped the side of the tent and looked down at my kiddos.

They had slept through the whole thing.

I breathed in deeply, letting the breath in and out slowly, trying to fight the rising panic in my chest that threatened to swallow me.

"Everyone okay?" My dad called from down the stairs.

I swallowed hard, steadying my breath.

"Yes!" I called in the direction of the stairs. "We're all okay down here!"

"Earthquake!" He only said.

"A five!" My bonus mom's voice trailed down the stairs. "Wow! That's a good one."

"When I said I wanted to experience all Alaska has to offer, I meant the Northern Lights!" I said loudly.

I went back to my bedroom, closing the door quietly behind me.

I gripped my knees to my chest, rocking back and forth.

"They're okay, Sandi." I said to myself, feeling the rhythmic sway of my body. "This isn't the hurricane. This isn't the hurricane. This isn't the hurricane."

I rock and rock. Repeating my mantra. Blocking out the images threatening to swallow me whole.

203

My ex holding me tightly. My children under a pillow fort we had made for them, their headphones blocking out the sounds of the monster just outside our window.

"I'm okay. They're okay. We're okay."

I rock and rock and rock.

Candles

"Please answer the phone. Please please please."

I paced under the carport. The burning in my chest erupts into a monster I almost couldn't contain.

"Please." I said again, running a hand through my hair.

"Hello?"

Relief flooded me, quickly choked out by the unquenchable panic reverberating through my being.

"Hi." I tried to say casually.

But the recipient of my phone call was immune to my illusions.

"What's wrong?" The godfather asked.

I heard my voice outside of my body. Each word feeling foreign, forced.

"My sister's friend just died. They think it's from an overdose. I was just with them at the beach last weekend. He… he played frisbee with Judah."

"Sandi, I'm so sorry. Do I need to come home?" He asked.

"No. Just…" I heard background noise. "Just tell me what you're doing." I took a deep breath. Another one.

"I'm at a store with Jacqueline."

"Perfect." I said, trying to slow my breathing. "What do you see?"

"Uhhh." There was a pause on the end of the line. "There's shelves, there's people."

"Okay." My pacing continued. I breathed towards the sky. "What's on the shelves? What are you buying?"

"Candles. There's candles and pillows..."

"I love candles." I said, tears started to well up in my eyes. A good sign. "Please tell me what kind of scents there are."

"Maple Honey. Sunset Serenade. Apple Crisp..."

He named off the scents and I listened, tears spilling over, my breathing slowing down.

I felt a small release. I felt my breath becoming more manageable.

I could let the godfather off the phone. I didn't want to bother him anymore while he was with Jacqueline.

"Thank you." I said. The tears were streaming now, hitting the concrete below me. "I just... it triggered me... that's how my ex..."

"I know." He said softly. "I know, Sandi." There was a pause. "I can still come home."

"No." I said, wiping my eyes. "No. But, could you pick the kids up from school today in a few hours? I'm going to head to the hospital."

"Of course I will."

We hang up and I weep on my way to the car.

Sit down

I'm a woman who gets the hell up.

I had my first child at 21 and suffered from Postpartum Anxiety.

"Get the hell up."

I did.

I got kicked out of church at 22.

"Get the hell up."

I did.

I had my second child at 23 and this time had Postpartum depression.

"Get the hell up."

I did.

I began caregiving at 26 for my ex.

"Get the hell up."

I did.

At 27 a category 5 hurricane destroyed my town.

"Get the hell up."

I did.

At 28 the pandemic hit and my life once again turned upside down.

"Get the hell up."

I did.

Then at 29, complete upheaval hit again with my divorce. Trauma layered on trauma. Years layered on years. Fights layered on fights.

An explosion.

Years of holding it all together crashed in on me. Years of getting the hell up and fighting. Years shouldering the burdens. Being the responsible one.

"Get the hell up."

.....

"Sandi. Get the hell up."

....

"Sandi?"

I haven't been able to finish a book in 6 months.

My songs are unfinished.

My brain isn't working like it used to.

I couldn't get the hell up.

Not this time.

The more I tried, the more depressed I felt.

The more I tried, the more I sunk into the bed.

"Sandi. Get. The. Hell. Up."

...

"You've been through worse."

And that's the point.

I have been through worse. I have been through so much worse and I still held it all together. Every single time. Without fail.

I pushed through. I grit my teeth and bore it.

I went to that space inside my mind where nothing else existed but my will.

My hair fell out and stopped growing.

I gained 30lbs.

I aged more quickly.

But I got the hell up. Every single time.

Every single damn time.

Now this opponent that wasn't even in my league, sent me to my knees.

And I couldn't get the hell up.

Months have passed in this energy. My mind and feelings disconnected from my body.

Going through the motions. Existing. Trying to find the joy in it all.

I've pushed and prodded myself to keep going, all the while moving more and more slowly.

What is happening to me?

Why can't I get past this?

I've faced so much worse than this.

Then I realized, all those years I was telling myself to get the hell up, I wish I would have had someone tell me to sit the fuck down.

"Sandi, sit the fuck down. Rest today."

"Sandi, sit the fuck down. I've got this today."

"Sandi. sit. the. fuck. down."

But I didn't have that.

I didn't.

But ultimately, that's my fault.

I'm making peace with that truth.

I'm learning to tell my own self to sit the fuck down.

Last weekend I went to the beach two days in a row and left the house a wreck.

Last night my kids had cinnamon rolls and eggs for dinner.

I've poured myself into art that has no purpose or monetary value.

I take the work I want and leave the work I don't.

I like to sit on my swing in the pecan tree and watch the light pass through the leaves.

I like to kayak instead of making sure the kitchen's clean first.

I take naps in the grass in my backyard.

I stare off into space for hours.

I roller skate in the park and I'm really bad at it. I can't stop. But it makes me happy.

There's baskets of laundry that have sat in my living room for two weeks.

I'm quick to walk away or pull back from people who can't reciprocate my energy.

I take my kids skating on Tuesdays.

And lately, I really like to use the word, "No."

I told myself to sit the fuck down.

I don't know how long I'll be down.

I'm tired. So, so, so tired.

A decade of work, a decade of getting the hell up, a decade of pouring out.

It's funny how stuff is still flowing my way though. Actually... maybe it's not funny at all. Maybe that's how it works.

Maybe you sow so you can reap. Maybe you pour out so eventually stuff pours in.

Maybe rest really is a part of the process.

I don't know. I'm trying it for a change.

And I can tell you one thing.

This time I'm not getting the hell up until I'm good and ready.

Chapter 16

Dirty thirty

"Hey darling." A man said to me as I counted out the tips at Papa Joe's. "Or should I say señorita?"

"Please no." I said under my breath.

"What are you, sweetheart? You look like you're foreign."

"Alien." I said, walking away and handing my bandmate the tips.

I had to rush to my car. I would work a double that night with a 6pm-9pm show at Papa Joe's and a 9:30pm-1:30am show at the Salty Hobo. I had just enough time to make it to my show with the godfather.

I waved goodbye to my bandmate and walked quickly to my car. I had half the mind to take off my heels so I could walk faster.

I arrived at my car and jumped in, slamming the door.

I was just about to press the start button when I heard a knock on my driver's side window.

I jumped, whirling around.

But the person who knocked had already walked away, waving before turning back to the group of people he was with.

Georgia Boy.

I turned on the car and buckled my seat belt, watching Georgia Boy join a crowd of people. He was standing close to a girl with long dirty blonde hair. He touched her back before pulling his hand away.

My eyes narrowed slightly as I backed up the car and headed to the Highway.

I put down the visor at a red light and opened the lighted mirror, taking in my appearance.

My hair was dark and unruly, my eyes lined with black. Spring was already bringing out more brown in my complexion, my skin absorbing the color easily. My red lipstick needed touching up.

I pulled out my lipstick and lined my mouth, giving them a pop to smooth the color.

"What are you, sweetheart?" The man had asked.

I slammed the visor back in place and continued my drive to the Salty Hobo.

I had to park at the marina, St. Andrews was packed that night.

I half ran towards the dive bar, my feet aching. I scolded myself inwardly. I should have brought my chucks to change into.

The godfather had already set up the stage. I stood next to him and leaned down with my hands on my knees, catching my breath.

"How was Joe's?" He asked.

"Just fine." I said.

I looked up, scanning the crowd. I was meeting someone at the bar that night.

I had three dates that week. It was my ex's turn with the children and I had stacked my nights. Another military guy who used to work in the rodeo; Antônio, who hosted events for one of the biggest resorts on the beach; and Peanut.

Rodeo was supposed to come watch me play that night.

We began our set and Rodeo arrived with a friend. He was blonde haired and blue eyed.

Truth be told, I was more attracted to his friend who had a dark complexion and long flowing brown hair.

Rodeo was not my typical type. Neither was Peanut. But I had been trying to expand my horizons.

I also had developed a few rules for myself.

No musicians. And nobody who resembled my ex or Sk8er Boi.

The only exception was Antônio, but he was insistent. And honestly, gorgeous in every sense of the word.

His black hair was well groomed, his teeth stark white, his beard cleanly maintained.

And his Brazilian accent was enough to make me swoon when we spoke.

So, I made an exception.

Beatdown on the Beach was fast approaching. The godfather and I agonized over our thirty minute setlist.

"We definitely have to do Zombie by the Cranberries." The godfather said.

"My niece Triniti would approve. What about Truth Hurts by Lizzo?"

"Absolutely not!"

"Come on!"

I was finally thirty. I had scheduled three gigs on my birthday, my mentality being that I didn't have anyone who would really do anything for me.

Not that my ex was ever super huge on birthdays. For my twenty ninth birthday I had to go pick up my own Tex-Mex food and a gallon of margaritas.

I got drunk and danced to the Across the Universe soundtrack while my ex stared at me incredulously.

But my thirtieth birthday started off with a bang. The godfather made me mimosas and coffee in the morning, my sister did my hair and make up.

"Beauty is pain!" She sang as she pulled a straightener through my hair and attacked my lashes with mascara.

My first show was at the Little Village that early afternoon.

By 2pm I was wasted.

But Greg and Michelle came to my show, surprising me with gifts. My sister came by with a cookie cake. The godfather sang in a bass voice as they joined the Happy Birthday chorus.

Then, the godfather drove me to our next show at the Taproom. I walked in absolutely hammered.

Jacqueline gave me daffodils. Georgia Boy greeted me at the gates. His beard had started to grow in.

"Hey girl! I hear it's your birthday!"

"Yep!" I said grinning. "We're all going bowling tonight if you want to come! My last show ends at 9pm."

"I'll see if I can make it."

The Taproom was packed. Monday Night Little Fest was hosting an all day fest that day and over twenty musicians took part. The godfather and I were scheduled to go on between my last show and my next one.

Greg and Michelle followed me to the Taproom.

"We're gonna follow you all day girl! This is your day!"

It was my turn to take the stage with the godfather. Bartender shoved a mimosa in my hand shouting, "Dirty thirty! Our girl!"

I took the stage and grabbed the microphone, ready to introduce us. But Kirk had other plans. He had the whole Taproom sing happy birthday to me.

I couldn't help it. I grinned from ear to ear and did a small curtsy.

Then I spoke into the mic. "Hello everyone! I'm Sandi MarLisa and this is the godfather, it's my thirtieth birthday, I've been drunk since 10am and I DON'T GIVE A FUCK!"

The crowd cheered, cell phones popped up recording the scene.

I could hear Bartender telling her friend. "Sandi is a whole vibe today."

I was. I was a whole vibe.

And, damn it. I sang Truth Hurts by Lizzo. The godfather be damned. It was my birthday!

We nailed our set, everyone applauding and singing along with us.

I hopped off the stage, Bartender handing me another mimosa. I walked up to join a crowd of people who all wished me a happy birthday.

Then, I dropped my mimosa.

"Sorry. I'm really drunk."

The godfather had another one for me in an instant.

We ended up making a video singing In Hell I'll Be in Company by The Dead South. Jacob sang lead, Jacqueline and myself sang harmonies, the godfather played guitar, Georgia Boy percussion and Boss Man even whistled the tune as he filmed.

Then, I was ushered out the door by the godfather for my next gig.

He escorted me all night. Greg and Michelle quickly on his heels.

The rest of the night was a blur. I performed my 80s act at Shore Shack Pizza for three hours while stuffing my face with pizza between songs.

The owner, Jim, just smiled at me, offering me more wine. "Happy birthday Sandi!"

Then, the godfather was driving me to Rockit Lanes, where my friends and I were bowling. Greg, Michelle, the Godfather, Sierra, Lauren and Michael were there.

"You know I'm here because I love you, Sandi." Sierra said, her eyes widening as she took in the loud sounds and the crash of bowling pins.

"And I love you for it!"

I was a true ham that night, my bowling terrible. But at least I was entertaining.

"Dude." Michael, who refused to bowl, said to the godfather. "Sandi is trashed."

The godfather only shook his head in my direction in response.

I looked down at my phone as the godfather walked me to the car. Two messages flashed on the screen.

One was from Georgia Boy. *Hey grl. You stll bwling?*

So he was hammered. I didn't bother responding.

And then... there was a text from Sk8er Boi.

I hadn't spoken to him in weeks, cutting off all contact.

Happy birthday, Sandi. The text read.

I quickly wrote back, against my better judgment.

Well, let's face it. My judgment was questionably incapacitated.

Thank you.

"Ready for a break?" The godfather said, setting down his guitar.

"Yeah." I said, putting down my microphone.

I grabbed my glass of Gin and took a sip, eyeing Rodeo. I was drinking more Gin these days.

Rodeo met my eyes and smiled, offering a small wave.

Tilting my chin up, I looked down at him beneath my eyelashes, my smile widening.

Then I stepped off the stage to meet Rodeo, absolutely dead inside.

Give me grace that screams

By the age of 8 years old I had read the book of Revelation a dozen times. I found the words hypnotic, fascinating. It had leviathans and dragons and beasts and angels and demons.

You find out Jesus has a tattoo.

It's wild.

It drew me in. And then the Left Behind series by Tim Lahaye came out. I read all 40 of the kids books and the entire adult series, ravenously.

When would the end of the world come upon us?

Was I ready to die for my faith?

I would pray to God every night that I was excited for Jesus to come back, but I'd ask if I could please get married first. Could I please have some kids? Could I grow up and enjoy life a bit?

Could I maybe not die a horrible martyr's death? If it wasn't too inconvenient.

Then I'd think that was selfish and try to take it all back.

Of course I wanted Jesus to come back. Of course I was ready to die for my faith.

And that's how you go about living your life, at least for the kids who are fully "sold out." The ones who take everything the preacher says seriously. They walk around their schools trying to convert their friends. They think about dying a martyr's death. They think about whether their thoughts are pure, or if their actions properly "represent Jesus."

At least, I did.

The end of the world was around every corner. Somewhere along the way, I lost who I was.

What did it matter? I was probably going to die a martyr.

I found the most involved, charismatic church I could have possibly found to fit my zeal. I spent 20-25 hours a week in services or volunteering.

I was ready to go out in the world and save all the lost souls, all the people who would end up in hell if I couldn't reach them in time.

Because if you can just imagine with me, truly believing with everything that you are that if you don't behave a certain way, speak a certain way or preach enough... you and all your loved ones could end up burning for eternity...

... wouldn't you be zealous, too? If you really believed it.

I mean, really. Deeply. With your entire being.

I was radical.

And I believe God met me in that place because he saw my heart. Or whatever you want to call the love that I think binds us all together. To me, it's an unnamable force that compels me forward.

But whatever "it" was, it met me. It opened my eyes to how misguided I truly was. How foolishly I was going about everything.

I started asking questions. I got kicked out of church.

My entire world came crashing in on me. Everything I had believed up until that point I was now deconstructing.

What was I supposed to do with all this zeal I had? That I had always had! What was I supposed to do with this belief that I was made for something more? Destined for some divine plan bigger than myself?

Because what if there was no planned trajectory for my life? What if I was the one responsible for creating meaning?

And, damn it, what if I didn't want to be a martyr? What if I didn't want to constantly be concerned about the signs of times and just LIVE MY LIFE.

MY LIFE. Mine.

Bit by bit I felt invisible walls crashing down around me. All the rules I had lived by just weren't working for me anymore. I decided to walk in love, starting with loving others the way I wish they'd love me.

It was so much easier to do. So much easier to keep up with.

It wasn't death, but life. True life. Even Jesus spent a total of only three days of his 33 years on the planet dead or dying as the story goes. So why did people talk about dying SO MUCH?

I wanted to LIVE!

When I got kicked out of church, I was ostracized by the community. So I built my own.

The world became my church.

I began reaching out like I had never done before. Going out to coffee with strangers. Inviting people out. Texting kind words. Writing essays about what I really, really thought.

And what I really, really thought looked nothing like I had been taught.

I stopped caring about whether or not the world would end, because I'm alive right now.

God, it's beautiful. Beautiful to be alive. Beautiful to breathe it in, each day a new chance to live and let live.

I ask you, what's so wrong with that?

Then, my husband got really ill. I became a caregiver. I thought I had to keep it all to myself.

It was the same martyr mentality that had followed me around my whole life, since I was 8 years old reading Revelation by flashlight.

I would pray to God for grace. "I'm 27 years old and I'm already a caregiver." Tears would run as silent prayers down my cheeks. "But all I can think about is how much I want to sing again. How much I want to do my own thing. How much I want to live my life out loud."

I decided I didn't want more grace to bear up under my burdens. At least not the grace that I was taught. The silent, stoic wife caring for her husband and children. The saintly woman working quietly and forsaking herself for those she loves.

"No!" My soul would scream, pounding at the door of heart. "Let me out! Let me out!"

And one day the doors flew open. I read to my husband the pieces I had written about being a caregiver and asked if I could share them. He agreed.

I began reaching out, sharing my struggles, talking about the people I love and how I love them. Opening up the church doors of my soul and releasing the purifying fire. It consumed everything and all of a sudden I wasn't alone anymore. People started seeing me, reaching out, connecting.

"Hey, I'm there, too."

"You're speaking my heart."

You mean this entire time I didn't have to be alone?

I didn't have to be a martyr?

I didn't have to try and mask myself with saintly grace from hell?

I could unleash the terrors within and use them as my materials to make something beautiful.

I no longer wanted to try and bear my burdens with grace. I wanted to cast off my burdens and be seen, to be understood and loved for what I am.

Being a saint is overrated.

I don't want my blood spilled until it cries out from the ground demanding justice. I want my voice to be the sounding board. I want to be alive to rend the heavens until it collides with earth, transforming it.

Give me mess. Give me the beautiful and the terrible. Give me grace that screams. Give me pain and joy. Give me the full range of the human experience.

That's my religion.

Los Antojitos

Peanut dug into his steak and asparagus as I picked up my taco to take a bite.

"You said you were so hungry and you only ordered one taco!" Peanut said.

I laughed, covering my mouth. "That's because I know I chow down on the chips and queso. Do you see the mess I've made?" I brushed the remains of the chips I devoured off the table.

"My kinda woman."

I looked outside to the deck of Los Antojitos in St. Andrews. There was a beautiful oak tree that the builders shaped the deck around, string lights lit it up at night.

"I did some electrical work here." Peanut said, absentmindedly.

I chuckled. "You're always pointing out places you've done work in."

"Part of the rules of being an electrician!"

My phone buzzed. I quickly glanced at the name that flashed on the screen.

"Shit." I said under my breath. I looked at Peanut. "Listen, it's work. I promise I'm not trying to be rude."

"No problem, beautiful."

I read the message from a bar owner nearby

Sandi. I double booked you and the godfather. I'm canceling you guys for tomorrow.

"Damn it." I said under my breath.

"Everything okay?" Peanut asked.

"Yes." I said with a sigh. "A bar owner double booked his dates. This is the second time he's done this to me."

Peanut finished swallowing a mouthful. "That sucks. You get any payment for his mistake?"

"No." I said looking out towards the window.

218

My head reeled. I really needed the money. The court costs to finalize the divorce were due.

My eyes went back to Peanut. A slow smile spread across my face.

"Hey Peanut." I said sweetly.

"Yes beautiful?"

I leaned over the table and touched his hand. "Remind me how tall you are again?"

"Six foot five."

I took him in. Peanut was a guy nobody wanted to mess with. He had that aura about him.

"You feel like getting into some trouble with me?" I asked, batting my eyelashes.

"Let me pay this tab, sweetheart, and you lead the way."

The bar was close by. We took a seat when we arrived.

The bar owner spotted me right away and tried to walk in the opposite direction. But I called his name, winking at Peanut.

Peanut took the cue, crossing his arms and flexing his prison tattoos. Scowling.

"H-hey Sandi." The owner said.

"Hi." I smiled sweetly. "I got your message and wanted to talk to you about it."

"I really–"

"This is the second time you've double booked me. And I know mistakes happen, but this is what I do for a living. I do have two children, you know." I looked at my nails. "And they're starting private school this year."

"Listen Sandi—"

"I'm not upset. But I can't continue booking with you if I'm going to continue being canceled, especially with hardly any notice."

"I…" The bar owner looked at Peanut. "I know I had to cancel, but I had decided to still pay you your fee… I was about to message you… since it was my mistake and you're a single mom and all…"

I smiled wider. "Oh? Well that is just so sweet of you. Thank you."

The bar owner left to go ahead and cut the check. I looked over at Peanut and smiled.

"You're a lifesaver." I said. "Great job."

"I tried to play the part." He said, uncrossing his arms. Peanut grinned at me. "You don't play around, do you?"

"I didn't get where I am by being stupid." I said, winking.

"No." Peanut said, reaching for my hand across the table. "I reckon not."

Beatdown on the Beach

I wonder if the shawl thing could be a different color. You know? Michael texted me.

I had sent him a picture of the outfit I wanted to wear to Beatdown on the Beach.

What about blue?

No

Not blue

Go with that one if blue is the only other option.

Lime green would be cool...

Dude. Lime green would be sick. Purple would be dope.

Literally fucking anything but blue.

Black and blue is literally so 90s business casual dude you'd need shoulder pads to pull that off and even then it's risky.

Wait is this for the fight?

God you make me laugh. And yes.

Good. Absolutely not blue.

"I love your outfit!" A woman said, passing me. "It's so... like retro meets hippie. You know? It just works."

"Thank you ma'am." I said, smiling. "I really appreciate it."

I sat on the stage with a good view of the boxing ring. The godfather was off searching for beer.

I looked around at the large crowd, taking it all in.

Tonight was a big one.

I secretly hoped Sk8er Boi would show up wanting to see me. But I hadn't heard from him since a weird Instagram message he had sent me. He randomly messaged me and told me he was moving to Tampa in a few months before blocking me completely on the platform.

I looked around for his face in the crowd, but I soon decided my attempts were futile.

"I wish the musicians had our own table." I said to the godfather as he walked to where I was perched on the stage.

"Are you kidding?" He said, sitting next to me. "I feel cool as fuck."

I smiled, thinking.

Earlier I had walked in through the back door as instructed, but was stopped by an armed security guard.

"Tickets?" He said.

"I'm with the band." I said, smiling.

The officer looked me up and down, taking in my sequined skirt, low cut crop top and heels.

"Good luck, ma'am." He said.

I continued walking in like I owned the place.

"Yeah." I agreed with the godfather. "This is cool as fuck."

"Sandi." Rob, the organizer of the event, approached me. "You guys are up next."

The godfather and I took our positions on the stage, breathing deeply. We had sound checked the day before with the sound technicians. They helped us set up and quickly left the stage.

The large screens on the walls flashed and my face was suddenly everywhere.

I stared straight ahead like I didn't see them. Waiting to be announced.

When people ask me how long I've been in the music scene, I tell them I don't remember a time there wasn't a microphone in my hand.

I was never pressed or pressured to be put on the stage. I was never shy. I was never quiet.

And I always knew I was good.

I always had a solo in every play. I went for the big roles.

I auditioned for the production of Annie. I wanted the role of Lily St. Regis.

Mr. Ron Holloman, who also taught theater for my son years later, took me aside.

"Sandi, you are eight years old. You're too young to play this role."

"But I want her solos."

"Then audition for Annie."

I rolled my eyes. "I don't want to be Annie."

I got the role of Duffy the orphan and there were a few quick solos that showcased my voice.

I would be approached later. Strangers praising me for my talent.

I quickly learned, it was usually strangers who praised me for my talent.

The people I considered friends would become jealous of me. I didn't know that's what it was called then. I thought they didn't like me because I was always a chubby kid.

And so, I fell in love with the stage. It became my home.

Music consumed me. I wrote poetry in math class instead of paying attention. My books were confiscated at the door of reading class.

"But this is reading class!"

"Yes. But you have to read what is given to you and answer the questions."

"God. What you give me is boring!"

My play was work. I sang in talent shows and won. I performed at the Martin Theater and Civic Center more times than I could count. I was selected out of choral companies to sing solos for larger choirs.

My voice was my power.

And I knew it.

There was nothing more natural in the entire world to me than performance. But beyond that, the stage was the one place I felt I experienced connection.

It was the one place I knew I would be celebrated.

Because I was volatile. I was a complicated kid. I had opinions and an inner desire to be great. I would go silent when uninterested. I would zone out when not stimulated.

My peers, especially young girls, felt intimidated by me. I didn't realize this at the time. But my confidence, my non apologetic attitude, my talent, made me lonely.

It was difficult to connect with other girls and this followed me into adulthood.

I didn't know it then. But this competition, especially amongst women, stems from the history of the token woman. The fact that there were not enough slots in the world for every woman to win in her passions.

I grew up thinking there was something wrong with me. I was bullied. I was incessantly picked on; for everything from my weight, to how I dressed, to how I talked.

But when I was on that damn stage. Everyone shut the hell up.

When I was on that stage, no one could touch me.

Because I was good. I was damn good.

And I worked my ass off. I took on more projects than anyone.

I treated my music like a job before I ever knew it could be a job.

In my spare time I studied sheet music for choral practice. I stood next to my mother in church and learned the harmonies she sang. Today, there isn't a harmony I can't sing by ear.

I could play the piano by ear. I have perfect pitch. I wrote songs and recorded them on this tiny two input recorder my parents got me for Christmas. I'd cry when six hours of hard work was randomly erased from the drive.

Once I wrote a song and started singing it and playing it on my guitar in the courtyard outside a chapel at church camp. To my surprise a small crowd began to form. Two boys with guitars watched my hands and picked up the chords. We played the song a few times.

After we were finished everyone cheered. One of the boys playing guitar said he'd talk to the band about me singing this song in front of the camp. Hundreds of kids. Something I would never try for myself.

It ended up happening. Afterwards, kids I didn't know were praising me.

Because strangers always did.

I was asked to sing my song at the next church service back home. It was a big church and a huge moment I looked forward to.

Right before I was meant to step on the stage, a church leader approached me and the two boys playing guitar.

"Sandi. I'm sorry. We're not going to play your song today. We just don't think the world is ready for Sandi Klüg yet."

Then I had to go sing back up for the main band.

My mother commented afterwards that I was singing for Jesus with murder in my eyes.

The words stuck with me. "The world isn't ready for Sandi Klüg yet."

My history with the church was always a complicated one. I was incessantly encouraged to cover up, to tone it down, to make my voice more simplistic.

I've been kicked out of one church. And I've left two ministries since then.

I probably will not return to the ministry after a decade of service.

I stopped singing. I spent six years alone raising my two children. I began to write essays that became popular. Once again, strangers clapped for me.

After my divorce, I was invited to a zoom call with the lead minister of a ministry I was a part of without any context.

I was then told that the life decisions I was making would possibly endanger the lives of my children. That he was blindsided by my divorce and I was possibly being influenced by the demonic.

This is, of course, when I had begun singing again. I began singing, dressing up and now I was getting a divorce.

A regular ole Jezebel. Nothing I hadn't been called before.

There was a woman in leadership on the conference call hearing everything this man was saying to me. There were no words for my defense.

So for the first time in my life, I defended MYSELF.

"I am completely uncomfortable with this conversation and frankly it is none of your business. I am not being influenced by anything other than myself, you have no idea what I've been through and I don't believe I can work for this ministry anymore."

I lost 70% of my income in a five minute zoom call.

Instead of support, I received judgment.

Nothing I hadn't experienced before.

I began pouring myself into my music again, coming out of a time period of spending six years alone.

Strangers once again began clapping for me. People I once considered my friends went silent on me.

No outward, obvious judgment. Just silence.

Just the withdrawal of approval.

Just the subtle disdain.

Again, nothing I hadn't experienced before.

Over the past year, I've begun to recognize myself again. Because of this, because of acting more like myself, the same old problems pop up. Shit I've been dealing with since I was eight.

I have cried in anguish for hours and then put on my makeup to go perform.

I have had panic attacks only to immediately put on my heels to dance.

Yes, I've spent more time in bars.

Yes, my lifestyle has changed.

Yes, my level of i-don't-give-a-fuck has been slowly approaching max capacity.

I am asked questions like, "Sandi, where did you come from? You seem to have come out of nowhere."

And you know what? That's because I've been nowhere. Nowhere and everywhere.

That's because I realized six years of silence didn't negate twenty four years of hard won experience.

I decided to say to hell with it all. I can't live like this anymore.

I can't try to fit myself in a box that was never meant for me, a box people sneered at me for being really bad at trying to contort myself into.

I can't continue on with placid smiles to appease people who can't clap for me when I start to win.

I started clapping for ME.

I started cheering for ME.

I started celebrating for ME.

Because I was tired of the strangers being the only ones who clapped. I was tired of not being seen for who I am and celebrated. I was tired of only feeling connected to others when I was performing.

I've since connected and reconnected with some really wonderful people. People who CLAP for me and they KNOW me. People who CHEER me and they LOVE me. People who simultaneously CELEBRATE my talent and my success without feeling threatened by it.

People who see me at my worst but it doesn't change their high opinion of me at all.

And it's a smaller group. I'm still met with snubs and sneers. It breaks my heart when people feel intimidated. It shatters me to know that not everyone can love me as I love them. Not everyone can celebrate me as I celebrate them.

But I'll be damned if I apologize for being talented and skilled—SKILL I EARNED—ever again.

I'll be damned if I ever play small in order to be well liked.

I'm learning to live under the gaze of disapproval and shine like a beacon of light for everyone else who ever felt unseen and unheard.

I'm learning to keep my head held high, to shoot every shot I can without backing down.

As a woman, I've always had to be three times as good to go half as far and listened to half as well.

So if people think I've lost my mind NOW.

Just you wait.

JUST YOU WAIT.

They ain't seen nothing yet.

"Ladies and Gentleman!" The announcer voice carried through the building. "May we introduce Bay County's very own Godfather and…"

I remembered it all. I remembered the world telling me it didn't want me.

That I was too much or too little of whatever they decided.

They weren't ready for Sandi Klüg yet.

But tonight?

Tonight I was…

"Sandi MarLisa!"

The spotlight shone on us as the godfather strummed the first chord.

And I became who I always was.

Stardust

Never let anyone tell you what you can and cannot do.

Never let anyone keep you in a cage.

Set your soul free and break out of every. single. damn. expectation that kept you from becoming exactly who you knew you always were.

Life is long as it is short. Set your goals like you'll live forever, live like this is your last moment.

Dream big and wild. Think improbably and impractically.

You can't do it unless you dream it up first, after all.

And what if it never happens?

On that day when you find out all the "what ifs," I dare you to look back.

Look back and tell me you regret any of it.

You won't.

I don't.

Love with every broken piece of your heart. Offer this world every scar, every bruise, every hell locked inside and every heaven—you keep your head in those clouds.

Because you? You'll keep this world guessing, and it's the questions they'll ask of you that will finally give you the answers you've been searching for.

Your soul is innumerous as the stars. If you pull on it, if you draw it up like water from a well, watch as more galaxies pour out of you. Watch as everyone stops and thinks, "Who is this person? They make me feel awake—alive!"

That. That, my friend, is how you'll know you made it. A connection with the divine. A portal between this world and the unseen.

The improbable. The impractical.

And maybe. Maybe, if you're lucky, you'll live to see where your stardust lands. How it transforms everything it touches. How your light makes the darkness beautiful.

So please. Promise me. Promise me this:

Promise me you won't settle.

Promise me you won't accept.

Promise me you'll be restless.

Restless like a river. Or an ocean. Or the stream I sat next to and read books that took me to worlds unseen.

Promise me you'll keep moving. Because stagnant water never helped anyone.

Unlock that door. Free yourself.

You were always the key anyway.

Chapter 17

Figure eight

I twirled and twirled on the ice, my boots slipping beneath me.

"Look mommy!" Lorelai shuffled past me, giggling and reaching out her little gloved hand.

I took her hand and we started to glide, a figure eight carved in the lake by ice skates just feet from us.

"Mom!" Judah shouted across the lake, running and jumping and sliding on the ice rink.

I laughed, breathing in the cold air.

A sound rumbled in the deep. It was the sound of drums.

The sound of ice cracking.

"Run to shore!" My dad yelled. He grabbed Judah's hand and ran. My bonus mom right behind them.

I yanked Lorelai by the arm, she immediately slipped on the ice but I dragged her by the hood of her jacket towards the shore.

"This is how you die." I thought to myself as the ice drums echoed through the mountains once more.

He sailed away

"Mommy! Can we go?" Lorelai whined from the couch at the Taproom.

"No baby. Not yet."

"This is sooooo borrrring."

It was Monday Night Little Fest and I had already performed, but I was determined to stay for the whole show. Judah was chatting up everyone in sight, asking deep existential questions to anyone who would listen.

"Dude." Bartender said to me. "Your son just asked me if bartending was my dream and, if not, what was the one thing standing in the way of accomplishing my dream?"

I heaved a sigh, putting my head down on the counter. "So you see what I live with?"

She just shook her head, utterly shook.

"Hey Sandi."

I turned to see who belonged to the voice. "Oh. Hey Georgia Boy."

He took in my face, studying it.

I had recently taken a trip to Asheville, North Carolina to see my best friend, Jessica, and my godson. The kids and I visited Biltmore Estate and we hiked a few mountain trails.

Jessica had made me an appointment to get my nose pierced. It was a change I wanted to make marking my thirtieth year, along with the tattoo on the cusp of my left ear Sierra had gifted me. Vines now framed my ear as if they had been stitched into my flesh and an Opal stud pierced the right side of my nose.

"I haven't seen you in a while." Georgia Boy said. He stepped closer to me, taking in my face. He pulled back the curtain of my hair to look at the tattoo. "You've got a tattoo and your nose is pierced." He stepped back. "It looks nice."

"Thanks!" I said. "Things I always said I'd do when I turned thirty."

I looked at Georgia Boy then, his face drawn.

Something seemed... off.

He wandered away, aiming for the fireplace closest to the stage.

Lorelai was talking to the godfather. Judah had found a new person to talk science with.

Boss Man stood next to me. "Your kid speaks better than I do."

I smiled. "Yeah. I know. Me too."

"So what happened with gorgeous Antônio?"

"Oh." I said, blushing. "He's too materialistic for me."

"And the tall guy?"

"Peanut, yeah. He was nice. We mutually decided it wasn't for us. He's still not really over his ex and I didn't feel that *thing* with him, you know?"

Boss Man nodded, setting his beer on the counter. "You know what you need, Sandi?"

"What's that?"

"You need a mediocre looking man who worships the ground you walk on. You deserve to be absolutely adored."

I sighed. "Yes, Boss Man. A girl can dream." I said wistfully, rolling my eyes at him.

I walked back towards the fires and looked for a place to sit. Georgia Boy was still at the first fire alone.

Well, that was unusual.

"Hey." I greeted, taking the seat next to him.

"Hey." He responded.

We sat and listened to the music for a while in silence.

"So what's up with you?" I asked without taking my eyes off the act.

"Hm?"

I turned to look at him. "You're sad." I said, matter of factly.

He laughed bitterly. "I've been sad, Sandi."

I cocked my head, squinting my eyes at him. "Well. It's obvious today. So what's going on?"

He sighed. "I took a boat here."

"I'm sorry?"

"I walked from my condo with my guitar on my back and made it to Papa Joe's. I met a boat captain at the docks and asked him to bring me here." He covered his face with his hands. "I told him I had a show I needed to make. I don't even have a show."

I stared at him incredulously for a moment, and then...

I laughed hysterically. I laughed and laughed and laughed.

"What the hell is so funny?" Georgia Boy took his face out of his hands and stared at me.

I couldn't stop. I couldn't stop laughing.

"You..." I said through tears. "You asked a random guy to sail you away to the Taproom."

Georgia Boy pursed his lips at me, eyes narrowed.

I burst into another fit of giggles.

"Mommy." Lorelai walked up to me, rubbing her eyes. "I'm sleepy."

"Climb up on my lap then." I patted my knee.

Georgia Boy looked at us. "She looks exactly like you."

"Mhm." I kissed Lorelai's head and stroked her hair, listening to the next musician.

It didn't take long for Lorelai to fall asleep in my arms. Her breathing became steady, her sweet face scrunched up in peace.

"So why did you do it?"

"Do what?" Georgia Boy took off his hat and rubbed his face.

He looked different, too. His skin was a deep tan and his hair had grown out, his beard filling in.

I rolled my eyes, sighing impatiently. "Why did you ask a random boat captain to sail you here? Why did you start walking?"

"Oh." He said, putting the cap back on his head. "I'm just going through it."

"Heard." I said, turning my attention back to the band.

Georgia Boy eyed me when I didn't say anything else.

"Hey Sandi." One of the musicians who performed that night wandered up.

"Hey! How's it going?"

The musician looked at Lorelai sleeping in my arms. "I think it's really cool how you bring them with you." He said. "Mine are still really young, but I want to bring them to my shows."

I nodded, smiling. "I try to bring them with me often. I used to write while bouncing them on my knee and sing while holding their hands."

"Sandi!" Kirk called from the stage. "We need you for the group photo. You too, Anthony!"

"Oh." I said, looking for a place to put Lorelai. "Here."

I picked up Lorelai and set her in Georgia Boy's lap.

232

"Uhhhhh…" He stuttered, making a cradle for her head with his arm. Lorelai stirred, looking at the new person holding her and then quickly relaxing her face back into sleep.

"I'll be quick." I said. "You're fine." I ran up to the stage to snap the photo.

Bartender made her appearance, getting down on one knee with her arms stretched out, grinning. I put my arm around Anthony, smiling at Kirk who held the camera.

Kirk stepped aside when the photo was snapped, moving to speak with one of the musicians.

And behind him was Georgia Boy who stood gazing at me, patiently waiting, and cradling Lorelai in his arms.

Momma, make them go with you

When I was young, my parents owned a baby store. I grew up entertaining myself and my sister with the big cardboard boxes. We made cities and homes with three bedrooms out of them. We came up with skits and performed them for the shop.

We played in the parking lot and watched our mother handle customers, organize her staff. We made friends with the other kids whose parents owned stores in our plaza.

I have a vivid memory of laying on one of the show beds, staring out through the front windows of the shop. The window washer was removing the old holiday paint and I thought watching him work was relaxing.

My mom caught me staring and lectured me about how it was rude to stare at people while they're working.

"If you have time to stare at him, why don't you walk outside and ask him if you can help scrub the windows? No? Then quit staring."

To this day when people are working, I avert my eyes.

My mom has done lots of things in her life. She was a waitress, a business owner, a teacher, a real estate agent, a correctional officer…

It always mesmerized me. I knew then that most people seemed to stick to one career and that my mom was a little different.

It showed me I didn't have to choose. People could be more than one thing.

It also showed me that women could work and bring their children with them.

I sometimes complained about being up at the store instead of at home watching TV, but my childhood is filled with memories of watching my mom work, helping receive customers, and proudly stating, "My mom owns this place" when people asked me where my parents were.

I even got my first job next door. I loved getting grilled cheese and a sweet tea at Key West Sandwich Shop and then walking to get cookies from JRs Ribshack.

Everyone knew me, but sometimes my parents wouldn't give me money for cookies. They said I shouldn't eat them every day.

Little did they know, me and the owner had a deal. If I went outside his lot and picked up all the trash, he'd give me a dollar so I could buy a pack of cookies.

This might have been one of the reasons I was a chubby, chubby kid... but I learned the value of trading services for money. And I got my damn pack of homemade chocolate chip cookies every single day.

As I'm writing this, I'm listening to my kids downstairs wailing, much to the dismay of their grandparents. The noise barely registers. You see, these kids built my business with me. I'm used to writing thousand word essays with a toddler pulling at me, used to sending invoices while my children do their homework at the kitchen table, accustomed to "getting in the zone" while my godson or nieces are over because the schools are closed that day.

In fact, my son grew up performing with me. I'd strap him tightly to my chest and stand behind my keyboard, playing and singing, daring anyone to make a comment. When he grew up a bit, I propped a chair next to my instrument, and he'd sit there, touching my thigh for comfort as the music built around him.

My life looks a little different than the days at my mom's baby store. The kids aren't lying on show beds, but sitting at picnic tables, eating pizza while their mom sings 80s music and flirts with the crowd.

My son took my heart and squeezed it the other day. He came home from school and I told him to sit down to do his homework.

"It's done already."

"Uh huh." I responded. I didn't believe him.

"No for real! I told my teacher my mom is a musician and she has a gig tonight, so she helped me do my homework during my break at school."

I had to walk away and dry the tears that slipped out.

"My mom is a musician."

Yes the hell she is.

And a writer. And business woman. And web designer, social media marketer and designer.

I tell my kids they built this with me. They were there when I taught piano lessons with two babies on my hip, helping me pound out the beat for my students.

They were there when I nannied, still trying to get my "little business" off the ground.

They were there. Always there.

"Tell me I can't do it," I challenged the world. "Tell me to leave them home. Tell me it's too much. Tell me this isn't how things are done."

No one ever said a word. I just got used to the staring.

But it's worth it when my daughter says randomly throughout the day, "Mom, I'm going to be a writer and singer like you."

Or my son says, "Mom, I'm going to be a deep sea diver painter ninja."

Because I made them go with me. I made them sit there and watch me do it, and they sometimes complain, but I can promise you one thing.

When someone tries to fit them in a box, my kids will be the first to stand up and say, "Oh no. That's not right. Because my mom..."

I made them go with me. I made them watch what a woman is capable of under pressure. I tucked them into bed and they witnessed me still working when they awoke again at midnight, looking for me.

Momma, make them go with you. Make them watch you. Make them be bored sitting there, watching you be you, watching you kill it out in the world. In whatever you decide to do.

Show them what women are capable of. Show them how we work. Show them how we don't bow, we don't bend, we don't break.

And how we damn sure don't give up.

Because as beautiful as motherhood is, it's not a personality trait.

I will not be a background character in their lives, but lead a story entirely my own.

As I sit here, staring out at yet another gorgeous river in Alaska, I think about the comments I received when I announced I was going to spend at least a month traveling... with my children who are eight and six years of age.

"How are you going to manage this with young kids? Why are you bringing them with you?"

And how I would just respond with a smile, every time.

"Because I've always made them go with me."

Chapter 18

Thawing

How many days until you're in my arms again? My boyfriend texts

6 more days. I answer.

I look to the right of my computer. Toast is sitting contentedly, watching me work.

He's had many adventures with me, but still no Northern Lights.

"There they are!" My father called the other day when we were driving back to Anchorage from skiing in the Chugach mountains. "Northern Lights!"

I look up and it's a road sign. *East Northern Lights Boulevard.*

I roll my eyes.

My phone buzzes.

I miss you! I hope you know we are really heading into an amazing year, Sandi MarLisa!

I smile and gaze out to the mountains beyond my window.

The ice is thawing.

The glacier doesn't fall far from the whale bolo

My father is characteristically an interesting man.

When I was fourteen years old, I got seasick for the first and only time in my life on his boat. He wanted to keep fishing, so he dropped me off on a random island off the coast of Destin, Florida.

"See you in a few hours," he said.

Okay, dad.

He's a minimalist. Lots of material stuff always stressed him out. It was always about the experiences.

Experiences that included hiking mountains, tubing down rivers, and always, ALWAYS taking the scenic route on vacations.

He married his second wife on a glacier in Alaska, wearing a whale bolo around his neck and ice cleats. My sister and I drank from rivers and lakes without names running through the glacier, and stood next to him shaking our heads as he walked down the aisle to "Another One Bites the Dust" by Queen.

Afterwards, we went to a bar with our bonus mom and new honorary aunt, the sun still high in the sky at 1am. We drank, listened to Alaskan folk music and laughed. We laughed a lot.

My dad got lost in the Canadian tundra for three days once and had to survive. I shared this story at his reception from my memory of what he told me.

"You always make stuff up." My dad said. "That never happened."

"Yeah it did." I replied, offended. "You told me this story yourself."

He paused for a minute before exclaiming, "Oh yeah! That's right!"

Only he would forget a story like that and consider it trivial.

He taught survival for the Red Cross. He loves to kayak.

So do I.

My dad and I didn't get along a lot while I was growing up. We were both stubborn and opinionated, and I was hell bent on doing my life MY way.

But something I learned about my dad is that he respects when people prove him wrong. I did end up doing my life my way and he brags on me, that creative kid of his.

Now I'm in Alaska again. This time in November, my kids asleep in the back of his truck, leaning on "Slinky," my bonus mom.

Alaska was the first place I ever went to where I thought to myself, "Wow. The world is big."

Everything looks different, and it's constantly changing. The leaves on the trees feel like felt, so unlike the waxy leaves I'm used to. And most icebergs are actually black, did you know? I only do because I jumped off one into a river after white water rafting.

And when you look down at a glacier you realize it's layered, like a crystal white geode.

The sun never makes its way all the way up to the top of the sky. It circles the mountains like a halo and at sunset casts an alpine glow, causing the trees to turn rose gold.

My children woke up excitedly this morning, pressing their faces against the window, squealing about ice crystals, begging to build a snowman.

I can see the appeal of living here, it's the perfect place for my dad. Adventures to be had outdoors everywhere you look.

He hated Florida, but lived there for over 20 years. Unfortunately, his daughters don't want to leave. We love our home, much to his dismay. Our brother is somewhere in Germany, because of course he is.

"Come to Alaska!" Dad cries, every time we get him on the phone. "Big money here!"

We always roll our eyes and make some joke.

"I know you like it in Panama City, but the world is bigger."

"We know, dad."

But as I ride down these winding roads, watching the sunlight sparkle like glitter on the snow, my sense of adventure awakens.

The mountains here are endless. Some look like clouds looming on the horizon, others look like warnings, jagged edges poking holes in a cotton candy sky.

Mountains have a way of making me feel safe, encased.

But I grew up on the Gulf Coast... and that stays with you.

The sea makes me feel free, like at any point I could hop in and sprout a tail and swim far away... to anywhere.

The water is a portal to everywhere. It's liberty. It's vitality.

"What did your family say when you said you were going to drop everything and travel for a month?" My therapist asked me.

I laughed. "They were exasperated, but no one was surprised. I think they just accept these things now."

My friends roll their eyes at me. "Why on earth did you decide to go to Alaska and travel in November, in the middle of a freaking pandemic and civil unrest?"

It's funny, because the 2020 election was last night with all its implications. But this morning was quiet and the snow still sparkled.

So I just smile at them. Because I don't know. The situation just seemed to call for it.

I needed to get out. I needed to see how big the world is. Remind myself of its vastness and inexplicable beauty.

I guess I'm like my dad in that way.

The Salty Goat

I sat at the table closest to the stage at The Salty Goat Saloon on Panama City Beach.

I was alone. It was 10pm on a Friday night and I had been planning to meet a friend at the bar after my show and watch Sons of Saints, but my friend had an emergency and had to cancel.

I figured I was already there and had decided to make a night out of it. I knew a few people already and was enjoying not having to be the entertainment for once.

Soon, Jacob arrived with his girlfriend.

"Hey Jacob!" I yelled. The bar was incredibly loud.

"Hey! We saw you were here on your Instagram stories so we thought we'd join you! The godfather and Jacqueline are on their way!"

I beamed.

Soon the table was full and we were screaming All the Small Things by Blink 182 at the top of our lungs.

"How's things going with Sk8er Boi?" Jacqueline screamed over the crowd.

I made a face. "We're talking again. I couldn't get him out of my head and the whole point of not talking to him anymore was to not think about him so…" I shrugged. "I don't know. I think about him less now that he's not totally off limits. He asked me to help him write a letter to get him into Helicopter Pilot school in Utah."

"I can't hear anything you're saying!" Jacqueline yelled again.

"I'll tell you later!" I said, laughing.

"Hey look! We got Sandi MarLisa in the house everybody!" Mason St. Germain called from the stage.

I sat up straighter and blew Mason a kiss.

"We got Jacob in the house!" Mason pointed in the direction of our table. "Remember to support Bay County Musicians everybody. Oh and—" Mason stretched out his arms before bringing the mic back to his mouth. "My friend Georgia Boy just walked in!"

I whirled around and sure enough, there was Georgia Boy waving at us, making his way through the crowd towards the bar.

Georgia Boy was friends with Mason St. Germain?

His beard had fully grown in. He wore a black ball cap backwards, a salmon colored oversized button up shirt and jeans with his famous red shoes.

"Does he own any clothes that actually fit him?" The godfather said to me.

I smiled. "I don't think so. But I wouldn't talk too much shit."

"Why's that?"

240

I turned to him and raised my eyebrows.

The godfather rolled his eyes. "Sandi. Seriously? Again?"

I gazed over my shoulder, watching Georgia Boy lean over the counter and speak with the bartender. "If he's into it. I'm not sure if he is. He's got a…" I cleared my throat. "… real nice body."

And considerable other things, but I didn't mention that.

The godfather sighed, staring back towards the band. "Just maybe don't sing Gives You Hell with him and we'll be alright."

I looked at him squinting. "Oh my god. That bothered you?"

He shrugged.

"Hey girl!" Georgia Boy nudged my shoulder and handed a drink to me. "I figured you'd be drinking Gin tonight."

"Is Gin Sandi making an appearance?" Jacob asked.

I sighed and stared up at the ceiling.

"Yes!" Georgia Boy pumped his fist in the air and offered Jacob a high five. "My absolute favorite of all alter egos."

I silently prayed for patience before squeezing my lime into my drink. "So embarrassing."

"No, it's great Sandi." Georgia Boy took a seat next to me. "I wonder what my alter ego would be."

"Whatcha drinking?" I said, looking down at his cup.

"Jack." He answered, shaking the drink.

"Well cheers, Jack." I held up my cup.

He smiled and winked at me. "Cheers, Gin."

We clinked glasses.

The band went on break, Mason jumping off the stage to talk to us. "Hey guys!"

We greeted him and hyped him up on how great of a show it was.

"Who's gonna get up there and sing one?"

"Not me." Jacqueline said.

"The last time I did that, I only did it because I was drunk off my ass." Jacob said, shaking his head at the memories.

"I'll do it." I said immediately. "What songs you got?"

Georgia Boy looked at me, smiling, before looking back at Mason. "Yeah buddy. I'll do one. Got a song list?"

Mason retrieved the song list from the stage and set it in front of us.

"Lots of 80s stuff on there, Sandi."

"Yeah…" I trailed off, considering. "Let's change it up. I want Mr. Brightside by the Killers."

"I'm stuck between What I Got by Sublime and Crazy Bitch by Buckcherry." Georgia Boy said.

"Up to you, man." Mason patted his back. "Let the band know. I gotta make my rounds."

Georgia Boy stared at the song list for a while, agonizing over his choices.

I watched him with my nose scrunched, my lips quirking up at the corners the longer he took.

"Just pick one!" I said, giving him a hard nudge with my elbow.

"Hey!" He jolted out of his concentration. "I'm just trying to pick the perfect one."

"Perfect is overrated!" I put my arms out, shaking them around. "Mr. Love is Overrated!" I took his arm and shook it before grabbing my drink. I was a little drunk.

"Sandi starts hitting people when she's drunk." The godfather said.

"I do not!" And I slapped him on the arm.

Georgia Boy burst out laughing. "Crazy Bitch it is then!"

"HEY!"

My so-called friends all snickered.

Georgia Boy bought me another drink, himself a shot of Tequila. My vision started to haze.

"You ready, Sandi?" Mason motioned for me to come up to the stage.

I took a giant step up, winking at the bassist, the legendary Mike Thompson, and smiling at Moe on the drums. Drew started playing the opening riff of Brightside on the guitar.

"Sandi MarLisa everybody!"

I felt the drums in my blood, the electric guitar like lightning in my veins.

The crowd stopped to listen, people nodding at Mason and Mike with approval.

I shouted, "One more chorus!" And started jumping, my fist in the air.

After it was over, Mike said into his mic. "Give it up for Sandi MarLisa!" Then he leaned over to talk to me as I made to jump off the stage, handing my mic back to Mason. "I want you on my radio show! Radio Cosmos Live!"

My cheeks hurt from smiling.

It was Georgia Boy's moment. He grinned at me as he stepped onto the platform.

As I sat at my table in the crowd, I had the thought that I had never seen Georgia Boy on the stage without a guitar.

Drew strummed the opening few chords and then...

"ALRIGGGGGHHHHHTTTT!!!"

Georgia Boy screamed into the mic, head banging.

My jaw dropped. I looked over to the godfather, Jacqueline and Jacob who lifted their drinks, shouting encouragement.

I settled down in my seat and watched him go. He was really going for it. If there was one thing Georgia Boy could do, it was bring energy. Even with just an acoustic guitar.

And yet, I couldn't shake the instinctive feeling that he really, really wanted a guitar right about now. I bet his acoustic was in his truck.

Georgia Boy finished the song to cheers, clasping Mason's hand and bringing it in for a bro hug.

I smiled as he approached the table, shaking my head slightly.

Mike Thompson followed, stopping Georgia Boy by grabbing his shoulder and shaking his hand. They talked for a minute—as I sipped my Gin—before walking over to me.

"Sandi!" Mike gave me a hug. "I hope I said your name right."

"You did just fine!" I said, releasing him.

"Sandi MarLisa." Georgia Boy smiled. "It's a mix of your mom's and Mema's name, right?"

I met his eyes. "Yes. How'd you know?"

He just took a sip of his Jack and Coke before saying, "My ears work just fine, too."

"You are a powerhouse, Sandi!" Mike continued. "The boys said, 'Sandi's gonna come up and do a song. You don't have to worry about her. She's really quiet and shy.' And then…" Mike made a big motion with his arms. "BOOM!"

I laughed, playfully touching Mike's arm. Georgia Boy took another sip of his drink.

"I'm shy everywhere else but the stage." I said. "The stage is home."

"The stage is home." Georgia Boy repeated.

"I want you both on my Radio Show. You have originals right?"

"Oh yes."

"Definitely!"

"You guys are welcome, too." Mike motioned towards our friends at the table. "If you have enough for thirty minutes."

"I only have maybe one." Jacob said.

"I have two or three." Jacqueline said, switching her attention to the godfather.

I looked at Georgia Boy, curiously.

"Yeah. I can do thirty minutes." Georgia Boy said, locking eyes with me.

"Me too." I agreed. "That won't be a problem."

Georgia Boy and I continued staring at each other.

244

"Cool!" Michael said. "I have you both on Facebook. So let's set it up." He walked back up to the stage, joining the band.

Georgia Boy and I continued staring at each other until our friends said they were getting ready to leave.

We walked out towards the parking lot. Jacob leaving with his girlfriend and Jacqueline and the godfather walking to where they had parked.

"Whatcha getting into tonight, Sandi?" Georgia Boy paused on the deck outside the bar.

I stopped, too, facing him. "Well, Georgia Boy, that depends."

Georgia Boy furrowed his eyebrows slightly. "And that depends on what?"

I found his hand, giving it a squeeze before looking up at him.

"On what you say next." I said finally, smiling widely.

He laughed and stared up at the sky, shaking his head before meeting my eyes. "Well then. Let's get out of here, girl."

I held his hand as he led me to the truck, opening the passenger door for me and helping me step up into the cab.

"My condo is right down the road." He said, closing the driver's side door.

"I know." I buckled my seatbelt and stared out the window. "I've been there before."

He laughed loudly, throwing his head back and grabbing my thigh as he drove. "You are something else, Sandi MarLisa."

I rolled my eyes, still staring out the window, the lights on the beach zooming past. A dinging sound rang through the cab.

"Ugh. That damn thing." Georgia Boy took out a seatbelt clip that wasn't attached to anything and stuck it in the holder.

I frowned. "You should actually wear your seatbelt, you know."

"Nah girl. I like to live life on the edge."

I squinted at him, heat rising in my cheeks. "That's not living life on the edge. That's just pure stupidity."

"Oh." Georgia Boy turned his face to me, smiling a mocking sort of smile. "Do you care if I live or die, Sandi MarLisa?"

"If you die because you weren't wearing a seatbelt," I said, rotating my head back towards the window. "I assure you I won't feel the least bit sorry for you."

"That wasn't an answer."

I wanted to smack that insufferable grin off his face.

Dammit. The godfather was right.

We arrived at his condo, Georgia Boy backing into a space. He let me out of the passenger side door before opening the second one behind me.

"Just gotta grab my guitars." Georgia Boy said. He emerged with his acoustic and another guitar case I hadn't seen before, locking the truck. "Let's go."

We walked in silence until we reached the elevators, Georgia Boy pressing the up button and stepping into the cab.

"You were off the chain tonight." Georgia Boy said, leaning up against the wall and smiling down at me. "You let loose a little bit."

"I like the drums." I said simply.

"You're starting a four piece band, right?"

I squinted at him. "That's the plan."

"Well." The elevator door opened. "Let me know if you ever need another guitar player."

I said nothing.

We rounded a few open hallways, the waves from the beach rolling with no rhythm, no time. Upon reaching the door to his place, Georgia Boy paused.

"Wait here." He said. "I won't be long."

I stood, curiously watching as he opened the door to his studio condo and stepped in. He emerged with a box of hard seltzers and a steel cup, still holding his acoustic guitar.

"I figured you could help me drink these. I don't like them."

I let him lead the way to the stairwell and we spiraled down to the bottom floor, a door opening to the beach.

246

We reached a trail in the sand. "Step where I step, Sandi. Okay? There's sand spurs everywhere."

I did as he said and we safely made it to the sugar sand, our feet squeaking as we walked. There were some wooden beach chairs right in front of where the sand turned from dry to wet. We chose two of them and sat down.

He set his acoustic case on a chair and the box of seltzers next to me. I looked around.

The beach was completely empty, the season not yet in full swing, the pandemic still keeping people away.

"Regular or extendo?"

I turned my attention back to Georgia Boy. He held out two joints to me.

I didn't know he smoked.

"Always the extendo." I said.

Georgia Boy put the regular back in his pocket and put the extendo in the side of his mouth, smiling as he lit it. He took a long drag, getting it started and then handed it to me.

"Drink up those seltzers." He said. I handed the joint back to him. "I don't drink them."

I looked in the box, several were already missing.

I wondered why he had the seltzers in the first place, thinking of the dirty blonde head of hair I saw next to him at Papa Joe's.

Jacqueline had mentioned the other day that she had seen Georgia Boy making out with someone at a bar, but that he was also seeing a friend of hers.

I opened one seltzer to be polite, but didn't drink it, setting it in the sand.

I wondered if they were all his "friends" too.

Georgia Boy gripped the joint in his teeth, opening the guitar case. "Do you mind if I play Hurricane for you?"

I bristled. But nodded.

I listened to what he had, humming along, the waves keeping time and the Gulf breeze singing harmony.

"What do you think?" He said, stopping his finger strum. "You want to write a verse for it?"

Absolutely not.

"Sure." I smiled, still looking out at the sea.

He started finger picking then, a beautiful melody.

My face titled towards him involuntarily, the cadence entrancing.

"...open the door..." He sang in a deeper voice than I was used to. "... step outside. I'm naturally high this time..."

I closed my eyes. Listening.

"... I'm dancing with disaster, come along for the ride, ain't making no stops this time..."

I kept my eyes closed for the remainder of the song. The melody was beautiful. The lyrics, honest.

"When did you write that one?" I asked. "Is it new? I haven't heard it before."

He smiled, putting the guitar back in the case. "I wrote it a long time ago. I don't really perform that one."

"Why not?" I asked. "It's a hell of a lot better than your other songs I've heard."

"Wow." He said, a laugh bursting out of him, cutting through the night. "You really say what's on your mind, huh?"

"Most of the time. Unless I don't think it's worth saying."

Georgia Boy nodded his head slightly, blowing out smoke. "You said I was a good songwriter once."

I remembered the night at Uncle Ernie's on Beck Avenue in St. Andrews. I closed my eyes at the memory. "Oh yeah."

He turned towards me, amused. "'Georgia Boy isn't much of a singer, but he's an amazing songwriter.'" He quoted. "You said it in front of a table of people." He blew out another stream of smoke.

I closed my eyes harder, wincing. "I had a lot to drink that night."

"No, it's okay." He shook his head slightly, putting a hand on my knee. "All I care about is songwriting. And I really like your honesty."

248

A thought struck me then.

"What?" Georgia Boy asked.

"Nothing." I said, hugging myself against the slight chill of Spring.

"No. You do that shit all the time."

I tensed at the tone. "What shit?"

He rolled his eyes, sitting up straighter and clasping his hands in front of him. "You look like you're about to say something and then the moment passes. And you don't say anything at all."

"Because I end up saying shit like 'Georgia Boy isn't much of a singer' when I say something." I said, wryly.

Georgia Boy laughed deeply, clasping his chest and leaning backwards.

I watched him, my lips pursed.

He settled down and caught my eye. "Oh. Don't look like that." He said, patting my knee. "Just tell me what you're thinking, Sandi."

I said nothing and stared off into the distance.

"Always so serious, Sandi MarLisa." I heard Georgia Boy say. I still wouldn't look at him. "Here, let's try this. Who are your musical influences?"

I rolled my eyes.

"Okay. Clearly I said something wrong." Georgia Boy laughed again.

I smiled then, looking at him. "No it's not that. I just can't really answer that question."

He frowned. "Why?"

My eyes glassed over a bit, thinking of how to form the words. "I grew up in a strict religious household. I was only really allowed to listen to country music and gospel. But I was also in choir... so classical music as well. I could get away with 1940s, 50s music. I adored the television shows of that time, I Love Lucy and others... I stopped listening to music actually." I grabbed the seltzer just to have something to hold. "I couldn't listen to anything I was really interested in anyway. So I wrote my own songs, because no one could tell me I couldn't."

Georgia Boy said nothing, his lips forming a small smile.

"What about you?" I said. "I'm guessing Sublime."

Georgia Boy looked surprised. "How'd you know?"

I finally took a sip of the seltzer. "I can tell by the way you sing."

He rolled his eyes. "Now we're back to my singing."

I threw a hand up. "At least when I hear your voice, I know it's you."

He furrowed his brow. "What do you mean 'you know it's me?'"

"I mean." I said, squeezing the seltzer too hard. "Your voice is distinctive. So many people sound the same. They try to imitate other artists. It's so BORING." I looked up at the starry sky, the wind ruffling my hair. "Your voice isn't perfect, Georgia Boy."

"Says the woman with perfect pitch."

I put my chin down, staring at him in surprise.

"I told you." Georgia Boy smiled. "I listen, too. You said it in one of your interviews."

I chuckled softly. "I didn't know anyone I know actually watched those things." I took another sip of my seltzer. "But yes. Your voice isn't perfect. But it's distinct. And what's worse?" I made a point to look him directly in the eye then. "To be boring and perfect? Or to be interesting but imperfect?"

Georgia Boy took a sip of his drink from the stainless steel cup. "Now we're getting somewhere." He set the cup down on the wooden chair. "I've got one for you."

"Bring it."

"Another influence of mine is Angus Young, the guitar player from AC/DC. All he wanted the whole time he was playing guitar was to sound like Chuck Berry. But when he played for a crowd, people would come up to him and say, 'What was that, man? I've never heard anyone play guitar like that!'"

I smiled.

"And all Angus wanted was to sound like Chuck Berry, but he couldn't. He couldn't do it. So Angus said, 'I don't know, man. I guess it's AC/DC.'"

I laughed, staring out at the Gulf, thinking about what Georgia Boy had said.

"What I was thinking earlier." I began, slowly. "Was that... I have never told anyone that they were a good songwriter before. Not one of my peers."

Georgia Boy waited for me to continue.

"I can't help but be honest about my opinion of music. I may not say what people like, and I'm not saying my opinion is law, but I'm always honest and I try to always be constructive. I don't offer my opinion if I don't think it's worth saying." I made myself make eye contact with Georgia Boy as I said sincerely, "You're a great songwriter, Georgia Boy. Just like your voice, all of your songs are distinct. Each one sounds different from any of your other songs. And the song you just played me, Dancing with Disaster?"

"Mhm."

"I think it's a great song."

Georgia Boy's smile broadened. It lit up his whole face, his entire body seemed to relax.

"Well." He said finally. "Look at Sandi MarLisa being so sweet to little ole me."

I rolled my eyes, shaking off the sentimentality.

We spent the rest of the night laughing. Somewhere in between we started kissing, exploring each other's mouths.

I got on top of him, unbuttoning his pants.

Then, we made love by the ocean.

"Don't look behind you." Georgia Boy said, his focus moving from my face to a point over my shoulder.

"Oh God." I said.

"That's not my name." Georgia Boy said, grinning.

I moved to get off of him.

"No no no. What are you doing? Keep going." Georgia Boy moved one hand from my hip to the sand.

Suddenly, I'm illuminated in light. Our visitors had shone a flashlight on us.

Georgia Boy puts his button up shirt over my shoulders, covering me up. "Just keep going. They'll get the hint and keep moving." He paused. "Think they want to join?"

I smacked his arm as he laughed.

But I didn't stop.

I picked up the box of seltzers and Georgia Boy grabbed his guitar, walking back up the sandy slope to the staircase. As we entered the small field right outside the entrance, the sprinklers cut on.

"Run!" I said, holding the box of seltzers to my chest.

"My guitar!" Georgia Boy shouted behind me.

We reached the door, me only wearing Georgia Boy's shirt, soaking wet, high and laughing our asses off.

"Sandi." Georgia Boy said through laughter after checking to make sure his guitar was okay. "Where are the seltzers?"

I looked down at the box and let out a cackle. The box was empty.

Georgia Boy looked back to where we had walked up the path. "We have to go get them." He started to move.

"Hell no!" I said, grabbing his arm. "Get your ass in here. You can find them tomorrow if you want."

We raced up the stairs, stumbling on a few of them, and reached Georgia Boy's room.

We started making out again, Georgia Boy unbuttoning his own shirt that was on me.

"This?" He said, tossing the shirt aside. "Is yours, girl. You earned it."

He led me to the bed and we went for round two in the sheets.

I awoke the next morning to Georgia Boy already awake beside me.

"Good morning, Sandi." He said.

I sat up in the bed, rubbing my eyes. The bed had moved to the middle of the floor again and my head ached.

"We woke up with sand all in the bed." I said, feeling the grittiness in the sheets.

"No." He said, laughing under his breath. "I woke up with Sandi in my bed."

I threw a pillow at him.

Georgia Boy got up and made me coffee.

It was awful. But I didn't say anything as I took a few sips and left it on the dresser.

I dressed to leave, trying to shake some of the sand out of my hair.

When Georgia Boy grabbed his keys, we both looked at the shirt he had thrown on the counter the night before.

I left without grabbing it.

Chapter 19

The Rising Sun

There is a house in New Orleans

"Do you need an ambulance?"

"No."

"Is he aggressive?"

"No."

They call the Rising Sun

"Are there weapons in the home?"

"I've hidden them."

"What's his name?"

It's been the ruin of many a poor boy

"They're coming, they should be there soon. Can you describe to me what happened?"

And God, I know I'm one

"Where are the pills now?"

"Hidden."

Oh, mother, tell your children

"They should be pulling in now."

"Yes I see them."

Not to do what I have done

"Could you step outside for me, sir?

Spend your lives in sin and misery

"Ma'am can you show me the bottle of pills he wanted to take?"

In the House of the Rising Sun

"He's admitted to the plan. We're taking him in for a psych eval. Who is he to you?"

"My husband."

"How long have you been together?"

"Twelve… twelve years."

Well I got one foot on the platform

"You should know, you did the right thing by calling. He'll thank you one day."

One foot on the train

"Can I see him before he goes?"

"Yes. We had to handcuff him ma'am. He didn't want to come. But he's calm."

I'm going back to New Orleans

"What exactly does he have?"

To wear that ball and chain

"How long has he been like this?"

"He was diagnosed 4 years ago."

There is a House in New Orleans

"He's in serious psychological distress. Thank you for calling. Here's my card if you need anything."

They call the Rising Sun

"Here he is ma'am."

And it's been the ruin of many a poor boy

"I love you. I just want you to stay with me."

And God, I know I'm one

The void

Maybe… maybe this is how I die.

Here, in the void.

It feels like I'm walking underwater. I take one step and I'm met with consistent pressure and resistance.

The water makes space for me, it doesn't say no to my steps.

It's like a dance.

Except I can't breathe.

My lungs feel like they're shrinking to nothing. Perhaps I'll sprout gills and get used to it here.

It's quiet. Here in the void.

My screams are absorbed into a watery abyss. I look up and see sunlight somewhere above.

But it's not for me. Not now.

I had a dream once where I was standing amongst a coral reef. Two dolphins swam past me and began moving in graceful figure eights. Then it started to snow. The coral was soon blanketed white and the dolphins beat snow flurries around and around in beautiful patterns.

It was a peaceful dream.

I do love my contradictions. I love duality. I love the idea of multiple ideas being true all at once.

Truth. I'm okay.

Truth. No I'm not.

I press forward still so slowly, moving towards... I don't know what.

The water makes room for me.

I'm wrapped in its warm embrace, waiting for my mouth to open and the sea to sweep through my lungs. Maybe it'll find a way to my heart.

It will burn. It's funny how people describe drowning as a burning in your lungs. A burning caused by water.

Contradictions.

Truth. I'm in control.

Truth. No I'm not.

There's beauty to be found in suffering, they say. There's good stuff in anything if you just look for it.

The good and the bad coexist together all the time.

But sometimes you get tired.

I stop moving through the water. I watch the bubbles settle.

Complete stillness. Complete silence.

I feel a scream building inside of me, knowing it's futile to let it out. I want to cry, but why? I'm surrounded by water anyway.

Truth. I feel like dying.

Truth. No I don't.

I look up towards the light of the sun and long for its warmth. I don't know how to get up there right now.

I don't know if I want to get up there right now.

I close my eyes and search for the small seed of hope I always carry with me.

I'm tired of planting seeds though. Seeds always have to die before they become anything. They always need water and sunlight. Constant maintenance and attention.

And sometimes... sometimes... the seeds are no good. It's just the way of things to not work out sometimes.

I find the seed and decide I don't want to plant it right now.

What I want is to be left alone in this sea. What I want is to slowly fade away as the water does its work on me like it smooths rock.

What I want no one can give me.

Hope is useless in the past.

And I keep looking there for hope. I keep looking to make seeds grow that cannot grow. I keep wondering and searching and grappling with all the things I could have done differently to keep me out of this endless sea.

Don't go looking for hope where there isn't any.

I open my arms to frame the sun, as if I could catch it and absorb it into my body.

Truth. I want to have hope.

Truth. No I don't. Not right now.

Right now it's all I can do to remember there's a sun.

I take another step forward, the water makes space for me.

There is a House in New Orleans

I dropped my kids off at their dad's and then began my drive home.

I felt like a failure. A disaster.

Turning up the music to drown out my thoughts, I held back the tears threatening to spill out.

Rage. Sadness. Contempt. Disgust.

Fear. Devastation. Loneliness.

I felt like my blood would boil out of my veins.

"Fuck this." I said, and pulled a coin out of the console.

"Heads rollercoasters. Tails New Orleans."

I tossed the coin and caught it in my hand, flipping it onto the dashboard.

"NOLA it is."

I arrived home and found some clothes, grabbing my make-up box and toothbrush in a rush. I threw it all into the passenger seat of my Highlander.

I knocked on the door of the master bedroom, stepping in to find the godfather at his desk. "Hey. I'm going to NOLA. I'll be back before our gig tomorrow."

He just sighed. "Is there a reason?"

"I need to get the hell out of here."

"Well, try not to die."

Nobody questions my decisions anymore. They just sigh in resignation.

Only took 30 years.

I stopped for a coffee at Wild Root and filled up my gas tank.

Then I was gone.

I opened the sunroof and felt the heat of early summer warming my neck.

I rode in silence for a few hours, thinking of everything in my life that's changed these past few years.

My brother called. I ignored it. Sorry bro.

I turned up the music, Rainbow Kitten Surprise blaring out of my windows.

My sister texted.

Are you really okay?

Lol. Yes.

I know there's a lot going on with both of us. I'm always here.

Love you.

Love you too.

I looked out the window and saw the Gulf Coast stretch before me.

Home.

A friend called. One whom I knew wouldn't question my decision.

"Hello?"

"Hey. What's going on?" Sk8er Boi asked.

"On my way to NOLA."

A pause. "Any particular reason?"

"If needing to get the hell out of Panama City for a while is a reason."

"It is."

"Good."

Silence.

"What inspired the trip?"

"Oh, you know. Dropped the kids off at their dad's and went into existential crisis mode."

"Because?"

"Because…" I swallowed. "Because I was supposed to give them better."

"Better?"

"Better."

"Better how?"

"Something stable. Something solid."

"Sandi. No one is more stable and solid than you."

"I just wish things were different."

"Different how?"

"What do you mean?"

"Well, if you wish they were different. That means you must have some sort of vision for what that would look like. Right?"

Another pause. "Not this."

"Sandi. Maybe your kids won't have the two parents who are still together with a white picket fence in their future, but, honestly, who wants that anyway? Boring. Small town rockstar for a mom, pretty exciting."

I smiled. "Maybe."

"So what's the plan?"

"Ah. I don't know. Drink bourbon on Bourbon Street. Dance to the music of a street performer. See a ghost. Stuff my face with Beignets. Perhaps I'll even find a witch who will tell me my future. The possibilities are endless."

He laughed. "I'll check on you later. By the way. Don't go to Bourbon Street. Go to Frenchmen Street. Tourists go to Bourbon."

I rerouted to Frenchmen Street and pulled up into a 24 hour parking lot. I stepped outside my car and shook out my hair, throwing on a headband —as is my way.

I clicked the lock button on my keys over my shoulder and set off towards Frenchmen.

I passed a man sitting on the sidewalk. "Hey darling. You look so good. I'll marry you right now."

"You can't afford me, sweetie."

I began to hear the sounds of jazz floating up the street, like a siren's call. I looked down at the sidewalk, there's paint splatters on every concrete square.

God, I love New Orleans.

I approached a storefront that said "Downtown Tattoo." I knew my first stop.

I entered the shop where I was greeted by the owner. "Can we help you?"

"Got space for me?" I asked.

"What are you looking to get?"

"A crescent city tattoo."

"We have 6 o'clock availability."

"Sweet. I'll be back then."

I followed the sound of music to a small bar and grabbed a gin and tonic, taking a seat at a high top.

I watched the band, complete with swing dancer, and soaked it in.

It's funny how we can hop in a car and be transported to another place, a different culture, a different way of life.

I checked the time and finished off my drink before heading back to the tattoo shop.

My artist's name was Pablo, and he knew an acquaintance of mine in Panama City. My tattoo is done from concept to completion within a half hour.

I paid for my new tattoo and asked the receptionist where the best place to eat was.

"I always say Coop's."

Coop's it is.

It's a 5 minute walk to the restaurant. I'm seated at the bar next to Sally and Logan from Cincinnati, and I ordered some specialty cocktail and Cajun seafood pasta.

I convinced Sally and Logan to get a tattoo. We're then joined by Blake and James, who are a couple from Chicago.

"Where are you from?"

"Florida."

"Oh, I'm terrified of Florida." James said.

"I don't blame you."

I finished the best Cajun seafood pasta I've ever had before bidding my new friends farewell and leaving the bar.

When I stepped outside, the sun had gone down. I began walking down the street looking at all the beautiful buildings, music following me everywhere I went.

My phone rang. It's Sk8er Boi again.

"Hey!"

"Well, you sound better. How's New Orleans?"

"It's aaaamaaaazzzinnnnggg."

"Is it?" He laughed. "So what conclusions have you arrived at?"

"What concluuuuusions?"

"You said you were having an existential crisis. Any revelations?"

"Oh my god. Oh myyyyy godddddd. There are vines all up and down this building."

"Had anything to drink, Sandi?"

"Why would you ask that?"

"No reason."

"Oh my god it's so pretty. String lights! There's string lights in this little courtyard and it's so pretty I want to die."

"String lights, huh?"

"I'm sending you a picture so you can experience this magical moment." I shot him a text. "I'm sorry. Did you ask me something?"

"Uh. Yes. But I think in a roundabout way I got my answer."

"What's the answer?"

"String lights."

"Oh my God. Yes. Yes. Exactly. Because… there's trash in the street, and you get hurricanes twice a year, sometimes thrice, and it kinda smells bad, and it's hot as hell, but there's string lights! And music everywhere! And vine covered buildings! And OH MY GOD. There's splattered paint all over the sidewalks. And someone drew chalk dicks, but that's besides the point."

"Yes. Because string lights are the point."

"You get me."

"Where to next?"

"I dunno. I'm just going to walk and see what happens."

The ruin of many a poor boy

I lifted up my head towards the sky and took a deep breath.

It smells awful in New Orleans.

I saw a house completely covered in purple, green and gold. A couple walked hand in hand down the street. A cook took out the trash to the road.

I passed a man sleeping on the sidewalk on top of cardboard boxes. A dog barked. Laughter erupted from every store front.

I studied the terraces and wrought iron fences. I passed a group of people listening to a man in a top hat giving a ghost tour.

And then I saw her. She's sitting at a table on a street corner with three decks of cards beneath stones placed in front of her.

I stopped. "You working?"

"Yes I am."

I sat down at her table.

"What's your name?"

"Sandi."

"Debra." She set down the joint she's smoking. "$15 for three cards or $25 for five. I can't read everybody. I don't tell the future, I don't believe in that. You pay at the end. If I can't read you, you don't pay. Fair?"

"Yes ma'am."

"The future is a silly thing to predict. But lately I've been everybody's therapist. Also, I cuss a lot. Three cards or five?"

"I tell you what Debra. It's been a life. Give me five."

"Choose a deck."

I chose the one in the center.

"Shuffle the cards well and then spread them out before you. Then pick a card one at a time and hand them to me."

I did as she said.

"Sandi. Sandi. Sandi. Hmmmmm." Debra looked into my eyes and held up the first card. "I love how you follow your intuition no matter what. But there's a problem." She held up the second card. "You're fucking holding back. Because..." She held up the third card. "You're delaying and procrastinating the completion of an old cycle that started to close about six months ago."

She tapped her finger on the fourth card, then touched the fifth. "You know what these tell me?"

"What's that?"

"These tell me that you care entirely too damn much about how your decisions impact other people. You've spent your whole life being kind and helping others. It's not a bad thing. It's good. But you need to embrace your ego." She held up the fifth card.

"No one's ever told me that before." I said.

"The ego isn't a bad thing like people say. You can have too much ego. You can have too little. You evade your ego and put others first. You've denied your ego too long." She set the fifth card in front of me. "But the ego is what makes you what and who you are. You have presence. It's time to be entirely yourself and do what you were fucking put on this planet to do. To hell with everyone else."

She smiled and winked. "That bar across the street sells the best Hurricanes."

I paid Debra and set off across the street to Lafitte's Blacksmith Shop. I walked up to the bar and asked for a Hurricane.

"Single or double?"

"Let's make it a double."

"What'd you get?" The bartender pointed to the bandage on my arm.

I pulled up a picture on my phone.

"Nice. Crescent city. Good choice." He handed me my drink.

I looked around the historical bar. It's lit by lanterns and candles. I spotted a piano surrounded by stools and took a seat.

Soon the pianist arrived. His voice was soft as he began to play and sing.

After he finished his first song, he said into the microphone, "Five dollars will get you any song you want. Nothing is a no. Anything is possible."

I asked for Tiny Dancer by Elton John and Purple Rain by Prince.

Soon I'm joined by Tammie and Claire. "I didn't know you could sit here!"

Shortly we added to our cohort with four girls, who couldn't be older than 21, and two blonde women. One was rather enthusiastic in her song choices.

Within twenty minutes we're all best of friends, screaming Baby Got Back by Sir Mix-a-Lot and Get Low by Lil Jon and The East Side Boyz with the piano man.

We looked around to the rest of the bar and demanded they all join in. Then we each took a candle from the piano and began waving it in the air as we sang House of the Rising Sun.

I heard Tammie scream across the piano to one of the blondes. "You're a teacher?! I'm a teacher!"

"Oh my gahhhh. I teach 1st!"

"6th."

I shook my head, laughing, and excused myself from the bar, voices and music following in my wake.

It's midnight and I thought I'd had quite the adventure. I began to enter the location to my car into my GPS, when I heard a strong, soulful voice singing Tennessee Whiskey by Chris Stapleton. It's pouring out of the bar I sat at earlier that evening.

I followed the voice and entered the bar. The crowd's enthusiastic and Paggy Prine was absolutely killing it.

I grabbed a gin and tonic and stood near the door, watching the entertainer do her thing. Paggy began walking around the bar with her microphone, singing to the patrons.

She came up to me and I started harmonizing with her on the chorus of Tennessee Whiskey.

Paggy stopped. "Ohhhhh." She said. "You're a singer." She pointed the mic at me.

I gave my head a shake. She nudged the mic closer to me.

Well, I'd had a few drinks.

And this is kinda what I do.

"You're as smooooothhhh, as Tennessee Whiskeyyyyy...."

The crowd gasped and clapped, and laughed hysterically when I changed the last line to, "And I doooooon't know the rest of the words to this sonnnnnnng."

Paggy and I took turns ripping the chorus. Then she told me to come up and do a song. Valerie by Amy Winehouse was chosen.

"Why don't you come on over Sannnnddiiiii." She sang, calling me up to the stage.

I wasn't a hundred percent sure on the song, but Paggy helped me.

And I had the time of my life with strangers in a random bar somewhere in New Orleans after midnight.

Afterwards, Paggy instructed the crowd to buy me a drink. "Sandi from Panama City, Florida everybody."

As they clapped, I was struck with a small realization.

I'm not just Panama City good, which I'm quite proud of.

I'm New Orleans good too.

I'm anywhere good.

And I tried to embrace my ego like Debra told me to do.

People came up to me and shook my hand.

"So if I come to Panama City, will I see you there?"

"Yes sir. I sing all around. You'll find me."

I met Serena and her boyfriend, they lived in Tampa and were celebrating their two year dating anniversary. They bought me gin and tonics the rest of the night.

We watched a man dance with a cane that was lit up with rope lights. Two other guest singers gave a good show. Paggy walked around with the tip jar.

We danced. We sang. We laughed.

And then the set was done.

Serena and I walked up to tell Paggy how wonderful we thought she was. Serena found out I'm thirty.

"Thirty! Thirty?! No way! I thought you were, like, my age."

"How old are you?"

"Twenty five!"

"Yep. I'm a bit older."

"There's just no way you're thirty. You look so young! I feel like I should ask you life advice."

"Oh honey, if only you knew."

"Heyyyy Sandiiiiii." A short and squat gentleman meandered over to me and looked me up and down.

"Hello."

"That was some real good singing girl. I'm Jonathan." He offered to shake my hand.

I took it.

He looked at me intently. "What's your sign?"

"Aries."

He rolled his eyes. "Of course you're a fire sign. I love me some fire signs. I'm an Aquarius."

I smiled.

"You got a man?"

Something told me not to lie. "I don't."

"Sandi." Jonathan leaned closer. "I need to tell you something."

"What's that?"

His silly grin grew to a look of sincerity. "Don't change anything about yourself." He looked to my hair that's always got a windswept look. "Your hair, the way you dress, the way you sing, or talk. And especially the way you carry yourself." He gestured widely in my direction. "You have an essence. When you walk into a room people notice."

He put his hand on my shoulder. "And I know you're not interested in me. But you should know that any man should consider himself lucky to have you. I would hold you in my arms and treasure you, because that's what you deserve."

I felt my soul respond in joy. "Thank you, Jonathan."

He took my hand, kissed it and walked away.

It's 2 a.m. Serena and her boyfriend offered to walk me to my car.

I had the feeling I found what I came there for.

Chapter 20

Not tonight

Hey Sandi. I see that you're in New Orleans. Are you still going to make it to the show tonight? We have you scheduled at 6pm.

The nozzle clicked on the gas pump. I typed out my reply.

Absolutely! See you at about 5:30.

I slammed my car door and put my aviators back on.

I was almost back home.

I arrived at Little Village with plenty of time for set up, the godfather eyeing me warily.

Jacqueline sat at a table as we played through our set. I sang Creep by Radiohead to cheers. It was becoming my most requested song.

I spotted Georgia Boy and Beanie walking through the front doors. I offered a shout out to the both of them as they sat at Jacqueline's table.

I joined them on my break, taking a seat next to Georgia Boy.

"Well how was New Orleans?" Georgia Boy asked. He pointed to the tattoo on my arm. "I... uh... I like your new tattoo."

I looked down at my forearm. "Thanks."

"Where did you stay, Sandi?" Jacqueline asked. "When the godfather and I went we had a really great spot."

"Tell them, Sandi." The godfather walked over with a new beer in his hand. "Tell them where you slept."

I scanned the table, my eyes resting on Georgia Boy.

"I rented a twenty four hour parking space and slept in my car."

Jacqueline choked on her drink. Beanie's mouth flew open. The godfather shook his head.

Georgia Boy's eyes flickered before he said, "Hey. I get it." He looked down at my new tattoo again. "Can I request a song?"

"Sure." I said, unenthusiastically.

"Drops of Jupiter." A ghost of a smile showed on his face. "And really let it fly."

After the show, we all remained for a while talking in the parking lot. I didn't participate much in the conversation.

"Hey! We're gonna smoke a joint." Georgia Boy called to the godfather and Jacqueline.

"Goodnight guys." I said, walking away towards my car.

"Wait! Sandi!" I heard voices behind me.

"Everything okay?"

"It's Sandi. She does that." I heard the godfather say.

I didn't look back.

Tropical Storm

"I keep ending up at a strip club!" I yelled into my phone to laughter.

"Are you sure you have the right address?"

"It's what he has on the flier! Musicians."

Sk8er Boi laughed.

"Okay. The bouncer or security guard guy is looking at me funny. I think I give up."

"Where's your next place?"

"The Salty Hobo. Some friends are playing."

"Isn't that outside? There's a Tropical Storm…"

"It's the Hobo." I shrugged, even though he couldn't see me.

"Well, have fun. I gotta go walk Bonnie."

I rolled my eyes, thinking he probably had a date to get ready for.

"See ya later Sk8er Boi."

It was easy to find a parking spot in St. Andrews, the tropical storm looming. It was a warm June night, but the wind made its way through my skin anyway. I could feel the rain coming.

I walked into the courtyard and waved immediately towards the stage. Then I stopped in my tracks, surprised at what I saw.

Georgia Boy was playing an electric guitar.

And he was good.

Damn good.

I grabbed a drink from the outside bar, Gin, and sat down at the nearest table to the stage, propping my chucks up on the table.

Georgia Boy smiled at me as he sang.

I stayed for the whole night, performing a song or two with the band. They even had a drummer again that night, Beanie on the bass.

Eventually, the wind blew hard and fast chasing everyone out of the courtyard. A light rain fell and lightning struck in the distance.

A few crowd members huddled on the covered stage with us. We screamed songs at the top of our lungs as lightning flashed and the thunder rolled.

"Let's call it." Beanie said. "Our time is about up anyway."

I talked with the band as they wrapped cords and hauled equipment onto buggies to take to their cars.

"So how are you doing, Sandi?" Georgia Boy asked as he dismantled his PA system.

"I'm fine." I said, leaning against a post on the stage.

"How do you feel about Jacqueline playing with the godfather?"

I frowned slightly.

My inbox had blown up ever since Jacqueline broke up her duo with Jacob. The amount of people wanting to work with me musically had seemingly increased once they saw that the godfather had scheduled shows to play with Jacqueline.

"It's fine." I said.

Georgia Boy winced, throwing an arm around me. "Is it though? Seems kinda…"

"Kinda what?"

"Fucked up!" Beanie said from the other side of the stage.

"Yes. Thank you, Beanie." Georgia Boy said.

"What you put on Facebook was hilarious, though. What was it? Open…"

"Open musical relationship, yeah." I finished for him. "I just wanted people to stop asking me questions about it."

Georgia Boy studied me. "So… you didn't run away to New Orleans because of that?"

My eyes narrowed. "I didn't run away."

"Sandi." Georgia Boy said, fixing his ball cap. "You ran away to New Orleans, slept in your car and got a tattoo."

"Sick tattoo, by the way!" Beanie interjected.

"Thank you, Beanie."

"You're welcome, Sandi."

"Walk with me." Georgia Boy said, gesturing for me to follow him to his truck. He carried his acoustic, electric guitar, bag of pedals and cords, and a small amp.

"So why did you go to New Orleans?"

I sighed, looking up at the sky. "Can't a girl just get away?"

"You slept in your car. So clearly it wasn't planned." He stopped in the middle of the road. "Shit."

"What?"

"My keys are in my pocket. Can you help me out?"

I stuck my hand in his front pocket.

"That's my dick."

"Oh my god!" I pulled my hand out like I had just touched a spider.

Georgia boy threw back his head and laughed before looking over his shoulder. "Oh shit. There's people waiting for us. Come on, let's get out of the road."

We shuffled to the side, my hand in his other front pocket now.

"My back pocket! Back pocket!" Georgia Boy said through laughter.

"Who the hell keeps their keys in their back pocket?!" I pulled out the keys.

"Just get over here and help me unlock the trunk."

I stuck the key in the lock and twisted it.

Georgia Boy burst into a fit of grown man giggles.

"What now?!" I cried.

"You would do that." He said, pulling down his truck door.

"Dooooo whatttt?"

"You would use the key and not just press the button to unlock it."

I huffed, incredulous. "Why are you so hung up on that?"

"Because you just… do these things…"

He began loading up the back of the truck with his equipment. "So you gonna tell me why you ran away to NOLA or what, woman?"

My stomach tightened at the last word. "I didn't run."

"Cut the bullshit and just tell me."

I involuntarily smiled, as agitated as I was. He had never been this candid with me.

"I dropped my children off at their father's. He thinks it would be best if the kids lived with him full time for the school year, since their new school is an hour away from me."

He slammed the door of his truck, turning to face me. "I don't quite get it."

"Well." I sighed. "You don't have children and I wouldn't expect you to."

"I can see it makes you sad though." He brushed some hair out of my face, the wind was still picking up. "Enough to run away to NOLA sad."

"Georgia Boy! Sandi!" Beanie walked up to us. Georgia Boy dropped his hand.

"We're at the Hobo in a Tropical Storm!" Georgia Boy said, clasping hands with Beanie and bringing it in. "Let's party for a bit!"

"Gin Sandi?" Beanie asked, tilting his head towards me.

"Gin Sandi! Gin Sandi!"

They made it into a chant.

"Fine!" I said, rolling my eyes and following them back towards the Hobo.

We nearly closed down the Hobo, laughing, talking and drinking, the thunder and lightning increasing every hour.

"No way that really happened." I said through tears.

Georgia Boy and Beanie stared at me.

"I'm glad my pain is funny to you." Georgia Boy said.

"Oh come on." I said, wiping my eyes. "You walk into Walmart, buying condoms for your…?"

"Younger cousin. Yeah."

I cackled, the thunder rolling in the distance. "And your ex walks down the aisle with the man she cheated on you with?"

I couldn't do it. I couldn't stop laughing.

"Sandi." Georgia Boy said, still staring at me. "I almost fought the man in the Walmart condom aisle. I almost couldn't keep myself from punching him."

I laughed harder.

Beanie and Georgia Boy stopped staring at me and instead exchanged looks with each other, shrugging.

"Write a song about it." I said, piecing myself back together. "You'll be alright. That's the funniest thing I've heard in my life."

Georgia boy shook his head, incredulous.

"You've gotta learn to laugh, Georgia Boy. Laugh at your pain." I calmed down, downing the rest of my drink. "It's the only way to make it through this thing called life."

Lightning flashed across the sky, one beam of light after another. A natural Florida light show fully on display.

Beanie looked at the lightning flashing across the bay.

Georgia Boy and I locked eyes then, him pursing his lips and shaking his head at me, trying not to smile.

I licked my bottom lip in response.

He bit his, rubbing his neck.

"I think I'm gonna call it a night, guys." Beanie said.

We stood. Georgia Boy shaking hands and looking off towards the stage. I gave Beanie a hug.

When Beanie walked off towards his car, I turned back to Georgia Boy. He was still staring at the stage.

"What's up?" I asked.

"I want that poster." Georgia Boy said. "It has my name on it."

I followed his gaze, seeing the weekly lineup of musicians posted on the back wall of the stage.

I shrugged. "Okay. I'll get it for you."

I started walking, Georgia Boy trailing behind me.

"Don't we need a diversion?"

"No." I said, not breaking my stride. "It's the last night of the weekly lineup and they throw these posters away anyway."

"Okay." Georgia Boy said. "I'll distract them."

I had reached the poster, removing it from the wall. "What? Wait. No."

"What do you call a Salty Hobo?" Georgia Boy said to a small circle of people talking in front of the stage.

They looked incredibly confused.

I turned back to my work on the poster, pretending like I didn't know him.

"A SALTY HOBO! SANDI! RUN!"

I had the poster in my hand. "What?"

"Run girl! Run!"

"Wait. Hold on!" I folded the poster quickly and put it under my shirt, protecting it from the rain.

Georgia Boy took my hand and started running towards the truck, leaving the confused people in our wake.

"A Salty Hobo." Georgia Boy laughed as he ran, gripping my hand. "It makes no sense!"

"WHY. ARE. WE. RUNNING?!"

Georgia Boy clicked his car keys. "Get in the truck! Hurry!"

We crashed into the car, slamming the doors behind us.

"Woo!" Georgia Boy yelled. "That was crazy!"

I sat, breathing hard in the passenger seat, retrieving the poster from under my shirt.

"I really could have just taken the poster from the wall, you know." I said, handing it to him.

"Oh my god." Georgia Boy said, ignoring me and staring at our stolen goods. "You stole a poster for me, Sandi. I'll treasure it forever."

I rolled my eyes. Amused.

Georgia Boy put the truck in reverse to the sound of rain drumming on the roof.

"Oh my god! That's my favorite tree!" I pointed as we passed Oaks by the Bay park.

"Your favorite tree?" Georgia Boy repeated.

"Yes." I said, settling into my seat. "The Sentry tree. I wrote a piece about it once."

Georgia Boy rolled the windows down and put on Vacation by Dirty Heads, rocking his head and swaying to the music.

"So, what are you about, Sandi?"

"Ummmm."

"Like, what are your dreams? What are your goals? Where are you going?"

I had no clue where any of this was coming from.

"I don't really know how to respond to that." I said.

"I've come to your poetry nights." Georgia Boy continued. "I know you feel pain. I know you feel it deeply. How do you get through it?" Georgia Boy put an arm out the window, resting it on the door and not minding the rain.

I looked at him then. He seemed to have come alive. He was loose, comfortable.

I thought about his question, letting the music play.

"I think…"

Georgia Boy turned the music down.

"I think we hang on to our pain sometimes…" I began. "…because we needed to know what we felt was real. And we somehow think allowing ourselves to heal from that deep pain means that our pain was inauthentic. As if healing invalidates our pain and how terrible or amazing it really was."

I stopped. Gathering my thoughts.

"Like… if you heal, then was it actually devastating? Was it really all that bad? Did you really even care at all?"

Georgia Boy turned his head slightly towards me.

"Pain, in a way, is a badge of honor for how deeply you allowed yourself to love. But I think it's better to heal."

"And why do you think that, Sandi MarLisa?"

I thought for a moment. "Because healing doesn't mean the hurt wasn't valid. It doesn't mean what you felt wasn't real. It just means you're choosing love over your pain."

"I don't believe in love anymore." Georgia Boy said. "My wife cheated on me."

Puzzle pieces clicked together in my mind.

Love is Overrated.

"I took a trip, like you." He smiled before it quickly faded away. "Only I was gone for about four or five months. I went to Nashville, Colorado, Las Vegas and all the way to the West Coast. Which, by the way, has absolutely nothing on the Gulf Coast."

I nodded my head in agreement. White sand was my home and I was ruined for all other beaches.

"What happened with you and your ex?" He asked.

Ah, the dreaded question.

"He has several mental illnesses, and I just couldn't continue on with him anymore. I have a lot of respect for him." I focused on the lights passing by the window. "I went to Alaska and North Carolina for a month after I left him."

Georgia Boy rolled up the windows, it had begun to rain much harder.

"You know what, Sandi?"

"What, Georgia Boy?"

"I think you're exactly who I think you are."

"Oh yeah?" I looked at him. "What do you mean?"

"I mean if it walks like a duck. Talks like a duck. It's probably a duck." He shook his head. "I think you're exactly who you appear to be. I'm trying to let that sink in."

I didn't understand a word he was saying.

"Here." Georgia Boy reached behind him and picked up a large book of CDs, handing it to me.

I laughed, looking at the thick book in my lap, unzipping the zipper. "I haven't seen one of these in ages."

"Pick one." He said.

I flipped through the plastic sheets filled with CDs. "Is this a test?"

"Yes!" He laughed. "I want to see what you pick."

I made it to the last page, I noticed an unmarked CD.

"I pick this one." I said, handing it to him.

He squinted at it, adding it to his CD player. "I don't even know what this one is."

The sound of wooden flutes filled the car and Georgia Boy lost it.

"Oh my god, you would pick this one, Sandi!"

At that point, nothing surprised me anymore about that night. "What do you mean?"

"I mean, it's Johnny Walkingstick. Oh my god. I met them at Little Village. It was a group of Natives playing their original music." He turned up the volume, the sound of wooden instruments and drums filling the truck. "You know what they said to me?"

"What?"

"I talked to them for a bit and shared that I was a musician and played guitar. Johnny Walkingstick said to me, 'Georgia Boy, do you know who you are?'"

We arrived at the condo. Georgia Boy backed in and put the truck in park.

"He said, 'You are a man who makes trees sing.'"

It didn't hit me at first. But I took in the words, letting them sink in.

"That's so poetic."

"Isn't it though?" All signs of tension left Georgia Boy's face. He could move through emotions so quickly. He turned the car off and opened the door. "Let's go!"

Arriving at his room, Georgia Boy set his guitars down on the floor.

"Ah shit." He looked around the studio condo. "I feel like every time you come over, this place is a wreck."

I peeked into the bathroom which was right by the entryway. The trashcan was full and the toilet seat was up, the counter full of products.

"Can you give me a minute in the bathroom?" He said, taking off his hat. His hair was growing out. "I need a shower after that show. I promise I'll be quick."

"Of course!" I said.

I sat down on the unmade bed for a moment before standing up and walking to the floor-to-ceiling windows that lined the wall looking over the Gulf. I opened the window and listened to the waves crashing on the shore, imagining Johnny Walkingstick playing his flute over the sound.

Georgia Boy was true to his word, coming out of the bathroom with just his shorts on.

"May I use the bathroom?" I asked.

"Of course!" He said. "Take your time."

I walked into the bathroom and shut the door.

I immediately noticed the trash had been emptied and the counters wiped off.

I smiled to myself.

I finished in the bathroom and walked into the main space. Georgia Boy had lit a candle, the bed was made.

He stood looking out the window I had opened. Hearing my footsteps, he turned around, taking me in with a joint hanging out of his mouth.

He walked over silently and handed it to me. I took a couple puffs, coughing, and handed it back.

"I'm so happy we're friends, Sandi." He said, sitting on the bed and inviting me to join him.

"Mmmmm." I said, accepting his invitation. I started kissing his neck, slowly making my way down to his shoulder.

He stood up abruptly, handing me the joint.

I eyed him curiously and took a couple more pulls before handing it back saying, "That's enough for me."

"You know what I've noticed about you, Sandi?"

"What's that?" I asked.

"You rarely turn down weed, but you're never one to light up a joint yourself." He wandered around the room, picking up a succulent. "Why is that?"

"So many questions." I said.

He smiled, awaiting my answer.

"I like my mind most of the time." I replied. "And smoking is terrible for your voice, but weed isn't so harsh."

"You like your mind." Georgia Boy repeated. "I like your mind, too."

Lightning lit up the room.

I laid down in the bed, hands cradling my head, a hopeful signal to Georgia Boy to finish his joint and get on with it.

"You hungry? I'm hungry." He said, putting out the joint in the succulent and setting it on the table before walking quickly to the fridge and opening the door.

I sat up on my elbows, watching him.

"Sorry about the mess in the kitchen! My dishwasher's broken. Oooooo." He turned around with a look of excitement on his face. "I have watermelon."

I chuckled at the expression on his face. "You look so excited."

"I ammmmm." He pulled the watermelon out of the fridge, kicking the door closed. "We about to have some watermelon. I'm excited!"

I watched him cut the watermelon down the middle, grabbing a spoon and one half of the melon before walking to me and sitting on the bed. He stuck the spoon in the middle.

"Do you like watermelon?" He asked.

I tried not to reveal my true feelings. "Oh yes. I love watermelon."

"Good." He said happily, scooping a big chunk right out of the center and holding it up to me, expectant. "Take this bite. The middle is the best part."

I smiled, shaking my head before opening my mouth.

He fed me.

"So what are your real feelings about the godfather and Jacqueline?"

I took another bite he offered me and swallowed before responding. "The godfather is my ride-or-die. We're wanting to form a four piece band anyway."

"That's not an answer about how you feel."

"Well, it's my answer."

"Need another guitar player?" Georgia Boy said with his mouth full.

"Uhhhh maybe." I said. I thought about the electric guitar he played that night. "To be honest, I have a lot of offers and I'm wanting to make the best decision."

"Well, keep me posted." He said, swallowing. He offered me another bite, but I shook my head. "I told ya, girl. We're gonna fuck this town up! I'll take you to the top!" He stood up to put the watermelon away.

I laid back on the bed again, Georgia Boy soon returning. He climbed on top of me, spreading out my hands with his.

"Hey Sandi."

"Hey Georgia Boy."

Lightning flashed, Georgia Boy's face illuminated as the thunder rolled.

His eyes left mine and grew wide with excitement. "Oooooo!"

He jumped off of me and I sat up again, looking to see what he was so damned excited about now. He held a small remote in his hand.

"I just got this lamp and it changes to all kinds of colors." He hid the remote behind his back. "Pick a color any color."

I laughed. "Okay. Orange."

He brought out the remote and pressed a button.

The lamp did nothing.

"Okay, let's try blue." He pressed another button.

He tried all the colors, growing increasingly frustrated as he hit different buttons.

"Well shit." He said, laughing and turning on the lamp manually. "I give up." He tossed the remote over his shoulder. "Come here, girl."

I crawled over to him, sitting on my knees and taking his head in my hands.

"What is it that you want from me, Sandi?" Georgia Boy grazed his mouth on my jawline.

Chills awoke on my body.

"What do you mean?" I said breathlessly.

I wanted him. Now.

He kissed that spot on the hollow of my neck whispering, "It's okay. I know what you want from me." Georgia Boy patted my butt and laid back. "I'm ready for you, Sandi. Let's get these clothes off you."

I climbed on top of him, straddling his hips and taking off my shirt, moving to unhook my bra.

"Hey, wait." He squeezed my hips with his hands before bringing them up and cradling his head saying, "You ain't gotta do it so fast."

So I leaned down and took my time, lightning filling the room with bright light.

We awoke late in the morning, the sun already high in the sky.

The bed was once again askew, Georgia boy's leg on top of my hip. He held me still.

"Shit." I said, sitting up too fast and gripping my head. "What time is it?"

Georgia Boy groaned and rolled over, unresponsive.

I got up and patted the floor, searching for my phone. I found it and stood up quickly, breathing a sigh of relief.

"Well good morning, Sandi." Georgia Boy said.

"Good morning, Georgia Boy." I set my phone on the side table and climbed back into bed.

"Soooo…." Georgia Boy said, looking at me sleepily.

"Sooo…" I repeated.

"About last night…"

"Oh God." I said, covering my face with a pillow. "What did I do?"

"Not what did you do. What did *we* do." Georgia Boy moved the pillow off my face and pointed.

I covered my mouth with my hands. "We broke the mirror."

"Yep." Georgia Boy burst out laughing.

I laughed, too, noticing how the sunlight through the windows lit up the blonde streaks in his brown hair.

"You have sunshine in your hair." I said, tucking a strand of hair behind his ear.

Georgia Boy shook his head at me, smiling. "The way you say things." He took in my face and said, "What do you say we go get some coffee?"

"Ummmmm…"

"Unless you need to go somewhere?"

I looked in the direction of my phone again. "I have a gig at the Taproom at 1pm. But other than that, I'm okay."

"Well let's go then!" He said, jumping out of bed. "I gotta head out early anyway. Going on a road trip to Georgia for Father's Day."

We got up and started getting dressed. I bent over to grab my chucks and felt something slap my butt.

"Georgia Boy!" I said, standing up straight and whirling on him.

"Oh ho ho." Georgia Boy said. "You ain't never said my name like that before."

I rolled my eyes and threw a shoe at him.

"I figured we could go to Lotus Cafe. It's right by my house." He said, handing me back my shoe.

"Okay." I said, untying one of my converse. "I know that place."

We arrived and placed our drink orders, taking our coffees outside to sit beneath the canopy of trees and tropical plants.

We sat in pleasant silence for a while, sipping our drinks.

"So I think I've discovered something about you, Sandi."

I turned to him. "Oh really? What's that?"

He smirked. "Sandi MarLisa has an accent."

I rolled my eyes before closing them and turning my face back towards the sun, allowing it to warm my cheeks.

"Don't worry." He said. "I know how to get it out of you now."

"Oh yeah?"

"Just gotta smack that ass."

I threw my napkin at him.

He dropped me off at my car with just enough time to run home and change for my gig.

I ran into the Taproom with ten minutes to spare, the godfather having already set up the equipment.

I opted out of drinking that afternoon, drinking water by the bucketful instead. A bar patron tipped me in a slice of pizza from Slice House just down the street.

"Georgia Boy." I said with my mouth full. "What are you doing here?"

He walked into the outside bar, his beard shaped up nicely and in clean clothes, carrying an empty glass jug.

He held up the jug in answer. "I'm gonna bring my dad some of his favorite beer. Oyster City!" He rubbed his neck. "And I figured I'd sit and watch you and the godfather play for a bit."

He filled up the jug and then stayed for an hour, waving at me when he left.

"You know he was here for you, right?" The godfather said, adding a capo to the neck of his guitar. "Just so we're clear?"

"Well yeah. He watched us play. But he wanted to get his dad that special beer or whatever."

"Sandi." The godfather said my name as if he were pleading with forces unseen to knock some sense into me.

I looked off in the direction Georgia Boy had left, pondering what the godfather had said.

Chapter 21

Forget I said that

Jacqueline and the godfather were in my living room when I walked in the front door sweating from kayaking.

"What does it mean when a man tells you that he loves you, but then tries to take it back? After he specifically said he just wants to be friends?" I asked.

"Again." The godfather said. Him and Jacqueline were seated on the couch. "A greeting would be nice."

"Hi. But seriously. What does it mean?"

"Who is this?" Jacqueline asked. "Sk8er Boi?"

"Georgia Boy." I said, walking into the kitchen for some water.

"Wait." The godfather said. "What? Was it like in regular conversation? Like, 'That's why I love you, Sandi.' How Sk8er Boi said it?"

"You had to bring that up? But no. He said. 'Because I love you, Sandi. Shit. Forget I said that.'"

"Oh boy."

"Yeah."

I thought back to the strange Monday night and subsequent day that had occurred.

Sierra and I had both needed to take some papers to the courthouse, which was located right up the street from her shop. So we met up, calling it a "court date."

I received an email that my divorce was finalized a few days previously, I had some fees I still needed to pay. My ex and I had filled out the papers ourselves without the use of a lawyer. Everything had so far been handled quite amicably, all things considered.

I sent out a mass text to all my friends. **Officially divorced!**

Sierra and I did what we needed to do at the courthouse and then I began my journey home. I was supposed to see a musical in theaters with Michael that evening. In the Heights produced by Lin Manuel Miranda.

I had made it a whole block before receiving a text from Sierra.

Drinks at House of Henry?

I groaned. Already knowing exactly how this night was going to go.

We're gonna end up at the Hobo, aren't we?

But I arrived at House of Henry, texting Michael.

Change of plans. Meet me at House of Henry.

Damn it, Sandi.

The first words out of his mouth when he arrived were, "I swear to god if we end up at the Hobo. Does Monday mean anything to you creatures of the night?"

We met a few people at House of Henry over drinks. A man who had moved to Panama City from NYC during the height of the pandemic. He now worked remotely for his company.

We also met a transgendered woman and her husband from Alabama. I complimented her nails and she took mine in her hands.

"I love yours, too. I'm trying to find a good nail lady. Will you share?"

I told her the nail technician I had been seeing for three years.

"You know, honey." She said. "I think I like you. But I need a week to decide."

Michael cackled.

Then we, and our new friends, went to the Hobo.

Lauren bought me drinks, Sierra speaking in deep conversation with her new friends.

"Hey girl." I heard a voice behind me.

It was Georgia Boy.

"Hey!" I gave him a hug. "What are you doing here?"

"It's Monday Night Little Fest!" He said, massaging his neck. "You were missed."

"Oh. Right, yeah. I had some work to do today and then I ended up hanging out with my friends."

I gestured to everyone at the other end of the bar.

"Well." He said. "You wanna go outside and talk for a minute?"

We wandered outside and headed for the pavilion by the water, but there was a homeless person setting up a shelter so we opted to walk down the sidewalk, bumping into each other as we walked.

Does one hold hands with their friend-with-benefits? I didn't know.

We stopped for a moment and gazed out to the water.

"Your poems at the last reading were interesting." He said.

"Well, thank you." I responded, leaning over the railing.

"They seemed a little pointed." He said.

I tilted my head. "How so?"

He didn't answer, just stared out into the water. Then he seemed to make a decision and turned to me.

"I… I was… surprised to get that text from you the other day. That you were officially divorced."

"Oh my god." I shifted on my feet, realization dawning. "You're mad at me."

"I'm not mad." He smiled tightly.

"Oh my god, you are." My jaw dropped.

"I got the text in front of my mother, Sandi!" He sighed at the sky. "We were at Los Antojitos and I choked on my drink and didn't speak for minutes! My mom asked me 'What's wrong?' And I said, 'Well, Sandi's officially divorced.'" He pointed at me. "You made me a motherfucker, Sandi!"

"Hey!" My mouth was still agape. "My marriage has been over for months. I didn't need a judge telling me that it was over."

"Well. This is news to me is all I'm saying. I'm from Georgia. It ain't over 'till those papers are signed."

"You didn't exactly ask too many questions when we first started doing it!"

"Would you stop?" He began to walk away.

"You're the one who asked me to come out here." I said, following him.

"Well, I've changed my mind."

I caught up to him and pulled on his shoulder, turning him to face me.

"Why are you walking away from me?" I asked.

"Because I love you, Sandi."

The words hung in the air for a moment. And then…

"Shit. Forget I said that." He put his hands over his face and walked away again.

I stood still, watching him.

"You… you love me?" A question.

He turned around again, leaning against the side railing. "I was gonna take that with me to my grave."

I walked up and stood in front of him, my brows furrowed.

"You love me." A statement.

"I…" Georgia Boy looked at me, clasping my hands. "Yes, Sandi. I love you. Now forget I said it."

"Oh." Jacqueline said.

"Oh." The godfather said.

"Yeah." I said, drinking my water. "Hey. Real question. Does it count if he said it at the Hobo?"

No one answered me.

Chapter 22

The countdown

How many more days until you're in my arms again, my love?

I check the date on the Calendar.

4 more, darling. Over 92,000 words. I've surpassed my last book.

I look at my computer, the typing indicator flashing.

Well get to writing. Because when you get back, you're all mine.

I set my phone facedown on the table and begin to type, butterflies trying to escape my ribcage.

Why do you like this damn tree so much?

"Hey! It's Sandi!"

I walked into the Taproom inside bar, searching for who called my name.

I saw a man with long blonde hair and a wide brimmed hat, crossing his legs and drinking white wine.

I approached and took a barstool next to him.

"Hey!" I said. Then I leaned over the counter and spoke to Bartender. She was seated on the ground. "Can I get a cabernet, Bartender?"

"Yes!" She said, popping up from where she was seated. "Thank God. Someone's ordering alcohol." She popped open a bottle of wine and poured me a glass. "These hippies aren't drinking anything."

I looked into the private event space. Lights were flashing and Electronic Dance Music blared through the glass doors.

"Everyone smokes weed and does psychedelics in this scene, Bartender." The man in the wide brimmed hat said.

Bartender handed the glass to me, grasping my hand in affection quickly before releasing it and pulling a bar towel out of her pocket. "Well. Boss Man's gonna be pissed is all I have to say." She walked away, calling over her shoulder. "Talk to your boy, Sandi."

"We love you, Bartender!"

She held up a middle finger, storming through the backdoors to the outside courtyard.

I turned my attention back to the man beside me. "Don't hate me, but I'm terrible with names. I know you've been at the poetry events."

"Johnny." He said, taking a sip of wine. "Hey. I'm surprised to not see Georgia Boy with you tonight."

I cocked my head, confused.

Taylor exited the private room, taking a deep breath as they closed the door on the blaring EDM sound. "It's a lot in there."

"How's our boy doing?" I asked.

"He's slaying. Of course he is." They said, walking up to give me a hug. "And Michelle looks like a pixie goddess. Because of course she does."

I smiled. Greg and Michelle were the most beautiful couple in the history of couples. Incredibly photogenic the both of them.

"You want to enter the fray with me, Johnny?"

"Yeah let's—" He broke eye contact with me and gazed over my shoulder. "Oh shit! It's Georgia Boy!"

I began to turn in my seat, but Georgia Boy was already next to me.

"What's up, Johnyyyyyy? Hey Sandiiiiiii."

He was hammered.

I greeted him, amused.

"What cha'll waitin' on?" He asked, walking to the private party room and opening the door wide. EDM blasted into the bar.

"Close the fucking door!" Bartender called, walking down the stairs. "I swear to god these hippie children."

I looked at Johnny and we took off after Georgia Boy, closing the door behind us.

Greg had outdone himself with his new project Fifth Density. Flashing lights lit up the walls and people dressed in festival clothes swung around LED poi balls and hula hoops. A few danced and swayed, smoking their vape pens and rolling their necks and hips. But most were lining the walls, watching everything unfold.

Michelle was at the front of it all, hula hooping and hyping up her man.

I walked over to her and waved, not wanting to disturb her by giving her a hug.

I stood on the side next to the DJ space. Greg bobbed his head and put his hands in the air. A large psychedelic powerpoint display illuminated the wall behind him.

It was loud, it was riotess.

It was beautiful.

My heart swelled with pride for my friend.

He didn't look up, he was so focused on what he was doing, in another time and space. So I turned back to the dancers and my mouth dropped open.

Georgia Boy had grabbed one of the poi balls, swinging it around and nodding at the people lining the walls, encouraging them to join in. His oversized teal fishing shirt seemed to glow in the dark.

I burst out laughing, watching him go. I looked to Johnny, but he was leaned up against the wall with Taylor, both shaking their heads.

Georgia Boy caught my eye and sauntered over to me, bobbing his head.

"This is wild!" He said, looking around. "Greg's killing it."

"Yeah he is!" I said over the music.

"I love the vibe!"

"The vibe." I repeated.

"Come on, Sandi." He said, handing the poi ball to me. "You know you want to!"

"I really don't—"

But he had left, finding another poi ball.

I started swinging the balls around, staring around at others for guidance.

They looked like magical fairies worshiping some light god.

I looked like I was lost.

Georgia Boy had found a friend of ours, Megghan, and was tangoing with her. They held the ball in front of their faces and ran after it like it was some will-'o-the-wisp.

I watched them in amazement. They took up the whole space. Some people left the walls to grab hoops or light whips.

I shook my head, rubbing the back of my neck.

"Alright!" Greg said. "I'm taking a quick break!"

He immediately found me in the crowd and gave me one of his infamous hugs. I felt like light was surging through my body.

"Hey you." I said, pulling away. "I wanted to come say hey but didn't want to disrupt you."

"Girl. I saw you as soon as you walked in the room. You don't just walk in the door and go unnoticed. You know that."

I smiled and touched his face.

"And that." Greg pointed towards Georgia Boy, who was still holding the poi ball and laughing with Megghan. "I like it." He grinned at me.

I didn't have time to respond before Michelle had whisked him away, the glitter on her face and curly black hair shining in the light, winking at me.

Georgia Boy found me. "Hey Sandi." He said, grabbing my hand. "Come outside with me."

He pulled me through the front doors to his vehicle that was parallel parked right outside the Taproom on Beck Avenue. Georgia Boy twirled me and I was suddenly up against his truck, his mouth on mine, kissing me deeply.

"Mmmmmm." Georgia Boy rumbled against my neck. "Sandi MarLisa." His voice was deep and heated.

He was very, very drunk.

"How about let's go to the Hobo after this?" He smiled and kissed me again.

Johnny joined us at the Hobo after Greg's show, Jacqueline and the godfather arrived, Beanie too.

We played darts and pool, talking about everything and nothing. Then we sat by the bay after a while, passing around a joint, laughing at the moon.

"I bet you I could swim and reach that building over there." Georgia Boy said, blowing out smoke.

Jacqueline and the godfather left. The godfather didn't come over to say goodbye.

I gazed after them before responding. "I don't doubt you."

Georgia Boy stood up and moved to take off his shirt.

"What the hell are you doing?" I said.

Johnny and Beanie burst out laughing.

"Would you please keep your clothes on!" I pulled him back down.

"That's the first time you've said that to me, Sandi MarLisa." Georgia Boy whispered in my ear.

My neck heated.

"What? You don't think I could make it across the way?" He said more loudly.

"No. I said I believe you. No need to prove anything if I believe you, now is there?"

Johnny and Beanie snickered. Georgia Boy handed the joint to Johnny.

"I've got to go, my friends." Johnny took one last hit and handed it to Beanie. "I gotta work in the morning."

"Me too." Beanie said, passing the joint to me without smoking it. "You guys be safe."

They left, leaving Georgia Boy and me by the water alone.

"You know what I think, Sandi?"

I sighed, getting used to his abrupt invitations for me to step into his deep thoughts. "What do you think, Georgia Boy?"

He took my hand and shaped it into a gun, pointing it across the bay. "I think you're like Jack Sparrow and his pistol."

He moved our hands towards the moon. "And you got one shot." He mock pulled the trigger.

"But you're saving that shot. You're holding onto it for a special purpose. And no one understands why."

My eyes started to ache. I blinked and removed my hand from his, taking a drag.

"What do you think?" He asked, searching my face.

"I think that's a lot of words for a man who's never even called me beautiful." I said, staring into the void below. I had half the mind to bring up what he had said the other night.

I felt something move on my arm.

"Ahhhhhh!" I yelled, standing up in a hurry. Brushing at my arm and dropping the joint.

"What? What?" Georgia Boy stood, too, surveying me for injuries.

"Get them off me! Get them off me!"

Georgia Boy found the culprits on my arm. "Okay. Okay. Okay." He said through laughter. "Would you hold still, woman?"

I tried to keep from spasming. Allowing him to pick the green critters off of me.

I had been attacked by rabid caterpillars.

Georgia Boy bit his lip as he removed them from my arms, carefully setting them free on the grass. "I don't want to kill them." He said.

"I don't want you to either, but can you hurry?!"

"Okay I think that's the last one." He said, bending over to set it free. He stood, taking in the expression on my face. "You freaked out!"

"Ughhhhh. I can't stand creepy crawlies on meeeee." I said. I started jumping around, brushing my arms and legs with my hands, jerking around before putting my hands on my knees, deep breathing.

"Would you come here?" He grabbed my hand and pulled, leading me across the street.

We reached Oaks by the Bay park and walked to the Sentry tree in the center, Georgia Boy determinedly trudging forward, tugging me behind him.

He twirled me and put his hands on my shoulders, then my face, straightening me.

"Okay." He said, gesturing to the tree. "Why do you like this damn tree so much?"

I gazed up at the looming oak tree above before meeting his eyes. I didn't understand what he wanted me to say.

"Sandi MarLisa."

"Georgia Boy."

He reached out for my face, framing it in his hands. "Tell. Me. Why. You. Like. This. Tree."

I twisted my head to get out of his grasp, taking a step back. "I don't understand."

He rolled his eyes and took my hand again. Before I knew what was happening, he had stood on top of the bench right outside the wrought iron fence that guarded the tree.

He hopped the fence and then held out a hand to me. "Come on."

"There's…" I gestured to the fence. "Spiky things everywhere. And hey! You're not supposed to be in there!"

"So you're telling me that you love this tree, it's your absolute favorite tree, but you've never leaned up against it and felt its bark?" He reached his hand out further. "Get in here. Right now."

I stomped to the bench and stood on it, letting him help me over the spikes.

Georgia Boy leaned up against the tree and grabbed my waist, pulling me close. "Okay. New rule." He said, looking up at the tree. "If we stand under this tree, we're not allowed to lie to each other."

I rolled my eyes, pulling away from his grip. "Let me go!" I wriggled.

"I'll let you go." He said, relinquishing his grip. "But stay. Please?"

I stopped fighting him then and heaved a reluctant sigh.

"Sandi. I never see you get excited about anything. I never see you feel *anything*." He took my hand and put it on the trunk of the Sentry tree. "But when you saw this tree the other night, your eyes lit up. You got excited." He leaned back and closed his eyes. "So feel this tree you love so much for the first time and tell me why you looked like that when you saw it."

I stared at Georgia Boy's closed eyes and then looked at my hand touching the tree.

"I…"

Georgia Boy gripped my hips and smiled, taking a deep breath.

"After the storm… I was devastated. Mainly about all the trees." I rubbed the bark beneath my fingertips. "I didn't break down and cry until I was fleeing Lynn Haven and passed Porter Park, where the Bailey Bridge is. I saw all the oaks had fallen and I…"

Georgia Boy opened his eyes and gazed at me.

"When I was safe, I went on Facebook and saw a picture of this giant oak still standing." I took a deep breath. "And I cried again for different reasons. I knew in my heart, in a weird way, that if this tree was okay— the Sentry—then my town would be okay, too."

Tears rolled down Georgia Boy's face, but he smiled. Sniffing.

"You're crying." I took my fingertips from the tree and caught a single tear.

"Yeah, Sandi." He said, kissing my neck and breathing into my ear. "And when I get cut, I bleed, too."

We stood, holding each other beneath the Sentry tree covered in resurrection fern.

"I think that's the first real thing you've ever said to me." Georgia Boy said finally. "And I stood here and listened even while ants were biting my feet."

I stood up straighter. "Ants are biting your feet?"

"Yes." He said. "Actually, yeah, it's hurting. Let's go someplace else."

We climbed the fence again, laughing, Eli helping me down before bending over to brush off the ants.

"Let's walk down to the bay." He said, grinning at me. All signs of tears were gone. "Bay girl."

We walked down an empty dock and quickly relieved ourselves of our clothes, jumping into the water.

It was warm, the moon glowed bright like one of the poi balls on a string.

"What do you see in the moon tonight?" Georgia Boy asked, putting his arms around my waist, his head on my shoulder.

"What do you mean?" I asked.

"I see a mummy. See the bandages?" He gestured with his hand. "What do you see?"

I squinted. "I guess maybe a pepperoni pizza."

"I wonder what it would be like? To spend your whole life reaching for the moon and finally landing on it."

"I think I'd probably be a little sad." I said, frowning slightly.

"What do you mean?"

"I mean, you spend your whole life working towards something and then you get it. Then what?"

Georgia Boy looked at me, incredulous. "I don't know, Sandi, you're on the fucking moon! Enjoy it, woman!"

I laughed a deep belly laugh. I wrapped my legs around him in the water. He kissed my neck.

It felt so good. So good.

"Hold your breath." He said, gently pushing us underwater.

And I freaked out, arms flailing. Georgia Boy quickly helped me up as I gasped for air, coughing.

"Are you okay?" Georgia Boy took my head in his hands, searching my face.

I couldn't talk. Couldn't breathe. Couldn't think.

"Oh my God." He pulled me close, holding me. "I scared you. I'm so sorry, Sandi."

He soothed me, holding me and rocking me until my breathing slowed down and I relaxed in his arms.

"I just didn't expect that." I said finally. "I didn't get a breath and saltwater got in my mouth. I felt like I couldn't breathe."

"It's my fault. That's my bad." He stroked my hair and kissed my forehead. "I'm so sorry."

We trudged through the water back to shore, I grabbed the kimono I was wearing and wrapped it around me, holding the rest of my clothes.

Georgia Boy walked me silently back towards the Sentry Tree, all lightheartedness gone from his face.

"Hey." I said, nudging him. "Cheer up."

He wouldn't look at me. "You really freaked out, Sandi."

I stopped abruptly, grabbing his arm. "Yes, I did. I wasn't expecting it and I didn't comprehend you telling me to hold my breath quickly enough. It was a mistake. You took full responsibility for it immediately. I'm okay." I nudged him again. "So cheer the fuck up sad boy."

He walked away, not looking at me. His head down.

I grabbed his arm and jerked him back.

"You know what I like about you, Georgia Boy?"

He didn't answer. Just looked at me.

"I like that you try shit and you're not afraid of making mistakes. I like that you grabbed the glowing ball tonight and danced, not caring if you looked foolish while doing it. You just wanted to support Greg and get people dancing. You don't care about looking silly as long as it makes other people feel more at ease. I like that you go after things." I pulled him closer to me. "And you're… you're allowed to make mistakes with me. I'm your friend. I forgive you."

He brightened, squinting his eyes at me.

"Oh." He said, seeing something as he gazed down at me, eyes wide. "You're fucked."

Then Georgia Boy took off running, taking my hand with him.

"Where are we going?!" I asked, panting.

He stopped right under the Sentry tree and got inches from my face. "Say what you just said to me again beneath the magical tree we can't lie to each other under."

I laughed. Rolling my eyes.

He pulled me to the bench and made me sit down, looking at me expectantly.

I sighed in exasperation. "You're allowed to make mistakes with me, Georgia Boy."

He breathed deeply, looking up at the thick branches filled with leaves.

"Ahhhhh!" I screamed.

"What now?!" Georgia Boy stood up, looking around.

I pulled yet another wriggling soft creature off of me. "These damn caterpillars!"

Georgia Boy laughed, helping me once more brush the caterpillars off, the sun beginning to rise over the bay.

Chapter 23

Bella Vista Restaurante

Clams swim in a white wine, lemon and butter sauce in the center of the table at Bella Vista Restaurante in Anchorage, Alaska. A vat of cabernet sits off to the side, three glasses already full.

A fireplace sits in the triangle of where three walls intersect. The walls are white, grape centerpieces sit on tables and in cubby holes.

My father tells a story about getting into a fight on a train in Alaska while on a work retreat. I stare up at the ceiling, shaking my head.

The Italian restaurant brings back a memory. My ex was in Chicago for his REU and I came to visit for a few days. He brought me to the Chicago Cultural Center on Michigan Avenue because he thought it would be my kind of place.

I walked in and my jaw dropped, tears of wonder filled my eyes.

The Tiffany dome was truly something to behold, not to mention the quotes that adorned the walls from famous authors and thinkers.

"A good book is the precious life blood of a master spirit embalmed and treasured up on purpose to a life beyond life." -Bacon

The beautiful masterpiece is made of individual pieces of glass shaped like fish scales and the signs of the zodiac line the top of the dome.

I wandered around for hours, my ex giving me space to experience the wonder of the place.

"I've seen a lot of things while I've been here." He said. "But this was the one place I thought you just couldn't miss."

I thought about how desperately I wanted to write in that building. The phantoms of the makers awakened my sense of inspiration.

It was like communing with the divine. I had never said that about a building before.

I wandered to an art gallery featuring a local artist's work. I studied the paintings and fell in love with one that was the picture of a window from inside a restaurant.

I looked at the title of the painting. "3 Arts Club Cafe."

My ex wandered over and I pointed at the painting. "Here. I want to go here."

"You want to go to a restaurant because you saw it in a painting?"

"Yes." I answered firmly. "Because if the artist thought it was worthy to paint, it must be a wonderful place."

He sighed. "Or maybe they just liked the aesthetic of the window, Sandi."

But we found some rental bikes and rode past Lake Michigan on that warm summer day in Chicago. We reached uptown and parked our bikes.

3 Arts Club Cafe was beautiful, but brunch was a two hour wait. We walked down the street to another restaurant and ate there instead.

"This was also depicted in one of the paintings!" I said as I ate the best blueberry scone I had ever had in my life.

We returned to 3 Arts just to walk around and experience the beauty of the place. A fountain sat in the center of many comfortable couches. Chandeliers hung from the ceiling and bow windows lined the far wall set into brick. Real trees sprouted from the ground and groomed green bushes decorated the space, making it feel like a garden.

I took my husband's hand and led him upstairs to the upscale furniture gallery that took over the next several floors of the space.

We walked around admiring all the handmade furniture we couldn't afford and looking entirely out of place.

But my favorite part of that day was wandering down the street as we searched for a surgical museum. We found an Italian restaurant nestled into a courtyard, the only ceilings were vines full of real green and purple grapes.

We ordered some wine and a small charcuterie board, enjoying the atmosphere and cooler temperature of the evening.

The waitress softly touched my hand as she poured more wine. "I have that same ring." She said.

I glanced down at the ring encrusted with black diamonds on my left hand. My engagement ring. We never could find a wedding band that fit it. It wasn't a ring made to be a wedding ring.

"Yes." I said. "It's a beautiful ring."

I woke up the morning before I was to leave for Alaska and shook my boyfriend awake.

"Wanna help me pawn my wedding ring for Alaska money?"

"Hell yes!" He snatched the covers off himself.

I pawned the ring for a whopping sixty dollars. The promise ring my ex had bought me in high school I actually pawned for a hundred. It was worth more.

I laughed as we left the shop.

"What is it?" My boyfriend asked.

"It's poetic, isn't it? The promise was worth more than the fulfillment."

My father is still talking, gesturing widely and musing aloud about how he was almost federally indicted because a guy pitched a fit about being in the wrong seat on a train.

I look at my bonus mom. I think about my father remarrying. His children were all grown though.

I think of my sister coparenting with her ex. She's on the same journey I'm on.

My kids ask me if I still love their dad sometimes.

"I will always love your father. I don't really have a choice in the matter. I was his partner in life for fourteen years. We accomplished many wonderful things together. We had you." I nudge them. "When you love someone, that doesn't just disappear and I don't want it to. Love was never the issue. The context of that love is just different now."

I pause, thinking.

"Just because it's over doesn't mean it was a failure."

I take a breath and sip my wine, taking a bite of the pizza in front of me.

God, it's good. Peppers, mushrooms, onions, pepperoni, fresh basil, homemade tomato sauce and raw tomatoes on top. The crust is crispy on the bottom and soft at the very top.

"You know. I don't usually have an opinion on pizza. But this one is damn good!"

"Told you!" My bonus mom says. "Isn't it way better than that other place we took you to?"

"It really is."

My father's mouth is slightly agape. "Don't have an opinion on pizza? You better get one. You're part Chicagoan."

I laughed. My dad was born and raised in Chicago; my mom born and raised in the Panhandle of Florida, and all of her children were born there, too.

I think about my parents. I think about the two worlds that collided when they made me.

Fire and ice.

I think of how they were two people on the same path for over twenty years, then the path shifted.

But did that make those twenty years a failure?

That would make me a failed experiment wouldn't it?

I shake my head, realizing the answer.

I don't have a guidebook for this next part.

But I will live the good. I will enjoy love while it's here. And it's always here, in many forms.

I'll take the bad when it comes, too.

But today? Today I'm eating pizza with my Chicagoan father in Alaska. The pizza is damn good and so is the wine.

I smile and glance towards my father's wine glass. There's a small fly in it.

"Dad. Just full disclosure. You've got a bug in your drink."

He rolls his eyes dramatically, holding up the glass. "Well, cheers everybody. Maybe this is how I die."

Divorce party

What's your mother's name again?

Marcia.

Right. Marcia. Marcia. Marcia. Like The Brady Bunch.

P.S. I hope the caterpillars aren't still looking for you!

I smiled, thinking about that night under the Sentry.

I suddenly remembered something someone had said to me months ago.

No. No Sandi, you're being ridiculous.

But I stared at the phone, considering what I wanted to say, ultimately deciding to say to hell with it all.

Maybe they're just looking for the butterflies I feel when I'm with you.

"I have a proposal for your son, Marcia. I'm going to ask him about it on our kayaking trip." I said.

Georgia Boy's mom had come to see me perform at Little Village.

"Do you think he'll go for it?"

I explained my proposal.

"Yes! Oh I'm so excited!"

Georgia Boy's reply came then. *You're so sweet.*

Georgia Boy and I had a kayaking day at Econfina Creek coming up. The night of our trip, I was hosting a divorce party at The Salty Hobo. Twenty of my closest friends would be popping in and out all night. Even Jessica was driving down from Asheville.

The irony wasn't lost on me that several of my friends who were at my wedding nine years previous, including the best man, would also be celebrating the demise of my marriage. Not in a church, but in a dive bar.

It was Georgia Boy who was late to our kayaking trip this time. He pulled his truck next to my driveway and rolled down his driver's side window, glancing towards the house behind me.

"You want to back your truck up into the carport?" I shouted across the lawn. "Easier to load the kayak that way."

He laughed shyly. This was the first time we'd really ever been around each other without the help of alcohol. "Uh. Sure. Yeah. I can park my truck in your carport."

I rolled my eyes. "If you're trying to make a sexual innuendo, I've heard better."

"Always so sarcastic, Sandi MarLisa."

He parked the truck and then met me on the lawn.

"I have a proposal for you today." I said by way of greeting.

"Uh… Oh."

"I'm gonna sex you up on the creek and then ask you."

We loaded the kayaks.

"We're strapping yours down securely this time, girl."

And headed to the small grocery store by my house, The Grocery Outlet, to grab lunch.

"Do you like chicken salad?" I asked. "Victoria's Last Bite right down the street has the absolute best chicken salad and they sell it here!"

"Uh…" He looked at the plastic container and scrunched up his nose, slightly backing away. "I brought some burgers for myself. You get what you want."

"Okay! Let me grab some apples. I love to eat it with apple slices!"

We even bought a watermelon to enjoy once we finished at the spring fed creek.

It's about a twenty minute drive to Econfina Creek from my house in Lynn Haven. Georgia Boy drove with the windows down.

Summer was in full swing. Creature Comfort by Arcade Fire blasted through the speakers.

"I like this song." I commented.

"Yeah?" Georgia Boy glanced at me before turning his attention back to the road. "It's a great song."

"So how'd that private party out in Destin go?" I asked.

He barked a laugh. "Oh God. Turned out to be a bust."

"Why?"

Georgia Boy put on the turn signal. "Me and Beanie got there and we had to walk down a huge slope. The party was apparently on an empty lot next to a House Boat on the Bay."

"Hahahahaha oh my God."

"Yeah. I said, 'Sorry, guys. Not feeling it.' I wasn't risking my equipment for that."

"I feel you. Sucks you lost out on a gig though."

Georgia Boy made the turn and straightened out the truck. "Oh we didn't."

"What do you mean?"

"I told Beanie we were going to drive around Destin and pitch ourselves to bars. And we weren't stopping until we found a gig that night."

I was impressed.

Very impressed.

I smiled. "And I suppose you found one."

"Yeah. At one of those axe throwing spots. It was really cool."

We arrived at the put-in spot. Georgia Boy exited the truck and pulled out our kayaks and supplies. I grabbed a few whole apples to put in the cooler.

"You wanted them sliced, right?" Georgia Boy said, pulling out a pocket knife.

I stared at the pocket knife. "You don't have to do that."

"It won't take me but a minute." He took the apples from my hand and bent over the cooler, slicing them with the knife.

I watched him work, the sun beating down on my neck. I snuck a picture of him with my phone.

"There's even a little baggie for them." He said, placing the now sliced apples in a plastic bag and standing.

He insisted on carrying the kayaks to the water himself. I trailed behind him holding the small cooler and carton of orange juice he had brought.

We loaded up the kayaks after putting them in the creek and paddled away.

The creek was lined with trees that were still recovering from the storm. But they were looking lush and fuller than the last time I'd been there.

We pulled into a small pool off to the side. It was crystal blue and a rock wall lined the shore, making a perfect hidden cove.

305

A soft rain started falling as Georgia Boy lit up a joint, protecting the flame with his hand.

He looked up at me and breathed in before slowly blowing out the smoke. The rain clinked on the spring water, the sun peeking through the clouds and casting a blueish light on his face and bare chest through the trees.

I wished I was a painter then.

But I thought to myself that one day I'd paint the moment in words, making him and the moment immortal.

I thought Georgia Boy was beautiful.

I looked down at my paddle, trying to hide my flushed cheeks.

"Where are these rope swings you've been talking about?" He tossed the orange juice carton to me.

I unscrewed the lid and took a big gulp, coughing after I was done.

"Oh my god. It's spiked."

Georgia Boy laughed, paddling closer to me. "Of course it is! It's rum."

"I'm gonna start calling you Captain Jack Sparrow." I said, tossing the carton back to him. "That's really tasty though."

"Well if I were a pirate, I'd tell you to surrender that boooootyyyy."

I rolled my eyes. "Okay. Maybe I'll just call you Captain Cliche."

He laughed, the joint sticking out of his mouth as he paddled with the current down the creek.

I followed him, taking in the beauty around me.

Wild Florida. There was nothing like it.

"So what did you want to ask me?" Georgia Boy asked, keeping a steady rhythm with the paddle.

"Oh!" I said, excited. "So... I want to see if—"

"Yes." Georgia Boy said.

"W-what? But I haven't even asked—"

"Yes, Sandi. Yes." He said again, letting go of one side of the paddle to take a drag. "Whatever you want from me. It's a yes."

I stared at him, recovering from the diversion in my speech.

"What I wanted to ask you is if you and Beanie would form a band with the godfather and me. You on the electric guitar, Beanie on the bass, both of you singing. Me as the lead singer on the keys and the godfather on the drums."

"I told you." He said, smiling around the joint in his mouth, puffing smoke. "Yes. Sandi MarLisa."

We found one of the rope swings. It was on a tree branch high up on a cliff.

"I can't climb up there." I said. "But here." I threw the rope at the end of my kayak to him. "Tie that to your boat and I'll hold on to a branch. Have fun."

He climbed up the cliff and took hold of the rope. He swung, falling down into the cold spring water holding up two rock signs.

We stayed for a while, Georgia Boy taking several turns on the rope, splashing me with water as he fell into the creek. I set my paddle beside me and took a few videos with my phone.

I looked up at the clouds and breathed in the scent of that Floridian summer.

"A butterfly!" I exclaimed, pointing at the flutter of wings that quickly disappeared.

Georgia Boy floated in place, working his arms against the current, watching the butterfly. Then he swam for his boat and climbed in.

"Uh. Sandi?"

"Yes?" I said, pulling the rope back to me.

"Where's your paddle?"

I looked down to my side where I had set the paddle. It had disappeared.

"Oh nooooooo."

"Sandi." Georgia Boy laughed, shaking his head. "You better toss me back that rope."

I kept looking up the creek, hoping to see the paddle stuck on a branch or a rock. "I can't believe I did that."

"I guess you're up the creek without a paddle."

I threw him the rope. "Here, Captain Cliche."

"Don't worry, Princess Sandi MarLisa." Georgia Boy said, tying the rope to his boat. "I'll rescue you."

A big sound rumbled in the distance. A bellow.

"What was that?" Georgia Boy asked.

"An alligator."

Georgia Boy paused his paddling and looked back at me. "What?"

"An alligator, Georgia Boy."

"You can't be serious. Where I was just swimming?"

I thew my head back and laughed. "Are we in water?"

"Yes?"

"Is it Florida?"

He rolled his eyes.

"Then there's gators or sharks in the water, Georgia Boy!"

We floated down the creek, tossing the rum and orange juice back and forth, laughing at everything and talking about nothing.

My next memory is coming to as I'm making out with Georgia Boy in his truck.

"Oh my god!" I pulled away suddenly. "I think I blacked out a little."

"Sandi." Georgia Boy said, shaking his head. "You've said that about nine times since we've been in the truck."

I sat up and looked around. "Oh my god! It's pitch black outside!"

Georgia Boy just stared at me, amused.

"Oh my god, what time is it?" I asked, looking for my phone.

Georgia Boy merely looked at the time on the dash. "It's 7:30."

"Oh my god! My divorce party starts at 8! I'm going to be late for my own party!"

"Oh my god Sandi." Georgia Boy said, putting his hand on my knee. "Nobody is going to be surprised that you're late. They expect it."

I swatted at him. He laughed.

"What happened?" I asked. "After I lost the paddle, things get hazy for me."

Georgia Boy paused, taking me in with an assessing gaze. "You... said a few things."

"Jesus!" I said, my head falling to my chest.

"That's not my name." Georgia Boy smiled.

"What did I say to you? Ugh. Why am I like this?" I put my head on the dashboard and pounded it a few times.

"Would you quit it?" He said, pulling me back. "It was nothing bad, just... telling."

"Tell me what I said!" I shook his arm. "I can't live like this!"

"Okay okay." He batted me away. "Where do you want me to start?"

"At the beginning! When you were pulling me in my kayak!"

He chuffed. "Sandi, were you ever even in the kayak? You kept falling out of it."

"Oh no." I covered my mouth with my hands as Georgia Boy let out a deep belly laugh.

"I called you a mermaid and you got so happy. I think you teared up a little."

"Please tell me what I did."

He paused, sweeping my face with his gaze. "Well. You drank most of that rum and orange juice."

I closed my eyes and put my head down, a hand to my forehead.

"And you said... things... a lot of things..."

"Yes. You've covered that. What things?"

"You told me that you loved me." Georgia Boy said. He kept his eyes on my face.

"Well." I said, removing my hand from my forehead. "That's... interesting."

"Interesting." Georgia Boy repeated. "That's what you have to say to that?"

"You told me that you loved me!" I exclaimed, throwing my hands up. "And then you never mentioned it again."

"Sandi, I had been drinking. It doesn't count. I was at the Hobo of all places." He shut his eyes.

"So it didn't count?" I whirled on him.

"You also said I was one of three men you had ever loved in your life."

I thought about that phrase. My ex was obviously one of the three. But who was the other?

Sk8er Boi?

Did I love him?

"Well. I had been drinking. It doesn't count." I mimicked.

He adjusted his ball cap, sighing. "Then you pointed at a ladder on a random dock and said, 'You see that ladder? Do me on it.'" He let out a bark of a laugh.

I merely put my head down on the dash again.

"Oh, don't look like that, girl." He wiped his eyes, putting a hand on my arm. "That was the most fun I've had in a long time."

He filled me in on my other antics as he drove, my face turning redder and redder.

When I walked into the Salty Hobo, everyone cheered. I put my hands up and yelled.

"Welcome to my night of debauchery."

More cheers rang through the dive bar. Strangers clapped.

Jessica took my hand and led me to a table by the pool tables.

"Happy divorce, Sandi!" Jessica said. She had bought me daisies and boxed wine. Another friend brought me a card that said "Congratulations on your marriage." But with marriage scratched out, replaced with divorce.

Another friend handed me a cupcake. My sister came up and hugged me. She had recently moved out of the house, I was sleeping in what used to be her room.

A few of her friends offered their congratulations. The bartenders gave me shots. I didn't have to pay for a single drink the entire evening. The Gin flowed like Econfina Creek.

Michael, Jacqueline and the godfather walked off to play darts. Georgia Boy wandered up to me holding a Jack and Coke.

"Everyone here is calling me River Boy."

I smiled, shrugging. "I'll just call you Jack."

"I won't remember everyone's names." He said. Georgia Boy seemed stressed. "I haven't met anyone here except Jacqueline, Michael and the godfather."

I studied him. "Don't worry. I doubt I'll remember the night at all."

I didn't remember the night. At all.

I only had flashes of memory plus texts and videos the next day, helping me piece together the events.

I woke up the next morning not knowing where I was. My hair was matted to my face. I touched it.

"Disgusting." I said. Vomit was crusted to my hair.

I sat up slowly, but my head didn't pound. I realized I was still a little drunk.

I found my phone and read the texts.

Dude. You disappeared for like an hour and came back with flowers and boxed wine. Michael texted.

Where are you? Georgia Boy is looking for you saying he's supposed to take you home. The godfather's text read.

I remembered then. The godfather had called me while I was riding in a car. Jessica handed me the phone.

"ARE. YOU. OKAY?" I heard the godfather's voice in the speaker.

I then threw up everywhere.

Let me know when you're awake. Jessica had texted. *We still got a Spring day today.*

She had attached three pictures of us at the Waffle House, we were laughing and looking very drunk. Our sweet designated driver, also named Jessica, had taken the photo. It was her car I threw up in.

I responded to my bestie and then shut my eyes, thinking I needed to pay to have the car cleaned.

I checked the time on my phone. It was surprisingly early, about 10am. Enough time to get myself cleaned up and grab the kids from their dad's for a day at Vortex Springs with my godson and Jessica's future stepchildren.

I shot off a text to Georgia Boy before hopping in the shower. **I got cuts on the bottom of my feet! Guess it was my turn!**

I checked my phone again after emerging out of the shower. It was Jessica.

I left your house key on the table. I had to half carry you out of the Hobo last night, you could barely stand up. I cleaned the throw up out of your hair the best I could and shoved ibuprofen in your mouth before I'd let you sleep. You better know I love you, hooker.

I laughed at my bestie's text, thinking to myself that this was exactly the reason she bore the title.

I owe you a night. We still get a few more days to party before you leave!

I then opened a message from Jacqueline. It was a video of me getting a lap dance from Bartender, Georgia Boy sitting beside me like a guardian.

A memory surfaced. Something Bartender had said.

"You're important, Sandi. Your friends talk about you when you're not around. You're respected." She kissed me hard on the cheek. "Happy divorce!"

I sent Bartender the video. She responded with a screenshot of a text conversation she had with Boss Man.

I wanna see Sandi kiss more girls!

I laughed and then remembered I had been propositioned for a threesome the night before.

I texted Michael the memory.

Someone asked me to be their third last night.

Well did you?

No. I feel in my heart that would be a lot of coordination. I did read a couple articles on it though. So if for some reason I have the inclination, I'll be prepared.

This is it.

This is who I am as a person.

Dude.

I'm fucking dying.

"My night of debauchery"

goes home and googles how to debaucher

A text arrived from Georgia Boy as I redressed in my bathing suit.

Ohhh nooo. Are you alright?

Oh yeah! It's not a big deal.

Haha that was a river adventure. Instant classic!

I'm sorry I disappeared on you. The godfather filled me in. I was absolutely trashed.

His response didn't come for an hour.

It was your divorce party at the Hobo… it's against the rules to apologize for a Hobo night.

I didn't respond.

Chapter 24

Love

"I got hurt in love, so now I'm afraid to love again."

Love didn't hurt you.

Rejection hurt you.

Bad choices hurt you.

A specific person hurt you.

Failure hurt you.

Codependency hurt you.

Bad habits hurt you.

Miscommunication hurt you.

Immaturity hurt you.

Anger hurt you.

Bitterness hurt you.

Love?

Nah. That's the good stuff.

Don't close yourself off to the good stuff.

My Mema

Applause filled the coffee shop.

"Thank you." I said to the small crowd. "Now, this next piece I hope to get through without crying. My Mema recently passed away… and I wrote this as a letter to her."

I thought of a letter I wrote to my Pa when he died all those years ago, how my Mema insisted my letter be buried with him.

My letter to her wasn't buried in her casket. It would be read to people she never even knew.

I shook my head, clearing my thoughts, and began to read.

Margaret Catherine

Well over a dozen people sat in your waiting room for hours, days.

It was a nightmare. A surgery gone horribly wrong.

That week I felt as if I were living in a haze. I couldn't focus on my work. I couldn't do anything but think of sitting in that hospital, waiting to hear that you were going to be okay.

"Not like this. Not like this."

I compromised by bringing my computer with me to work at the hospital that week. Your friends and family all had the same look of determination on their faces. All of us repeating the same mantra in our heads.

"Not like this. Not like this."

This isn't how Margaret Catherine was going to go.

We knew we couldn't ask God for you to never die. But we could ask Him to give you a death worthy of the life you lived.

And when it was your time to go, it wasn't going to be in a cold hospital after a bad surgery.

Oh no.

Margaret, that's not how you were going to go.

Margaret. That name that's half of mine, the middle name my mother, Lisa, chose for me.

MarLisa. Two names put together to make a whole new one.

I used to try and get friends and family to stop calling me Sandi and call me by MarLisa instead. It never worked.

It's now the name I use for the stage and my writing.

I remember you beaming when I told you my daughter, Lorelai, would have your middle name, Catherine, as her own.

I remember so many things, Margaret. Mema. My Mema.

I remember you sitting me and my sister on the counter so we could help you cut the dumpling dough.

I remember sleeping in your bed with you and sneaking in the middle of the night to turn off your TV.

I remember you hiding the peanut butter from Papa. You threatened us with our lives if we told him where it was.

I remember you instructing me to go pick a pint of fresh blueberries so you could make my favorite recipe; blueberry pie.

I remember you watching me take care of my brother, Luke. You told me how you helped raise your youngest brother, too. "He was my first baby."

I remember the B-Romance novels you loved to read; you signing every book you bought me with "Mema (year)."

You read your Bible every day, as long as you could. You prayed for your grandkids and called to tell us so.

You were the first woman Assistant to the Dean at Chipola College.

You had your Monday card game. You wouldn't let me come spend the night on a Monday because you were with your girls.

You took trips with your siblings quarterly.

You organized the family functions, gathering us from the four corners of the world for a celebration.

When I asked you if you ever considered remarrying after Papa died, you said, "No. It's too much to learn another man's habits."

You came to my choir performances. You laughed with my friends and remembered their names. You loved telling people I was a writer.

You taught me how to find blackberries on the dirt roads, and how to make jam.

You helped me catch tadpoles and fireflies in jars. You helped me carry the bucket to feed the fish.

You taught me how to sew, how to vacuum a carpet correctly, how to cook good southern food...

... and how to love. Oh, Mema. You taught me how to practically love people.

Because the biggest memory I have of you is that hospital waiting room. The people you loved all silently praying on your behalf.

"Not like this. Not like this."

It was then, if I didn't know already, I knew I wanted to be like you.

Loved.

Mema, I want to love and be loved in return. Just like you.

And you didn't leave us that day. Oh no. You lived to see your 80th birthday and one year after.

You lived to allow your children the privilege of serving and taking care of you, just as you had for all of us.

The hands that once held us all were now being held.

You lived. God, you lived. You loved your people well, Mema. You sure did.

You have planted infinite seeds into the lives you touched; with your cooking, with your phone calls and cards, with your warm welcomes and hugs, with your quiet dignity.

And your wit. Oh how you could make me laugh.

"Baby, what do you want for breakfast? I have bacon, eggs, toast..."

"Now Mema. You don't have to go through all that trouble for me."

"... Well, I didn't say I was the one cooking it!"

You made my mother promise to take care of your "mustache" or you would refuse to lie still in the coffin.

The only thing I've ever been angry at you for is the fact that you are not immortal. This pain of losing you I will carry with me the rest of my life.

But I will carry it gladly. We all will. Seeds have to die after all, they have to germinate. And you've planted so many seeds.

We promise to grow, Mema. We promise to take these seeds of love and do right by the one who planted them.

I took your hand and kissed your forehead one last time today. I whispered the words, "Well done."

I came home and received a text from my sister. A video of the family you created singing, "It is Well With My Soul."

Each family member took their part of the chorus in the living room of your warm, inviting home that's known nothing but love; the harmonies slowly sending you into the arms of the God you served your whole life.

I imagined Papa snapping and clapping in time, excited to see his bride once more. I saw Pa and Ma beaming at their eldest and only daughter.

I smiled to myself as I listened and thought it wouldn't be long now.

A few minutes later, my sister called. And I knew.

"Is she gone?"

"Yes. It was peaceful."

And all I could do was smile, just faintly, and whisper, "Yeah. Exactly like this."

Christmas in July

"That piece about your Mema tonight, Sandi? It hit."

"Thank you, Johnny." I said, breaking down my PA system. "And thanks for reading some of your song lyrics for us. They read just like poetry."

He put his hands together and bowed.

Georgia Boy sat at a bar top with Beanie, laughing. He wore an oversized short sleeved button up. It had images of different colorful martinis on it.

I shook my head at his shirt, silently laughing to myself. Then I looked at Johnny and took in his style. He wore a wild patterned shirt, but it worked with the open button at the collar, vest and boots he wore.

"You think we can team up and burn Georgia Boy's shirt?" I said jokingly. "Maybe buy some clothes that fit him?"

Johnny rotated his head to Georgia Boy and back to me. "Nah." He said. "That's Georgia Boy. He does that. That's him. Change one thing about him and you have to trade it for something else." He put his hands in his pockets and looked at me, assessing.

The comment struck me. Johnny had cut to the chase, calling me the fuck out.

I nodded, smiling slightly. "You know what, Johnny, you're right. I wouldn't change a thing about him."

Johnny smiled, nodding at me with approval. "I'm glad you recognize that, Sandi."

Georgia Boy walked over and helped me pack up. I thought about the text I sent him earlier.

I formally invite you to the Taproom Christmas in July party as my plus one. Wanna come with me after my poetry event?

I'll let you know in a bit.

He hadn't confirmed with me. Things had been a little weird between us since divorce party day.

"I've gotta go get my car and swing it up front." I said to no one in particular.

I walked out the door and down the street. I found my car about a block away and pulled it around to the front of Wild Root.

My door flew open and there was Georgia Boy, he jumped in the passenger seat laughing hysterically. I saw Johnny and Beanie out front shaking their heads.

"Take me for a ride, Sandi!" He said, standing and gripping onto the top of the car. "Surfing USA!" He yelled into the night.

I rolled my eyes and took him for a ride around the block before parking.

The boys helped me load my equipment and then we stood around talking for a moment. The night was muggy, summer in full swing.

"Alright boys. I have a party to get to."

"Ooo after party. Where at?" Johnny asked.

"Sorry Johnny. I'd invite you, but it's a private party and I can only bring a plus one."

I turned to look at Georgia Boy. At that moment, I decided then I wasn't taking no for an answer. "And that's Georgia Boy."

Georgia Boy's mouth gaped open before he quickly closed it.

"Oh." Johnny eyed Georgia Boy. "Well have fun you crazy kids!"

"We can take my car, Georgia Boy." I walked away and got in the car, watching Georgia Boy say bye to his friends before joining me.

We reached the general location, but couldn't find the actual house.

I called Bartender.

"I'll come out to the road and direct you!" She said.

We took a turn around the block again and then turned at a stop sign after a cop car.

Bartender came off the side of the road, flagging the cop car down.

"Oh my god!" We heard her say. "No, not you officer!"

She walked quickly to our car, pointing to a parking space next to hers. "I've never been so excited to see a cop!" She quipped.

We walked inside the home, and it was a home not a house. Boss Man greeted us at the door to his den.

"It's Sandi! Oh… and she brought Georgia Boy."

Georgia Boy winced at the small slight and stayed close to me.

We played White Elephant, Boss Man providing the gifts. Boss Man's wife, Lily, brought me a glass of wine and Georgia Boy grabbed a beer from the cooler.

The attendees moved to the beautiful backyard where string lights hung from vines heavy with purple and white night blooming cereus flowers.

"I believe this one is called, 'Queen of the Night.'" Boss Man took a bloom and laid it on the table in front of me.

Georgia Boy scooped it up and tucked it behind my ear, putting his arm around me.

"Where are all the musicians?" Georgia Boy whispered in my ear.

"I don't know." I said, whispering back. "Would you like another beer?" I asked.

Georgia Boy looked at me affectionately. "No Sandi. I'm okay. Thank you."

Bartender found a scooter and rolled around the backyard on it.

We laughed and talked through the night. Lily spoke to me about how she had encouraged Boss Man, at the beginning of the Taproom, to make it a safe haven for local artists.

"So you're the visionary behind all that Taproom does? All the art gallery events and live music?"

She smiled at me. "Art is so important for the community. I wanted Taproom to be a welcoming space for creatives."

I rose from the table to grab a bottle of water from the cooler, Georgia Boy grabbed my hand as I stood.

"Can I get you something, Sandi?" He said, squeezing my hand.

I looked down at him. His face was softer somehow that evening.

"That's sweet. But no." I said smiling. "I'll be back."

I grabbed a drink from the cooler and walked inside, finding some cheese and grapes from the charcuterie board and snacking.

"Hey Sandi." Boss Man walked in, looking around to see what food needed to be replenished.

"Boss Man."

He walked to the fridge and grabbed some cheese, coming back to lay them out on the spread.

"So you and Georgia Boy?"

I swallowed before answering. "No. He asked to be friends."

He bounced his head. "Good. Good." He organized the cheeses. "He's a dirty musician. Not good enough for you."

I rolled my eyes. "I'm a dirty musician, Boss Man. And I have a feeling nobody is ever going to be good enough for me according to you."

He nodded, not looking at me. "Yes. Well."

I gave him a pat on the shoulder before walking back outside.

Georgia Boy and I left the party late in the evening, walking out with Bartender.

"That was fun." Georgia Boy said, closing the door to the passenger side of my car.

"Yes, it was." I smiled.

I always loved my life, but sometimes I felt it more.

Tonight was one of those nights.

"Thank you for inviting me, Sandi."

I turned to him to respond and Georgia Boy touched my face, stroking my cheek with his thumb, grazing the flower in my hair. Then he lightly grabbed my chin and pulled me closer, kissing me.

And I couldn't shake the feeling that, all other kisses be damned, Georgia Boy and I had our first kiss that night.

Chapter 25

Salty Oak Brewing Company

I pulled into the Salty Oak Brewing Company parking lot, nicknamed the SOB.

I opened the driver's side door, changing out of heels and into my flip flops. I was wearing high waisted shorts, a crop top and a kimono. Out of the corner of my eye, I spied Georgia Boy walking over to me alone, his hands stretched out.

"Hey hey, Sandi!"

"Hey!" I said, shutting the door.

Georgia Boy kept walking until he was inches from me, sliding his hands around my waist under my open kimono.

The touch felt tender, intimate.

"I've missed you, woman."

"You're touching my waist." I said, breathlessly.

"Yeah." He ran his mouth over my jawline. "Is that okay?"

My breath hitched in response. Something fluttered in the bushes behind Georgia Boy.

"Look!" I cried. "A butterfly!" I ran over to examine the monarch in the bushes. Georgia Boy watched me silently.

He then took my hand and led me into the brewery. Beanie was there playing guitar. Mason St. Germain sat watching with a friend.

After a couple of sours and the boys' having several beers between them, we were singing Under Pressure by David Bowie and Queen and Sweet Dreams by Eurythmics, Mason and I switching back and forth between harmonies and melodies.

"We're jamming!" Georgia Boy said, playing his guitar. Beanie had brought out his bass, he played it like a lead guitar.

"Come out to the truck with us." Georgia Boy said after the show.

We all stood between his truck bed and a fence, a joint passed around. Georgia Boy turned the joint around in his mouth backwards and motioned for me to kiss him.

"Breathe in." He said.

So I did, inhaling the smoke. Beanie and Mason exchanged looks.

Afterwards, I joined Georgia Boy in his truck. The weed had left him contemplative. I moved to start kissing him but he drew back, assessing me.

"So. I've been meaning to talk to you about something. About what you said at the river."

"Mhmmm." I said dreamily, stroking a hand up his thigh.

His breathing hitched slightly, affected by the touch. He grabbed my hand and stroked the inside of my palm.

I took a deep breath, feeling his touch permeate my being, my soul.

"Sandi. You told me that you loved me and then left me at the Hobo."

I removed my hand, my mouth slightly agape. "I told you I was sorry and you said everything was okay."

He put his head down and drew in a breath, taking off his ball cap and refitting it. "I know. I know. But you told me that you loved me and then left the Hobo with someone else."

"Jessica." I said, infuriated. Did he really think I left with another man? "I left with Jessica."

"Well I didn't know that at the time!" He said, throwing up his hands. "I didn't know where you went. No one did. I searched for you for like an hour."

I crossed my arms and looked out the window. "Jessica is my best friend. She said I could barely stand up and no one noticed so she took me to the car. I was clearly at the point of trashed beyond even the Hobo's standards." I threw my hands up. "I even threw up in this poor girl's car!"

"Well, I'm just saying that all I could think was, 'Well. Georgia Boy, you were right. Love really is overrated.'"

I couldn't roll my eyes further in the back of my head. "I can't stand that song. Keep telling yourself that love isn't worth anything, Georgia Boy. See how far that gets you in life. You'll be a bitter person at the end of it!"

"You left me."

"I was drunk!"

"And I was drunk outside the Salty Hobo when I told you that I loved you. And you were drunk on the river when you said you loved me."

"What do you want, Georgia Boy?" I rounded on him.

He closed his eyes. "I don't know."

"Well." I said. "Do you want me to throw up in your car?"

He shook his head, bewildered. "What?"

"Do. You. Want me. To throw up. In your car?" I enunciated each word with a clap.

"No Sandi! Please open the door!"

I threw my hands up again in frustration. "You know who took care of me the night I got really drunk? Jessica. She cleaned throw up out of my hair after taking me to Waffle House and then drove me home safely, shoving ibuprofen down my throat. You know who called around making sure I was somewhere safe? The godfather. He managed to get ahold of Jessica and confirm." I turned to him. "My friends. My friends took care of me."

Georgia Boy looked completely confused.

"I don't know what this is between you and me, but it's definitely not friendship. And if you want something more, it's gonna be your responsibility to clean the throw up out of my hair. Do you want that? Do you want that responsibility, Georgia Boy?"

A pause.

"I just don't understand why you're talking about throwing up in my truck!" Georgia Boy said.

"Ugh!" I stormed out of the truck and slammed the door.

He followed me, grabbing my arm. "Why are you walking away?"

I turned on him. "It doesn't sound like you want a relationship right now. And that's fine. You can't even manage to say that I'm beautiful or anything that actually indicates that you want something more than friendship. I don't even know why I'm upset, honestly. All you care about is how I can benefit you musically. So, *I'm*—" I got close to his face, my tone biting. "—going home. We can be friends with benefits or whatever the hell we are."

"You're going home." He repeated.

"Yes, Georgia Boy. Yes. I'm going home. And you should go home and rethink everything you've ever thought about love and get over it, Mr. Love is Overrated. Everyone gets their heart broken. There's nothing unique about it!"

"What is it that you want from me, Sandi?"

"A date! A date, Georgia Boy." I opened the door to my car. "A real one!"

"That's what you want. That's what you want from me? A date?"

"Yes, Georgia Boy! Or do I really mean that little to you?"

"I… you…"

I got in the car and slammed the door. A butterfly fluttered off my window when I started the engine.

Part Three

Chapter 26

The hill

Judah gripped the small root that stuck out of the ice, crying.

My dad had sent us up the steep hill to sled, not knowing the very top was slick with ice.

We moved up the hill with no problems, but when we hit the ice we fell, gripping onto the side.

We couldn't move. And it was a long way down. We risked broken bones or worse if we let go and raced down the hill without a sled. I took a peek at the bottom and gripped the ice wall tighter with one hand, the other held the sled. Our salvation.

"It's okay, baby." I turned my head to the side. I had the thought that I could manage to shimmy to the side and help Judah.

"Okay, listen. Hold tight, just like you are. I'm going to go to the side and help you from there."

"You're leaving me?!"

"No baby. I'll just be right over there. I can't help you from here."

He cried harder, gripping the branch tighter with his gloved hand. "Don't leave me, mommy. Please! I'm scared!"

My heart cracked at the terror in his voice. "Baby, look at me in the eyes right now."

He turned his tear stained cheeks to me. His chubby face squished under his hat.

"I would never, ever leave you. The only way out of this is for me to get to the side and help you from there, or sliding all the way down."

Judah hyperventilated.

"Judah, you have to stop. You have to conquer your fear and be brave. There's no way around it. There is no choice. So breathe with me and calm down. You have to calm down to get out of this."

"I don't want to die!"

"So be brave." I said firmly, keeping all of my own fear out of my voice. "Now breathe with me and conquer your fear."

We breathed together, deeply and slowly.

"Keep breathing!" I said, swinging the sled to the side. It thunked in the thick snow, catching in a thicket. I breathed a sigh of relief, beginning to shimmy. "In and out, son. Come on!"

I took my eyes off of him and concentrated on rescuing myself. I safely reached the side and found a tree branch. I took off my gloves and stuck them in my pocket, holding on to the end of the branch with one hand and reaching the other out to Judah.

"You have to move, son."

"What?" His head swung to me in terror. "No! I can't! I'm scared."

"You have to be brave, Judah." My eyes were immovable from his. I would not let him see my panic, my terror.

It was a gift I had. My therapist told me once that my emotions never matched the look on my face. It was due to the years of trauma I experienced. I learned to keep a poker face quickly.

I was actively working on being able to express my emotions outwardly.

But now? Staring at my terrified son?

That warped gift of mine served me well.

"You can do this." I said. "Being brave means doing things even when you're crying. Even when you're scared. You can do this scared. Just move. One hand after the other."

Judah said nothing for a time. "I'm trying! I can't make my arms move, mommy!"

"One hand after the other." I said again. "It's only a couple shuffles and then mommy's hand is right here. And Judah?"

He stared at me, eyes wide.

"I will not let you fall. You hear me, son?"

He took a final deep breath and moved, shimmying quickly until…

"That's it!" I grabbed his hand and pulled him across the ice. When his jacket was within reach, I snatched his hood and hauled him into the snow.

We held each other for a good while, still breathing in sync.

"Okay." I said, refusing to let the tears that wanted to come out spill over. "We have to sled down now."

"What?!" Judah said, wide eyed. "No!"

"We can't walk down, it's too icy." I picked up the sled I stored under a tree. "So come on. Just don't think too hard."

I set the sled at the top of the hill and sat down, reaching for Judah's hand. He breathed a shuddering breath and then took it, nestling into my lap.

"I'll be brave, mom."

I smiled, securing the hood on his head and mine before pushing us off the ledge.

We zoomed forward and hit the ice patch, spinning around completely. I felt the sled slide out from under me as we raced down the hill, our heads leading the way.

I curled into Judah, protecting his head. I straightened my legs and tried to spin us the other way.

"This is how you die." The thought raced with me down the hill.

Down with the sickness

I felt like I was dying. I hadn't been able to move from the bed in days.

All I wanted to do was sleep. My body ached. My breathing labored.

Covid-19 is a bitch.

My smell and taste were gone, the worst symptom of them all in my opinion.

My house was quarantined and I was alone.

The doorbell rang and I groaned, rolling to my side. Wondering if they'd just go away if I laid there long enough.

I put on my robe and shuffled to the door, my hand on my forehead.

It's my ex.

I flung the door open. "Hey. Is everything okay?"

"Yes. Uh." He held up a pharmacy bag. "I heard you were sick and I brought you some medicine."

He looked good. His skin a deep brown, his eyes had light in them, his black beautiful curly hair styled. He wore a button up and khaki shorts with flip flops.

He looked healthy. I hadn't seen him this way in years.

"Thank you." I said, taking the bag. "I'd invite you in. But I'm pretty sure it's Covid. I lost my taste and smell."

"It's okay. I'm fully vaccinated. As a teacher I got it ahead of everyone else. Plus, we don't have classes right now for the summer. And anyway, I just wanted to drop that off." He started to walk away.

"Wait." I said, taking a step forward. "Come talk to me for a minute if you're not busy."

He flexed his hands before answering. "Okay."

We sat on the couch and soon we were laughing hysterically.

I didn't realize how much I had missed him. We talked intelligently, about ideas, about the world, about what the future held.

He smiled broadly, his whole face lifting up with his laughter.

He looked like our son.

He looked young.

This was the person I had fallen in love with. This was the man I partnered with for fourteen years.

I tried not to weep at the sight, tried not to run over and tackle him in my joy.

My heart swelled with pride for that boy I fell in love with at the fast food restaurant we worked at together. I wanted to jump out of my skin and zoom across the room, shouting my thanks to the universe and forces unseen.

"So who's Georgia Boy?" He asked.

I looked up and a ghost of a smile was on his face. "How do you know about him?"

"I'm not completely oblivious." He said, shaking his head at me and chuckling. "And while we're on these subjects." He stared at me with a mock serious expression. "A divorce party? Really Sandi?"

We spent three days together. He took care of me while I was ill.

"Returning the favor." As he put it.

We talked about trying our relationship out again, but ultimately decided against it.

"I… there's so much pain. Years of pain. I am still triggered by certain memories. I still have PTSD from my experiences. There would be so much to unpack and I don't think either of us have the emotional energy to do the work it would take. Plus…"

I sat next to him, somber expressions on both our faces.

"Plus…" I began again. "I think I'm just familiar to you. And you're familiar to me. We need to keep growing, even though it's painful."

We fought some, arguing about past hurts. But months down the line, we both ultimately got the most incredible poetic justice.

I received a text from my ex.

Need to have a conversation about the future. A few life updates that you need to know about. Free half-hour soon?

Can we talk like now? You know I hate ambiguity.

Jesus.

Just a phone call.

Like do you have a girlfriend? Is she moving in?

I'd rather talk in person if possible. You know I get misunderstood easily especially on the phone.

FaceTime then

Jesus

I can't live like this

Okay. I'll call in a second.

I answered the call on the first ring and demanded he get straight to the point.

"Do you remember that professor I worked with for my REU in Chicago?"

"Yes. Of course."

"Well... he looked over my work in France."

"Right. The groundbreaking stuff."

"Long story short. He said if I wanted to write a dissertation, he would support me in my right to defend it."

My breath caught in my throat. "And?"

"And... well... long story short... I defended it and I now have a PhD in Physics from the University of Chicago."

I burst into tears, sobbing over the FaceTime call.

"I..." He cleared his throat. "You were one of the first people I wanted to tell. I wouldn't be here without you, Sandi."

I breathed heavily, struggling to not just outright weep at this news, at the lightness and freedom in my chest because of it.

Many times, the universe winks at you.

Many times, it even smiles.

But sometimes... just sometimes... it reaches through time and space and whispers, "Well done."

And on even rarer occasions, it reaches out its hand and asks you to dance.

Wildly. With abandon. With an open heart and mind.

Forgetting the past. Forgetting the pain.

An invitation to reach for what lies ahead, forgetting what lies behind.

And dance upon this barren land, your tears watering the ground and bringing newness of life.

I was ready. I was ready for that wondrous dance.

A story well told. A story for the ages.

"I am so proud of you." I said. "And I'm so happy you're alive."

With that, my spirit was at peace.

A chapter closed.

It was time to write a new story.

The blue marshmallow

Deep footprints were etched in the ice, practically fossilized. Snow, then rain frozen over.

"Watch out. Someone could twist their ankle on this path." My dad called.

We were on our way to see a glacier and ice cave in Alaska. But it was quite a hike ahead of us.

My son and daughter actually enjoy hiking. I always brag on my daughter.

"She hiked all the way up Stone Mountain when she was three. I didn't carry her once."

She always beams at this story.

Then she reached a steep hill in Alaska.

"I can't do ittttttt." She cried.

"I thought you wanted to climb a mountain?"

"I DIDN'T MEAN ITTTTTTT!"

My daughter was born with a soul she'll grow into someday. It's so big for her little body right now that I watch her struggle with it. I observe her fighting with her emotions and trying to keep them under control.

She's a ticking bomb. Cross her and find out.

I held her hand, helping her keep steady on the icy path. She wore a matching teal jacket and snow pants while the rest of us wore black. We called her the blue marshmallow.

I looked down and sighed. "Baby, your boots are on the wrong feet again." She's insisted on wearing her shoes on the wrong feet since birth.

"I know." She said. "I like them."

"That can't be comfortable."

"It's fine."

We stumbled along the path for a while, until I realized a change in strategy was in order. "I think it might be better if you have your own spike pole."

My dad handed her one and she took off, taking the lead of our group. I noticed as she walked away that she had chocolate stains all down the back of her teal trousers.

"Look at her go." My dad said.

"I know. She just needed her own stick."

The trail wound through the mountains, the world in greyscale. Except for the blue marshmallow.

She stuck out against the black and white, taking on the wilderness with her vividness.

Because my daughter? She fills the world with color.

The tantrums she threw as a toddler were impressive. I'd sit with her in the room as she screamed for 45 minutes straight. Mostly exasperated and exhausted with her, but there was a not-so-secret part of me that was always impressed with just how long her will could hold out.

I'd always tell her, "You've got a strong will, baby. But so does mommy, and I've been alive longer with more practice and I promise you won't win this."

It didn't stop her from trying.

She still hasn't listened to my lesson that the secret to a strong will is pacing yourself.

Holding out that will over time. Beating down the stone walls like a river beats down rock.

She'll learn, soon enough.

That's how she hiked. Her will driving her little legs up the slopes and through the trees. Eventually, she tuckered out and fell to the back of the line.

"Mommy. I'm so tired." She whined.

"I know."

"Just a little while and there's a bench up here where we can rest." My dad said.

We reached the bench and Lorelai lost it. She refused to sit with the rest of the group and folded her arms, sulking on a distant boulder.

"Oh boy." I said under my breath.

"I'm honestly impressed she made it this far. I don't think she'll make it to the caves. We still have a while to go, and it's up rocky terrain."

I looked up and scanned the landscape. To get to the ice caves, we still needed to climb up a large pile of boulders covered with ice and snow, then cross a small river and hike up a steep slope littered with slick rocks.

"Yeah, probably not." I agreed.

My bonus mom, who the kids call Slinky, scouted out our path and returned with a report.

"I don't think any of us can make that trip." She said. "I'm not going to do it. You can try it out with your dad though."

So Slinky stayed with the, now angry, blue marshmallow and my dad, my son and I continued on the second leg of the journey.

Thick snow covered the boulders as we forged ahead. More often than not, our boots fell through the snow and hit the rocks. My dad pointed out the safe routes as we picked our way over the mountainous pile.

Judah slipped on a patch of ice.

"Put your hood on." My dad said to him. "Protect your head. And put on your gloves. Ice cuts, you know."

My right leg fell three feet through the snow, I had to drag myself out.

"Try to stay on top of the snow."

"Yes, that would be ideal." I quipped.

My son liked to talk more than he liked to pay attention to what he was doing. As he made conversation, I steadied him when he lost his balance, or nearly fell into the river.

He kept us laughing.

"Grandpa, did you sleep naked last night?"

"What? No?"

"Well, I saw your pants on the floor next to the couch."

"That's because I went out late to see if there were any Northern Lights."

"I'm just saying it's suspicious."

From boulder to boulder we hopped, the sun falling further behind the mountains. It reminded me of my childhood in Florida, climbing the rocks to the end of the Jetties and jumping off the end into the Gulf of Mexico.

Except, the end of these "jetties" consisted of more ice.

Finally, we made it to the other side of the boulder wall.

"Alright. Now it's just up this slope." My dad said.

I could see the glacier above us, defined by the specks of blue set into the mountain. There were four ice caves just below it, sparkling like crystals.

"Yeah. Lorelai probably couldn't have done this." My son said.

"Probably not."

I thought back to when I took her hiking once and she insisted on wearing a purple princess dress with a crown to match. I drew the line at her plastic high heeled shoes, for practicality's sake. So she opted for pink cowboy boots instead.

She hiked all three miles in that damn puffy purple dress.

The caves were finally drawing near. We huffed and puffed our way up the rocky slope until we reached the wide mouth of the largest cave.

"Go on and lick it." My dad challenged my son.

So he did.

I felt the walls of the cave. Yep. Ice.

"Look at the rings in the ice." My dad pointed out. "It looks just like the rings of trees. It shows the passing of time."

In the walls we could see thin lines of dirt and blue. Almost like a clear marble. We could see some jewel-like stones settled deep in the rock, hear the whistling of the wind through the cave.

We took our pictures, we stared for several minutes down the interior of the cave.

My dad looked up at the sky. "A snowstorm is on its way. The girls are waiting on us back at the bench. Time to go."

I turned to go back the way we came and was stunned by the view. We were looking down at the valley we just hiked up from. The boulder wall blocked our view of where the girls were.

I thought of how upset Lorelai would be when I got to her, began to think through the process of validating her disappointment, encouraging her for the fact she got as far as she did.

"Oh my God I don't believe it." My dad said, awestruck.

"What?"

He simply pointed in answer.

My son turned to look, too—his face lighting up—and started whooping.

Because blazing over the boulder wall, coming straight towards us, was the blue marshmallow with her chocolate covered snow pants and wrong-footed shoes. Slinky in tow!

"I don't believe it." My father said again.

I could.

"Oh my God. She actually did it." Judah cried, waving both arms in the air.

"I'll go meet them." My dad said. "We'll have to hike back up to the caves. That girl has earned it."

My son lowered his arms and sighed, shaking his head. "She's kinda amazing."

Damn right she is.

A soft sound traveled up the slope, growing louder all the time, riding the wind. It could have been a bird.

And then...

"I. Am. Not. Afraid!" I heard the blue marshmallow's voice echo through the valley, crystal clear. "I am brave! I am strong!"

And I just shook my head, watching the little blue marshmallow pick her way over the snow covered rocks, her teal coat defiantly shining like a beacon through the white.

"Yes you are." I whispered. "Yes you are."

Chapter 27

No Name's

Hey girl. You feeling any better?

It was Georgia Boy. I hadn't heard from him in weeks after our come-to-Jesus meeting in the SOB parking lot.

I sent a selfie.

Feeling much better.

Are you still okay to perform in the All Original Monday Night Little Fest?

I rolled my eyes. So that's why he was texting.

Yes. I'll be there.

My first show back after being sick was at No Name's with the godfather.

I arrived and opted for Gin and Tonic.

Not that I could taste it.

The night was hot and sticky, my hair expanding in the late July humidity.

I let loose, my vocal chords almost sighing with the release.

This. I had missed this.

Ashley Feller was there, a local musical legend and St. Andrews Jezebel Podcast host. Jacqueline sat with her.

And then, there was Georgia Boy, throwing up rock and roll signs to me as he joined the group.

The Gin had set in, so I wandered over to the picnic table where he was seated and sat down.

I looked into his eyes and sang Creep, touching his face and grabbing his chin.

He didn't look away.

I walked through the crowd to grab another drink, spotting a man sitting alone at a table. He looked sad. I bought my drink and walked over to him.

"Hey!" I said. "Enjoying the show?"

"Yeah!" He responded. He had black hair and a mustache. Military then.

"Waiting for someone?"

"Oh no. Actually this is my first night in town. I just got stationed here."

"Well enjoy the show!"

He mumbled something.

"What?" I asked. "I couldn't hear you over the noise."

"Are you Jewish?" He said more loudly.

I sighed. "Not that I know of."

"Your hair is like mine." He said.

"Well." I looked over towards the table where my friends were seated. I noticed Georgia Boy watching me before quickly turning away. "Jacqueline is Jewish. Come sit with us and we may find some other things in common, too." I winked at him before walking back to the stage.

Military Guy sat alone the rest of the performance. We finished the show, Gin Sandi making her full appearance, and began packing up the equipment. Eventually, I was told to sit down by the godfather. I took a seat across from Georgia Boy.

"Hey Jack." I said, pointing at his glass.

He smiled. "Hey Gin."

I saw Military Guy move out of the corner of my eye. He sat down next to me.

"Hey Sandi. Can I buy you another drink?" He then looked around the table. "Anybody else want another drink?"

Everyone shared their drink orders except Georgia Boy.

339

"I'm meeting my brother after this." He said.

When Military Guy returned, he easily put himself in the conversation after passing out the drinks.

"I actually just moved here from being stationed in Alaska." He said.

"Oh!" I said. "Interesting, my dad lives in Anchorage."

We talked for a while, Georgia Boy eventually excusing himself and leaving to meet his brother.

Military Guy was on it with the drinks. He left to go buy another for himself, the rest of us passing this go round.

"Sandi." The godfather said when he had left.

"Yes?"

"Are you sleeping with him tonight?"

"What? Who?"

"You know Military Guy wants to sleep with you, right?"

"I–What?"

"He wants to put his penis in you!" The godfather said more loudly.

I looked off to where Military Guy had wandered away.

"You walked up to him when he was sitting alone. You invited him to talk to us. He's buying you drinks. That's why Georgia Boy left. You realize that right?"

"I...." I stammered. "He... Georgia Boy is meeting his brother... and I was just trying to be nice! He looked sad!"

"Well, Jacqueline and I are leaving." He motioned in the direction of the door to the inside bar. "Good luck with that."

They left me sitting perplexed at the table.

Military Guy arrived with his new drink, sitting down.

"So where do you play next?"

I was startled out of my thoughts by his question. "Oh uh. I'm at Monday Night Little Fest at the Taproom. It's all originals." I put my hands on the table and stood, realizing something. "I've gotta go... really nice to meet you!"

I power walked out of the bar and made it to the safety of my car, shutting the door and putting my head down on the wheel.

I didn't want to sleep with Military Guy that night.

Or any other guy at the bar.

Because I wanted to sleep with Georgia Boy.

And he had left.

Cool as fuck

The Taproom was packed, but I couldn't get the crowd's attention.

I was already under scrutiny, the neighbors had been consistently complaining specifically about me because of the St. Andrews sound ordinance.

Boss Man had received a text from a neighbor who particularly liked to voice her opinion.

Can you turn her mic down? She's talented, but too fucking loud.

It had become a running joke.

But no. *This* was a joke. My body was feeling back to normal and I wanted to put on a performance, not be background music.

I'd had enough.

I stood on one of the pillars with my cordless mic. A few people looked up from their drinks as I sang.

It wasn't enough for me.

So I walked to the bar top, patrons watched me as I marched, my chin held high.

I gripped a barstool and put my knees on it, then I hoisted myself onto the bar.

I sang from a seated position, finally grabbing the attention of more people.

Bartender played affectionately with my hair for a while. I encouraged people to tip her.

But it wasn't enough. I wanted to go higher.

Needed. I needed to get higher.

So I stood on the bar, my hands wide, my head tilted back.

I sang my heart out. People couldn't help but stare.

Boss Man walked outside and saw me there and put his head down before finally accepting his fate. He brought out his phone and started recording the scene.

I walked and danced on the bar, people cheering loudly after each song.

"Do you want to walk?" Boss Man said, reaching his hand out to me.

Yes. Yes I did.

I took his hand and walked the bar. We reached the space where there was a small gap, the other bar top a few feet away.

I looked at Boss Man and nodded.

I jumped the gap to cheers. Boss Man helping me down and giving a slight bow.

"Reminder, I got two kids in private school, folks!" I said into the mic. "If you want to tip us, the tip jar is on the stage. Or you can raise your hand and I'll come to you. I do like to be accommodating."

A man came up and offered me a five dollar bill from a wad of cash. A twenty fell to the ground as he handed the five to me.

"It's a sign." I said seriously.

He smiled and bent over to retrieve the twenty, pressing it in my hand.

"Thank you, doll." Then I leaned over the bar. "Bartender, could I get another sour?"

I accepted more tips while Bartender made my drink. I took the glass and walked back towards the stage, people offering me bills the whole way.

I reached a bar couch and laid down on it. Singing into the mic and lifting my glass in the air.

Greg and Michelle walked in at that moment. Greg tilted back his head and laughed, pulling out his phone to record me.

They sat on the next bar couch hyping me up and cheering for me.

I looked up and a pair of officers walked in, in full body armor, looking so damn serious.

So I yelled, "Hey look! It's officers Cool As Fuck! Hey guys. Welcome." I silently thanked that country singer all those Monday nights ago.

The cops looked around, trying to find out where the sound was coming from. They finally saw me lounging on the couch and they burst out laughing.

"Come on guys the sound ordinance is ridiculous! Tell that neighbor I said hey though. HEY NEIGHBOR! MAYBE DON'T LIVE IN A THRIVING MUSICAL COMMUNITY IF YOU DON'T LIKE MUSIC!"

"It's too loud darlin'." And they turned to walk away, smiling the whole time.

"Yeah we'll turn it down!" I said into the mic.

Bartender leaned over where I was lying on the couch. "Hey, uh, Sandi. You're talented but too fucking loud."

I laughed and kissed her hand.

I stood then and spoke into the mic, "Well, we're Denuvo, your favorite too-loud 80s duo. That's my bandmate over there on the synths!"

Cheers rang through the bar.

"And I'm Sandi MarLisa!"

I flung out my hand to meet the cheers, friends and bar patrons smiling at me.

Then I took the stage, throwing the tips I had collected in the jar.

Well. They were all listening now.

Crazy bitch

"What's the weirdest thing you were ever tipped?" Military Guy asked, throwing a dart.

I thought about it for a minute. Military Guy went to retrieve his darts.

"Probably here at the Salty Hobo. I got tipped a pocket knife and a Safeway card." I stepped up to the line and threw my first dart. "We don't even have a Safeway."

It was after Monday Night Little Fest. All the musicians had walked down to the Hobo. Jacqueline wanted to play darts, so the godfather teamed up with her and Military Guy teamed up with me.

Georgia Boy was around somewhere. We had our first band practice with the full band, dubbing ourselves "The Letdowns."

Boss Man and Bartender had heard the name and insisted it be revisited. They wanted "Sandi and The Letdowns."

But Boss Man agreed to book us our first show in October. We had plenty of time to practice and get our sets ready.

With our first show being in October, our timing was perfect. We'd be able to get a few gigs in the off season and then come next year we'd be set up to rock!

The band practice went extremely well. Even my kids joined in. As we practiced Under Pressure, I motioned for Lorelai to stand in front of my keyboard.

Two notes. Two notes was all she needed to be a part.

Dun-dun! She hit the infamous high chimes right on cue. The godfather smiled widely as he played the drums, I put my hands up behind her and became her hype woman. Georgia Boy and Beanie smiled, grooving with her.

Georgia Boy had even stopped me after band practice.

"I heard there was a movie you wanted to see." He said, holding my hands in his. "How about I take you to see it?"

A date. A real one.

A lot of Georgia Boy's friends had shown up to the Monday Night Little Fest. He had organized a great line up as host.

Kirk had been slowly inviting other musicians to host their own Little Fests over the past several weeks. I admired his vision to give a voice to local musicians, and continue that vision by inviting other hosts, ensuring its legacy.

"We're so close, Sandi!" Military Guy shook my shoulders. "We could win this thing!"

Military Guy was nice enough. He had invited us all to his new condo unit on the beach for a pool party.

But he had been showing up to all my shows, insisting on buying me drinks. He even sat through an open mic I had hosted at Wild Root, wanting to stay and talk to me afterwards.

It wasn't lost on the godfather, who poked fun at me every chance he got.

"He's got a nice mustache." He said, twirling his own that he had recently adopted.

"I'm just not interested." I always said.

I threw a dart and the board lit.

We had won!

Military Guy brought it in for a hug, jumping with me up and down.

"Woooo! We make a great team!" He shouted.

"Yeah! Way to go part—"

But I had been dragged away. Someone gripped my arm and was leading me to a small hallway next to the dart room.

"Excuse us!" Georgia Boy called over his shoulder. "This is me and Sandi's song."

Georgia Boy twirled me and I backed up a few steps, regaining my balance. I looked up and glared at Georgia Boy.

"You're crazy bitch…"

Georgia Boy was singing the lyrics of the song he had screamed at the top of his lungs at the Salty Goat. It had come over the jukebox.

He turned around on his heels and hip thrusted, looking right at me as he sang.

My gaping mouth closed and then I was giggling, rolling my eyes with my hands on my hips.

He took my hands and danced with me, giving me a long slow thrust with his hips and running his hands down my back.

345

Georgia Boy then led me right in front of the doorway to the dart room and kissed me in full view of everyone. Then he bit my neck and grabbed my ass before putting his arm around me, leading me through the doorway, right past Military Guy.

"I see your dart game is over." He said over his shoulder, walking us toward the red front doors of the Salty Hobo and out onto the street. "So what do you say we get out of here?" He only stopped when we reached the sidewalk, turning me until I was in front of him and cupping my chin. "I want to see Sandi MarLisa's house tonight."

So, I took Georgia Boy to my home in Lynn Haven and invited him in.

"You have roommates?" He asked.

"The godfather lives with me." I answered, opening the door to the spare bedroom where I was currently staying. "My sister and her two children used to live with me and they recently moved out. I haven't had a chance to move into the master yet, so…" I gestured for him to come into the bedroom. "This is where I'm staying. It used to be my office."

He briefly looked into the bedroom and then walked back into the living room, surveying his surroundings.

"Your piano?" He asked.

"Yes." I answered. "The one I learned on."

He spotted my two paintings on the walls and gave me an inquiring look.

A lion. And a butterfly.

"Oh." I said, smiling. "I like telling people about those. I got them before the children were even a thought. But…" I trailed away.

"But what?" He asked.

"But… my two children. Judah, you know, like 'the lion of Judah.' And we call my daughter 'Lorelai the butterfly.' So…" I shrugged. "It's like it was always meant to be. Even before they were born."

He walked to the back door and looked out before turning and smiling at me. "Sandi's swing."

"Well, it's my kids'." I said.

"No. It's yours. You said you wrote your song Atlantis on it."

I tilted my head. "You really have listened to my interviews."

346

"I always pictured you having your coffee out there." He said, looking back out the window. "Sandi's house." He rubbed his neck. "But anyway." He walked towards me. "You know what I really want to see?"

"What?"

"The bridge. Your bridge. What was it called again?"

"The Bailey Bridge?"

"Yes!" He walked straight out my front door. "You can walk to it right?"

I ran after him, closing the door behind me. Georgia Boy was already in the road.

"Which way is it?" He called, looking both ways up the street.

"What are you doing?" I called back.

"Take me to your river! Show me to your shore!" He put his hands out wide. "I don't know how else to say it, girl. Just come on!"

So I did.

Chapter 28

The gift

I got you a gift.

Really??? Tell me.

I smile. **No. You'll have to wait.**

A few more days.

Toast sits in my backpack, ready to go back home.

I'm ready, too.

Hurricane party

I had been cooking all day.

And cleaning. And keeping the kids entertained.

And stressing the fuck out.

The tropical storm system that was Fred was supposed to turn into a hurricane.

A category 1 to a Floridian is nothing.

But a category 1 to a Floridian who survived a category 5?

I stirred the spaghetti with vigor.

My father was in town and so was Georgia Boy's dad. I invited them and Georgia Boy, the godfather and Jacqueline over for a hurricane party.

"George, meet George."

My kids were over, but I figured they had been around Georgia Boy in a group setting before for band practices and shows.

Everyone arrived, gathering in the living room until dinner was served. Georgia Boy walked in quickly and led me to my laundry room where we shut the door and made out desperately.

The friends with benefits thing was becoming harder to keep up. The kisses were sweeter, the gazes prolonged.

And the sex...

Well.

Plus, Georgia Boy was becoming more openly obvious in public.

He pulled me into his lap when we were hanging out with friends. Mason turned to Beanie and asked, "Sooo... how long they been fucking?"

I found myself hoping for him to show up to my shows.

And he did.

We spent more nights together than seemed reasonable for our arrangement. He took up so much more space in my thoughts.

We made love in the Gulf and walked to Pineapple Willie's to meet Beanie for lunch. Georgia Boy couldn't stop staring at me, to the point where it made Beanie shift in his seat.

He took me to Art Break Day which is a national event hosted locally by Floriopolis in St. Andrews. Every business participates, displaying some art project people can craft for themselves.

We arrived at a tent for the LGBT+ alliance in Bay County. Friendship bracelets were the project.

Georgia Boy and I made one together, lollipop instead of a joint sticking out his mouth.

It was the sexiest thing he could have done for me.

We walked to the Taproom and the craft was creating a paper raindrop to put around an umbrella a local artist and muralist, Sara Griffith, had crafted. The prompt was to create a raindrop that reminded you of someone.

I held mine up after I was done. I had drawn a picture of a guitar with golden rain falling around it.

Georgia Boy held his up and he had drawn what appeared to be my face on the raindrop.

"I thought that's what you were supposed to do!" He said, as Boss Man, Bartender and I cracked up laughing.

It began to rain, a Florida summer shower, and everyone moved to help carry the bar couch cushions inside. Afterward, I walked back under the open sky and put my hands up.

"Sandi!" Georgia Boy called from the safety of his umbrella. "You're gonna get all wet, girl!"

"That's the point!" I yelled back, not taking my eyes off the sky.

Before I knew it, he was standing in the rain with me, staring at the same sky.

Georgia Boy looked tired one night at a bar and disclosed to me he hadn't eaten in three days.

"Oh my god!" I shook his arm. "Let's get you some food! What the hell, Georgia Boy?"

It was then he shared with me his deadly food allergy. In fact, most food was unsafe.

He couldn't be in the room while this particular food was cooked or he would have a serious reaction. Utensils used by cooks at restaurants were a risk because they might have touched the allergen.

Mexican restaurants were usually safe. He knew specific items on the menu at a few other restaurants that he could order.

But most items at restaurants were off limits. He often had to refuse other people's cooking and he tried to do so without explanation.

"If I tell people about my allergy." He said. "The whole conversation is centered around food. I'd rather talk about other things and just not eat."

I tried to wrap my head around it. Putting myself in his position.

But… it was like me having gone through a category five hurricane. It was like me caregiving for my mentally ill spouse.

It was like being a woman in a male dominated entertainment industry.

It was like being a single mother.

No one could ever really understand unless they lived it.

I could try though. I put my hand on his knee. I could try to understand.

"It's why I drink a lot of beer." He said. Our pizza we ordered arrived at our bar table. "Beer keeps me full and I know it's safe. Food scares me still." He stared at the pizza. "Pizza is usually safe." He took a bite of a slice and moved it slowly around in his mouth. "Weed helps me not feel so sick all the time. It helps encourage me to eat. I grew up on a chicken farm in Georgia."

"Oh my god." I covered my mouth with my hands. "Georgia Boy. That's terrible."

"They couldn't figure out why I kept getting sick." He took another bite of pizza. "I spent a lot of my childhood in hospitals. I got scared of eating." Georgia Boy set down the pizza and pushed it away from him. "I don't want anymore."

I made sure from then on that he ate while he was with me. The conversation made me feel closer to him.

So, he had experienced trauma, too.

Then, I felt ashamed.

Why did I have difficulty bonding with people emotionally until they shared about their trauma? Why did I suddenly trust people more once I understood their pain?

It was a question I kept in my heart, to be dealt with another day.

Georgia Boy played a show at The Salty Goat with Mason and Beanie. I showed up, grabbing a Gin before settling in at the bar.

Georgia Boy jumped off the stage with his wireless electric guitar and walked over to me, asking me to dance.

I stood, putting my arms around his neck, careful to keep myself from brushing up against the guitar strings. The band played Save Me by Jelly Roll.

We swayed, Georgia Boy resting his forehead on my neck.

"I can't wait to take you home with me tonight." He said into my ear.

"What's got you thinking such dirty thoughts?" I teased.

"I don't know." He sighed. "Maybe it's the location of my right hand."

I looked down and saw where his hand was playing his guitar, then threw my head back and laughed. He kissed my shoulder.

"Georgia Boy!" Beanie called from the stage. "If you're gonna dance with Sandi, you've gotta at least stay on beat, man."

"Sorry Beanie!" I yelled.

"Come sing Creep for us, Sandi." Beanie said.

I took the stage, singing to Georgia Boy the whole time.

Then I walked over to his side of the stage and planted a kiss right on his lips, in front of God and everybody at the Salty Goat. I pulled away and his mouth had dropped open.

We walked outside the bar for his break, laughing and talking. Then it started raining and Georgia Boy took my hand, running me inside.

Mason hung out one of the windows, speaking to bar patrons. He shouted, "You guys look like a teen movie!"

We went on our date to the movies and kept catching each other's eyes during the funny parts. We went out for coffee and he took me to the bay behind Buster's Beer Bait & Tackle on Thomas Drive.

We sat on the dock, drinking our coffees.

"You know." Georgia Boy began. "I never drank iced coffee until I started hanging out with you."

"What?" I said. "But you get iced coffee every time we go out!"

351

"Well." He smiled. "You never drank the coffee I made for you in the mornings. You'd always leave the mugs full, so I started taking you out for coffee in the mornings instead."

I stared at him, expressionless.

"Is this more your style?" Georgia Boy asked, quickly changing the subject.

I smiled. "I love the beach." I pointed my iced coffee in the direction of the bay. "But the bay is home to me. It's a portal to the beach." I nudged him. "It's a portal to everything."

We went to Newby's Mothership with Mason and Beanie and a few of our friends, and we danced to a band that played Sins not Tragedies by Panic! At the Disco.

A woman came up to me, drink in hand, and motioned for me to come closer to her so I could hear.

"You know." She shouted over the noise of the bar. "I'd do some questionable things to have a man look at me the way he looks at you."

I looked over my shoulder at Georgia Boy dancing to the music with Mason, then back at the woman. I squeezed her hand and nodded before Georgia Boy took my other hand and led me away, screaming out the lyrics to the song.

We danced and danced, until Georgia Boy saw something in my face and pulled me away from the crowd, leading me to a small bridge in the woods.

He leaned against the bridge and pulled me between his legs. The sound of the band echoed across the parking lot to us.

"What is it?" Georgia Boy touched my face.

"It's nothing." I said, putting my hands on my favorite part of his body. I loved squeezing his lats.

"It's something."

I knew he wouldn't let it go.

"It's just normal stuff." I said. "My life is heavy right now. I miss my children when they're with their dad. I'm in debt from the divorce. My Mema just died. I've got a few clients I'm doing work for on top of gigging and somewhere in between there I'm trying to write a book." I heaved a sigh. "It just... it just feels overwhelming sometimes. But it's normal stuff. I can handle it most days, but today was stressful. I paid the first payment for my kid's tuition and it's... expensive. We get the tuition discounted because my ex works there and I just can't justify not trying to make it work. I...."

He lifted up my chin and looked deep into my eyes. "Sandi, you know how you told me I'm allowed to make mistakes with you?"

"Mmmmmm."

"Well." He said, squeezing my thighs. "You're allowed to feel things with me."

I smiled. "Where's the Sentry tree when you need it?"

We heard a familiar voice traveling over a warm breeze.

Our eyes snapped to one another.

"It's Mason!"

We ran through the parking lot, bypassing the security guards at the entrance and weaving our way through the crowd until we found Beanie at the foot of the stage. Anne Cline, one of the hottest musicians in town, was front and center at the base of the stage as well, rocking back and forth to the music.

We jumped up and down, Mason finding us in the crowd and grinning, clasping our hands as he sang All the Small Things.

I made a bed for us in the backyard beneath a full moon that night. Georgia Boy and I made love until he paused and said, "Your ass is going on that swing."

We then rocked ourselves into sweet oblivion.

My sister found us asleep on a pile of couch cushions in the living room when she had come over for a few of her things. I was in the middle of switching from the spare room to the master and lacked a mattress.

"So, who's Georgia Boy?" My sister asked.

It became everyone's common refrain.

Anywhere we could get our hands on each other, we launched one another into ecstasy.

I had become hopeful.

I didn't look for anyone else. Didn't want anyone else.

Sk8er Boi would call and I started ignoring it. I wrote a letter to get him into Helicopter Pilot training in Utah to explain his poor former grades. He'd been accepted.

I thought of another personal statement letter I wrote for someone else. How that letter eventually helped lead to a PhD.

I thought of myself. I thought of all the work I constantly put into others.

I knew what I was capable of when I threw my full weight behind a mission.

I thought of how I was ready to embrace my own story and not just be a side character in another's.

I had been more selfish this past year. I had taken chances for the sole purpose of seeing what would happen.

I went out more. I laughed more. I talked more.

And… I cried less.

Happiness felt as if it would visit me. I was on the brink of taking a deep breath.

I could see the light just beyond the surface of the void.

My heart cracked open for Georgia Boy. He had reminded me of a time before I experienced so much pain.

We *played* together.

And I suddenly had a whole new appreciation for the expression 'playing music.'

But I wouldn't let myself fall all the way into trust and hope.

I couldn't. Not yet.

We exited the laundry room, my cheeks flushed. I called for everyone to come make their own plates.

We spent the storm playing board games and drinking beer and wine. Hurricane lamps sat on the table, a cooler of water sitting just in front of the sliding glass door.

"You okay?" Georgia Boy rubbed my back as I looked out the window.

I tried to calm my breathing.

I awoke in my bed with a panic attack when Georgia Boy stayed over one night.

I sat up, breathing heavy, my body covered in sweat.

"Shhhhh." He had soothed me, rubbing and kissing my back, pulling me back into his embrace.

Memories still haunted me sometimes. There were some hurts that would take an entire lifetime to heal properly.

If I lived that long.

His arms felt so safe. Like I had spent my whole life looking for his embrace.

He touched me, not just sexually. He stroked my hair and caressed my face, along with gripping my body and slapping my ass. He took his fingers and traced my lips, my collarbones, my stomach, my breasts.

Lower.

He hadn't told me that he loved me again, but I could feel it in his energy. I could see it in the way he looked at me, in the way he treated me.

I found out new details about his life. He had a Bachelor's degree in business from the University of Georgia. He also was a former store manager at the biggest music store in town before the pandemic shut it down. He had worked in insurance and international business for a time before longing for something more and chasing after it. He had a full solo album out already and had even created his own type of blueberries, agriculture being a main focus in business school.

He surprised me every day. The more I found out about him, the more I wanted to know. The more I understood, the more questions I seemed to have.

I wanted to be his.

And I wanted him to be mine.

Georgia Boy, his dad, Judah and myself played Rummikub. Judah had a blast, he loved the game and did well.

He looked over to Georgia Boy. "Are you staying the night tonight?"

I smiled. My son loved to ask my friends that question. He was so used to having people live with us, he thought everyone was staying the night.

"No." Georgia Boy said. "No, I'm just here for the party."

The storm ended and everyone filed out, Georgia Boy hanging back.

"You have a hickey on your neck." My dad said as he left.

I put up a hand to cover it, wincing.

I shooed the children to bed, giving them hugs and kisses before quietly shutting the door and finding Georgia Boy. He led me outside to the backyard and I shut the door, reaching for him.

He backed up, pulling a joint out of his pocket and lighting it.

"You okay?" I asked.

"Hm?" He said. "Oh yeah, Sandi. I'm fine."

He pulled on it for a long time, letting out a steady stream of smoke. He offered the joint to me and I put up a hand, refusing. Georgia Boy stuck it between his teeth.

"I'm happy that you came over. I had a fun time."

Georgia Boy didn't look at me but smiled around the joint. "Well Sandi. We've done a divorce party together. I figured we should do a hurricane party, too."

I looked at him, patiently waiting for him to explain his weird attitude. "Is something wrong?"

He straightened and looked at me through squinted eyes, taking a drag and blowing the smoke out of the side of his mouth.

"Do you even know me?" He asked. "Or are you just hanging around me because it feels good?"

The question took me by surprise. "What?"

"Judah asked me to stay the night."

"Okay?"

"I don't want to be someone he looks up to. I don't want him looking at me like that."

Understanding hit me. It stung.

Lots of people assumed what my home life was like.

Small town rockstar and a mother... there were always assumptions.

My neighbors thought my house was a drug house after all. They saw all the cars in the driveway and assumed.

I wished people would assume that I'm just trying to make my mortgage payment. I wished people would assume that two extra adults in the house meant more money to send my kids to private school.

"Oh. Listen. He doesn't know who you are to me. He's just used to having people over all the time and he was having fun with you. So he wanted, like, a sleepover. That's all."

He took another drag and backed away. "I just want to be honest with you, Sandi. That's not me."

"What's not you?"

"I'm not looking for a relationship. I told you. I want to be friends."

My stomach dropped, my hope deflating like a balloon.

Again.

It was happening *again*.

So I stood up straighter, flinging my internal walls back up like a fortress.

"Don't worry. You've made yourself clear. Lately I've thought we've been spending way too much time together anyway."

"What do you mean?"

"I mean, I'm putting a lot of energy into a man who just wants to be friends."

"What's that supposed to mean?"

I rolled my eyes. "Exactly what I said."

Georgia Boy backed away, took a drag and blew smoke up to the stars. "Now you're mad at me."

"No, not at all." I said, looking towards my tree swing. "We can be friends. See you at band practice."

He sighed. "That's not what I'm saying."

"Then what are you saying?" I flung my hands up. "What is it with men and wanting to 'just be friends?' Then I start treating them like a 'friend' and they get mad! My *friends* see me once every other week for coffee if I'm lucky!"

"Sandi I just can't—"

"Oh don't worry, Georgia Boy. I really don't need your speech. I'm not wasting anymore time on a guy who can't even call me beautiful, or says he loves me and then takes it back." I snorted. "How absolutely *childish*."

"You see." He pointed at me. "The fact that you want me to say it so bad is exact—"

"Exactly what?" I said, my head bobbing, my hands brought together in front of me. "Exactly what, Georgia Boy?

"There's that fire, Sandi. There's that passion." He said, moving closer to me. "I like that."

I took a step back. "I didn't realize I needed to yell in order to be heard."

"That's not what I'm saying." He rubbed the back of his head.

"What are you saying then? 'Cause right now it's a whole lot of bullshit."

"Wow."

"Why can't you admit to yourself that you love me?"

"I love…"

I crossed my arms, waiting.

"... my guitars?" He finished lamely.

"Wow. That's incredible."

Georgia Boy looked like he was pleading with the moon. "That was supposed to be funny."

"No Georgia Boy. No. It's not funny. It's boring. I am bored with this."

He put his chin down to level with me. "You're bored with me."

"I'm bored with this situation. It's a tired old story. Man gets his heart broken and now refuses to love another woman who makes him happy ever again! How original! Dear God roll the fucking credits! This. Is. Cinema! We have an award winner!"

Georgia Boy put out the joint and flicked it into my fire pit. "Do you always have to be so sarcastic all the time?"

"Do you always have to avoid your feelings?"

"I just think we're two people with huge holes in our hearts and that's not healthy for anybody."

"Speak for yourself." I paced, putting my hands on my hips and sighing to the sky. "I've done my healing. It wasn't exactly glamorous or graceful, but I've done it! I did the fucking work, cried my tears, went to months of therapy. It's normal—extremely normal—for me to expect affection from a man who claims to love me!"

Georgia Boy flung his hands up. "I just want to be your guitar player!"

"What the hell are you talking about?"

"Your kid asked me to stay the night, Sandi. It's too much."

Too much.

I was too much.

My life was too much.

My greatest fear confirmed.

"Fuck off."

A pause. A dog barked in the distance.

"What?"

"Fuck. Off."

"Fuck off." He repeated.

"Yes." I said, infuriated. I stood to my full height and raised my chin, trying to gather my dignity.

I would never beg for another man to love me.

Ever again.

"My children are the kindest people you will ever meet and how *dare* you take my son's innocent question and make it something gross. I have *never* had men I'm romantically interested in over to this house when they're here."

Georgia Boy put his hands up, placatingly. "Sandi…"

No. I would not forgive him for the insinuation. I would not.

Being a mother and a small town rockstar came with its fair share of judgment. I usually brushed it off.

But Georgia Boy had hit a nerve. So this is what he thought of me? He thought I had random men over all the time for 'sleepovers?'

I was hurt.

I had definitely been more free this year. I had definitely gone out more, drank more, smoked more weed than I ever had in my life.

I thought of what my big client had said when I dropped them.

"You're at risk of endangering the lives of your children if you keep going down this road."

I seethed. I fumed.

Nobody.

Nobody fucks with my kids.

Nobody gets to question my judgment concerning them.

Especially not in my own goddamned house.

I shielded those kids from literal and figurative storms. I read them every bedtime story, gave every bath, sang every song, made every meal, walked them to school, calmed their fears, dried every tear, took them to parks and libraries and on adventures to Alaska.

And I did it all while taking care of my ex husband and running my own business.

I felt self righteous for the first time in my life.

Because if there's one thing I've done right in my life. If there's one thing I'm confident in.

I'm a damn good mother.

"You were invited because you're over here all the time for band practice and you're around them at shows." I continued. "They're familiar with you in a group setting. You will never, *ever* stay the night here when they're here unless we're in a deeply committed relationship. How dare you question my judgment."

"Sandi, I—"

"No!" I took a step back. "I am extremely protective over my kids and you came into my house and made me feel as if I did something wrong. As if my son had done something wrong just because he was kind to you. You looked at something innocent and made it feel dirty."

"That's not—"

"Fuck off, Georgia Boy. Fuck all the way off."

"Fine." He threw up his hands and walked to the sliding glass door, opening it and storming to the front of the house.

I followed him to the front door, watching him open it and leave, closing the door firmly behind him.

I walked to the kitchen and started scrubbing pots and pans before giving up and grabbing a glass of wine, wondering what the hell just happened.

Chapter 29

One more day

You're almost back in my arms!

I grin, taking a sip of coffee. It's my last full day in Alaska.

A red hat sits on the desk next to my computer. Toast beside it.

I'm ready to be home.

A text comes through from my bandmate.

I hope you're ready to come home hitting the ground running! We have a show the night you land.

YEP! I miss the stage.

I lean back in my chair and stretch my back. My parents are taking me to an art museum and F Street Station before I leave as a last hurrah.

My flight out of Anchorage leaves at 4pm tomorrow. I arrive in Panama City Beach at noon on a Friday and have a few hours before my show at six.

I think about arriving at the airport with my kids after our Alaska trip together the year previous.

"Mom!" Judah said, looking into an airport gift shop. "Can we buy a souvenir?"

I looked down at him and squeezed his hand. "Son, this is where you were born. You *are* a souvenir."

My children. Fifth generation Floridians.

They're also fourth generation musicians.

My daughter sings and plays piano. My son plays an acoustic guitar.

Their hair matches mine, their skin is sun kissed even after a week spent in winter, their dark eyes hold depth, their minds and hearts beat with wild Floridian spirit.

I take them kayaking. I take them to climb mountains. I take them to my shows.

My little adventurers. My little wildlings.

Yes.

Yes, I'm ready to be home.

You're a musician, Judah

"Oh shit." My son is a musician.

I watched him move around on the stage at his concert, ukulele in hand.

He wasn't shy. He wasn't tense.

He was confident. Loose.

At one point he pointed at the crowd.

At one point he looked at his friend singing and gave him a head nod.

Shit.

"He loves it."

Shit. Shit. Shit. SHIT.

My second thought. "Is he any good?"

I watched him strum the ukulele amongst the other kids. His band mates were doing well. They hit downwards on the beat.

But my son had a full strum.

I watched his hands move between chords. He didn't look at where his hands were moving. He felt it.

Oh no. He's a natural.

I watched him finish his song in awe. Watched him whoop and holler after the song was done. Watched him pat his bandmates on the back, telling them they did a great job.

And he's a leader too.

Oh boy.

As he made his way through the crowd to me, I started putting pieces together.

He begged me to help him make a music playlist. The past year or so, he'd find a new song and get so excited to share it with me.

"Mom. This song is exactly how I feel right now."

They'd be big songs. Songs that felt too big for my little boy.

But his soul has always been old. And he's been through way more in his life than a 9 year old should.

And it all clicked.

Oh God. He loves music like I love music.

He loves music like his soul needs it.

He loves music like it makes him feel something.

He loves music like it makes him come alive.

I caught him at the piano looking up a tutorial on YouTube on how to play a song. His self motivation surprised me.

His brain is always so busy. He's easily distracted. Video games keep his attention. So do documentaries about the ocean.

It's difficult to get him to be motivated for anything unless he has direction and clear instructions.

But this he was doing on his own.

"Look mom! I found a game that will teach me how to play piano!"

He loves orchestral music, specifically movie soundtracks.

363

He'll put on a seven minute piece and exclaim, "Okay mom. Get ready. This is my favorite part!"

Then he'll air guitar to the flute.

One thing I tried to do as a parent is give my kids space to figure out what they like. And let them show me what they're about in their own time.

Of course, I have an affinity for the arts. They're around it all the time. But I always wanted their interests to be theirs. I wanted them to tell me who they were.

When I was dating and my kids were brought up, one of the first questions asked was, "Do they play any sports?"

And I'd smile and say, "Their dad is a physicist and their mom is an artist. What do you think?"

My son is a lot like his dad, who is also a musician, as was his father and his father before that.

And like his dad, my son likes science and big questions. Hanging out with my son I have to mentally prepare.

Because he doesn't just ask me questions. He asks me big questions.

"Mommy. Do you believe in sins?"

"Mommy. There's no right or wrong answer. If you had a lever in your hand to switch train tracks, and the train could go one way and kill your mom or the other way and kill 5 strangers, what choice would you make?"

Yeah. He really asked me that.

So when I told him I thought he did a great job at his rock show, I wasn't surprised when he stopped me and took a deep breath.

He looked at me and said, "Are you saying that as my mom? Or are you saying that as a musician?"

My son.

I smiled. "How would you like me to give you feedback?"

"I want your honest opinion."

And I could see my answer would mean everything to him.

So I paused and told him the truth. "As your mom, I think you absolutely murdered the stage tonight."

He grinned.

"As a musician," I continued. "I think you're a 9 year old kid with natural talent. But more than that, I can tell you really put in the work. You were doing stuff the other kids weren't doing. You had confidence and flair. You moved around and really felt it. The truth is though, being a musician is about learning more than just one song and rocking it. I think you have what it takes to be good."

He nodded, an acceptable answer in his eyes. "My teacher says I can learn acoustic guitar next semester. So I'm going to do that."

I could see the passion. I could see the drive in his eyes. I could feel his soul.

Well, shit. My son is a musician.

I turned to my acoustic guitar that I learned on knowing it was my son's now; already thinking about how I could wrap it to not make it look like a guitar.

It's an Alvarez, my father's guitar passed down to me about 20 years ago, and it resonates beautifully. But the guitar was never my favorite instrument. Piano and voice were where I hung my hat.

I thought of the years I've spent studying music and performance. The work that never looked like work to anyone.

The work that makes me roll my eyes when people talk about my "natural" talent.

I thought of how I always thought I wasn't intelligent. How I spent 9 years slowly completing my Bachelors degree just so I could prove to myself and everyone else that I was smart.

How I spent a decade in marketing to prove I could do it if I wanted.

I thought of Brian May, guitarist for Queen, and about how he's a published astrophysicist. But he chose music above all.

And I thought about my son.

Judah.

Judah David.

I named both my children after music. Judah means praise and King David was a skilled musician and psalmist who ruled a nation.

And I laughed wondering why I was so surprised.

My mother always said, "I gave you your name, it's up to you to keep it."

Sandi MarLisa. The name of three generations of Floridians.

I looked at my son, becoming so excited for Christmas morning when he gets his very first guitar. Passed down from a family of musicians.

I don't know what he'll do. I don't know who he'll be.

Maybe it'll be a career. Maybe it'll simply be the first passion of his life that opens up many others.

But my son is a musician. There is no doubt.

All I can do is hand him the legacy of his family.

It's up to him what he does with it.

Rock on, my boy.

It's not a mess, it's art

Despite my best efforts throughout the week, my kids' room is a mess by Saturday.

It's mainly my daughter, by her own admission. She's a funny little creature.

I've never had to limit TV time with her. She's a self regulator. She'll watch it for a bit and then turn it off, ready to create something.

What does she create? None of those $3 crafts you can buy at the Target dollar section.

From about 3 years of age, I picked up on what she likes to do. It's not organized activity, but no less meticulous crafting.

She has a craft box that is continuously getting bigger and bigger. Every so often, I pick up felt, stickers, glue, colored paper, etc., and stick it in her box.

She has a doll she tucks in every single night under a blanket she made. The blanket is crafted out of a dried out wet wipe and stickers. The doll's bed is an empty Dunkin' Donuts box. Her pillow a small frog stuffie.

My daughter's room is littered with small pieces of paper at all times. These are the leftovers of her best creations.

I go to pick it up and it's, "No, mommy! That's for a project I'm working on!"

Or it's, "Mommy! I'm crafting!"

Every Amazon box that comes through this house is automatically claimed by her. Out of the boxes she makes three story homes for her dolls.

I bought her a doll house once, but it's now covered in glue, stickers and nail polish to get it "just right."

And the books. Oh the books.

She never let me read to her when she was small. She ripped the book out of my hand and demanded she read it herself, babbling nonexistent words as she turned the pages.

She claimed my nice copy of *The Hobbit* as her own. She liked it because the pages were gold filigree and there were lots of maps inside.

And it was pocket sized. Perfect for tiny hands.

For years, she's carried that book around in her purse when we go out. I don't understand why she has about ten purses, her mommy never carried one.

But I guess she sees her mommy carrying a book and wallet around with her. A purse is, of course, much more efficient.

"I want to be a writer like you!" She says to me.

"You don't have to be a writer like me, you know." I reply.

"Don't worry. I'm not going to have kids though." She says. "Judah will have kids and I'll come watch them. Kids are a lot of work."

"I see."

"And I'm going to go other places."

"Yeah?"

"But I'll come visit you sometimes."

"That would be nice."

"Mommy?" She cocks her head.

"Yeah?"

"Why don't you wear pretty necklaces? Why don't you have earrings?"

I smile, looking at the earrings she made for herself. They're little bubble stickers with Ls on them. For Christmas, she wore little Christmas tree stickers.

"I had my ears pierced once. I had three piercings actually. I could never keep up with the maintenance. And I just don't really like to wear necklaces too much. I wear rings though. Always have." I show her the four rings on my hands.

"And headbands!" She looks up at my hair.

"Yeah. I like those."

"Well I want to get my ears pierced," she says.

"Okay. As soon as you can take care of them yourself. Your mommy won't remember."

Then she asks me to help her craft. But, of course, I'm doing everything wrong. Per the usual, I sit with her while she crafts. Her enjoying my presence, me watching her work.

I see myself in my daughter. It's impossible not to. I see her dark hair and her love for creating.

She can even sing. On pitch. All natural.

I asked her once if she'd like to be on stage. I could get her lessons, she could sign up for the talent show.

"No mommy," she said. "I just don't want to do it in front of other people."

This is foreign to me. So foreign. I was on the stage at 4 years old and I lived for it.

And I almost pressed her. I almost asked again. She has talent, after all.

I tried her out in dance classes, but she was always frustrated that she couldn't dance the way she wanted to.

So now she dances at home, in her own way, when she feels like it.

Because even though she looks like me, she's not me. Even though she loves the things I love, she has her special way of loving them that is entirely her own.

I follow her lead.

So I buy her more craft supplies from the Dollar Tree. I buy her another dress up outfit to fill her box that's overflowing. I let her paint her own nails. I watch as she hangs her pictures with tape in the foyer (the fridge wasn't front and center enough).

I ask permission before I throw away trash. After all, it could be important.

And I tolerate the scraps of paper that always leak into the living room and overflow her bedroom floor.

She's my daughter, after all. And I know...

It's not just paper.

It's not just stickers.

It's not just a messy room.

It's magic. Her brand of magic.

I'm privileged to witness the beginnings of it all.

And I wonder, I wonder, I wonder...

Like a connoisseur looking at a painting...

what it all means.

Chapter 30

Slam poetry

Good luck tonight! I'm gonna miss the poetry reading!

I rolled my eyes at Georgia Boy's text. How did he get off trying to ignore the fight we had last night?

Too bad. One of them's about you.

A pause.

You gonna do me like that?

Liar

I told you I thought you were beautiful and you said you didn't believe me

I was offended because I don't lie

Except that one time when I said I liked watermelon

But you looked so excited about it

And you were so cute telling me how much you loved the middle of it

You fed watermelon to me by spoonfuls

So maybe it wasn't a lie, I just only like watermelon when I'm with you

Call me a liar one more time

I remember when we first met

I was singing and you were sitting at a table with a AC/DC hoodie on in January and you looked so depressed

I didn't know you had just gotten divorced like I did

You came up and put money in my tip jar and smiled at me

And your eyes said so clearly, "This isn't the last you've seen of me, girl."

You told me later you knew you were in trouble then.

You were somethin'

Call me a liar one more time.

You came off the stage once and danced with me at your show, still playing your guitar

I put my arms around your neck, laughed and said, "Why do I feel like this is a metaphor for our friendship?"

"What do you mean?" You said.

"A guitar in between us." I responded. "But I don't mind it."

The singer yelled from the stage that if you were going to dance with me you had to at least stay on beat.

You whispered, "Is this our first dance?"

Call me a liar one more time.

We went to the beach late one night

You put a box of hard seltzers in my arms

We sat on the beach and shared a joint

Laughing more than I had in a long time

When we went back to your condo the sprinkler system cut on

We ran and when I got to the door you looked down at my arms

"Where did all the seltzers go?" You asked

We looked behind us and there was a trail of seltzers leading towards the beach

We laughed. Barefoot and soaking wet. Seltzerless.

Call me a liar one more time.

Your bedroom has windows that open to the Gulf

I remember a lightning storm when you made me sing to you a song I wrote

And you cried

You took my hand and pressed it to your cheek

Saying I was so sweet

371

The lightning lit up your face that night

with light

I fell asleep to the sound of wind, rain and your steady breaths rising and falling on your chest like music

I remembered the oath I took with myself to never date another goddamned musician and I smiled

Call me a liar one more time

We looked up at the moon and you asked me what I saw

I said the moon kinda looked like a pepperoni pizza

You said you saw a mummy

"How would you feel if you spent your whole life trying to get to the moon and then suddenly you're there?"

We were very high.

I paused and thought about it. "I'd be sad."

"Sad? You're on the freaking moon."

"Yeah but like, then you have to figure out what's next. Like, you made it to the moon but now what?"

You looked at me incredulously. "I don't know, Sandi. It's the MOON. YOU'RE ON THE MOON."

And I laughed hysterically.

Call me a liar one more time.

I mentioned my favorite tree and you made me take you to it and explain

You said I rarely got excited about anything but when I talked about the damn tree my face lit up

So I told you why

I explained that the tree was over 250 years old and after a really bad hurricane, seeing it still standing gave me hope

If the tree was okay, then my town would be okay too

You teared up. Then you made up this entire narrative about how we couldn't lie to each other if we were standing under the tree

Then a caterpillar crawled on me and I screamed

You got bit by ants and we ran like hell to the bay

Call me a liar one more time

After a show we sat at the water's edge with some friends

And I swear a hundred caterpillars crawled on us that night

The next morning you texted me and said, "I hope the caterpillars stopped looking for you."

And I shot back, "Maybe they were looking for the butterflies I feel when I'm with you."

I could feel the pause through the phone.

Call me a liar one more time

You told me you loved me outside the trashiest bar in town

You went beat red when you said it

You blamed me for getting it out of you

Like I had done anything else but just smile at you

You said you meant to take that with you to your grave

You just wanted to be friends

Call me a liar one more time

We went kayaking and I got so drunk

I lost my paddle 45 minutes into the trip

You had to tow me the rest of the way

I kept falling out of my kayak so eventually I gave up and floated along downstream

You called me a mermaid

You said I smiled and teared up

But I don't know. I was so drunk.

It started raining and you pulled us to the side and kissed me in a cove

I told you I loved you back

You froze

Who's the liar now?

Flooded roads

You gonna tell me how your slam Georgia Boy poetry went?

There was no slamming of Georgia Boy.

I thought that's why you were so secretive of it?! Why else would you not want to tell me what you said?

To bother you, Georgia Boy. To get under your skin and bother you like you bothered me.

To be petty.

It's been bugging you, huh?

Me? No…. we men don't get bugged. We squash bugs. ;)

I sense sarcasm here. But yeah. You left my house after being mean to me and I wrote a damn poem. If you don't like it, maybe don't date artists.

You told me to fuck off, Sandi!

AND I MEANT IT.

We had a nice evening and then you wanted to bring my kids into it. YOU PICKED A FIGHT FOR NO REASON.

I wanted to be honest with you! And when they asked if I was staying the night, I felt a wave of guilt or something. But then you really yelled at me and I didn't want to run away... but after like the third fuck off I was like ok... I guess I will since that's what you wanted so bad!

Those are my kids. I don't fuck around with them. I don't like being questioned about them. They have nothing to do with you right now. So you let me worry about them. Literally all you had to say was, "No, I'm not staying." They just like having people over. They think it's fun. It wasn't anything deeper than that!

I just wanted to be honest with you.

Well, I appreciate your honesty. But then you went on and on about things completely unrelated to the point.

I am jaded by relationships and you are a freaking amazing person. That really shook me up!! I haven't been that depressed driving in the flooded roads since the last hurricane, and that was the day of my divorce...

Oh.

I thought about his song, Hurricane.

"...on the day love left, there was a hurricane..."

I didn't realize he meant it literally. Usually lyrics are veiled in truth, but he just stated things so plainly.

So the hurricane triggered him.

I understood more than most how a hurricane could be triggering.

Triggers take away all rationality. They make us erupt into the worst versions of ourselves, where the only parts left are fear and our worst experiences.

It just brought back a lot of darkness and made me question just about everything.

I got up off my couch and walked to the kitchen to get some water. My phone dinged in my hand.

Come see me on my lunch break?

I smiled.

I met him in the parking lot of his day job at a local marijuana dispensary. We sat in his truck and hashed out our argument. He went over his fears, I went over mine.

And then we decided to drop the issue, promising to communicate better the next time something like this came up.

I had double gigs that Saturday back to back and then I showed up at House of Bourbon in St. Andrews that night for Georgia Boy's show with his band. I wore a black leather skirt, black heels and a turquoise off the shoulder, low-cut top.

The band immediately invited me up to sing Creep and I performed the song to a full house. Georgia Boy offered me his hand to help me down the stage after it was over.

He wandered down from the stage with his wireless guitar soon after and let his gaze follow my curves up and down, taking his time on every section of my body.

Then he looked me in the eyes and said plainly, "You look so fucking beautiful."

A blush erupted across my face, a smile blooming in its wake.

Georgia Boy smiled widely, tilting up his chin and walking back to the stage.

He walked me down to his truck after the show and pressed me up against the passenger side door, kissing me deeply.

"You are so beautiful tonight, Sandi MarLisa." He kissed me again, biting my bottom lip. "Maybe it's that dress you're wearing. Maybe it's the way you sang Creep tonight. Or maybe it's just because you're Sandi."

He opened the door for me and helped me step into the cab. Then he leaned over the passenger seat and started the truck, turning on the air before touching my face affectionately.

"I just have to help the boys load the equipment. You got the air on so you'll be comfortable." He kissed me. "I'll be right back."

It was those little things he did that stood out to me over and over again.

We arrived at his condo and he lit candles before climbing on top of me and kissing me tenderly.

We were in a mess of white sheets, sprawled out on the bed, the window open and the waves lulling us to sleep.

"I didn't just write a poem about you." I whisper to the darkness.

"Hm?" Georgia Boy grunted.

"I wrote you a song."

He sat up straight in the bed. "You what?"

I laughed. "I wrote you a song."

"Sing it to me."

"I'd need my phone."

"No, just sing it to me just as you are."

"I don't memorize lyrics easily and I just wrote it. Plus, I need a piano."

He was on his feet and to the closet in seconds.

"Don't tell me you have a..."

He did. He had a battery operated keyboard.

"I don't even know why I have this thing." He said, laying it across me. Georgia Boy found my phone on the dresser and brought it to me. "I never play it." He laid down on his side, facing me, and waited expectantly.

I sat up in the tangle of sheets, naked and unashamed.

And began to play.

Someday

Maybe I'm reading too far

Into all these signals you're sending my way

I don't think so though

Not when you smiled like that today

You say I make you happy

But you're not ready to love again so soon

Well what am I supposed to do

When…

You had me at
Hey baby you're something special
I just wanna be friends because I
need you in my life but romance dies
And I want you forever

You had me at
Hey let's make love in the ocean
Then we both fell over and cracked up laughing
Then you gave me your shirt
And we ran like hell back to your room
For a second round

Hey baby
You had me at someday
Just not right now

You took me by surprise
Your clumsy charm and those kind eyes
And the way you smile and shake your head
When I do things my way
You said I'm too much love for one man to handle on his own
All I heard is that you wouldn't try to cage me in

And then

You had me at
Putting up with my drunk ass self
Taking my hand and saying, "Let me help."
And letting it go when I refuse
Rolling your eyes and sighing, "you do you."

You had me at
Giving me space to figure it out
All the while you have your arms wide open
Your heart broken a time or two
But you say, "Girl I might take a chance on you."

Hey baby
You had me at someday
Just not this soon

You didn't have me at hello
You had me at let's take it slow

You had me at
Why do you like this damn tree so much
You never get excited about anything
But when you see this goddamn tree you light up
So tell me what the hell does it all mean?

You had me at

Girl tell me about your dreams

And can I be a part of that beautiful scene

You paint so well

Oh dammit to hell

Girl, you got me going crazy

You had me at someday

Someday

Someday

Just not right now

Surprise guests

Georgia Boy couldn't speak. He just looked at me with eyes of wonder.

He was beautiful. And I couldn't help but love him.

He asked me to play the song for him one more time in our own private concert before he made love to me all over again, even sweeter than before.

We awoke the next morning and wordlessly started kissing. The sunlight streaming through the windows.

My eyes were closed, moving my mouth down his neck, to his shoulder.

"Don't freak out."

"What?" I said, opening my eyes.

"There's people watching us."

"Hm?" I turned around.

And let out a scream.

"I told you not to freak out!"

I covered my face with the blanket, breathing hard.

Because right outside the window were window washers on a boom, squeegeeing water off the glass.

"You can't make this shit up." I said beneath the blanket, awestruck.

Georgia Boy only laughed and tried to convince me to make myself busy while I was under there.

Chapter 31

It's not broken

I pulled into the parking lot of Georgia Boy's condo and shot him a text.
Here for coffee.

I sat for a while in my car, waiting. After ten minutes I called him.

"Sandi!" He said.

"Georgia Boy! Ready for coffee?"

"Uhhhhh…." He started. "Yes. I'll be right down."

Soon, I spotted Georgia Boy walking across the parking lot, he wore a button up shirt but it was opened up completely.

I furrowed my brow and studied his face, walking over to him.

"What's wrong?" I asked immediately.

"Nothing!" He said, smiling. "Can we take your car?"

I pulled back his shirt and saw a large hump on his shoulder.

"You're hurt." I said.

"It's really fine."

"We're going to the ER." I said, taking his good hand and leading him to the car.

"No we're not! We're getting coffee."

I crossed my arms. "I'm not going anywhere until that shoulder gets looked at. You play guitar, Georgia Boy. You want to screw up your arm until you can't play anymore?"

He reluctantly followed me to my car, wincing as he sat down. I gingerly helped him buckle his seatbelt at his protest, but I insisted.

I didn't ask him how he sustained the injury. I just started my vehicle and backed up into the parking lot.

"We need to call your mom." I said.

"My phone is dead."

I handed him my phone. "Type in her number please."

We arrived at the hospital. I wasn't allowed in because of Covid-19 regulations, so I waited in the car.

I spent the time texting Georgia Boy's mom, letting her know what was going on. Then I found the number for his other job at the marijuana dispensary. Georgia Boy came out to check on me. I had him call his work and let him know I spoke with his mother.

He came out to check on me two more times. I had a feeling he just wanted to know if I was still there.

They let me into the hospital room when he got one. His arm was dislocated. They discharged him with a pain prescription, sling, basic exercise instructions and told him to keep the arm in the sling for two weeks.

"My sister is a Physical Therapist Assistant." I said, driving him back to the condo. "I'll speak with her and get you a proper exercise regimen."

He just looked at me.

I took him to the store to get his prescription and helped him choose some basic groceries. Then I drove him back to his condo and helped him into bed.

"I have to get my kids from school." I said. "I'll be back to check on you later."

He said nothing as I left.

I came back that evening before my gig and made sure he had everything he needed, preparing dinner and washing his dishes.

I received a text from Sk8er Boi as I ran the water.

So…. probably no helicopter school.

He had attached a photo of his bandaged hand.

What happened?

I shot myself while cleaning my gun.

I hung my head.

I thought about my last conversation on the phone with him.

He told me he had a girlfriend, but it was a temporary arrangement. She was a travel nurse and was only in town for three months.

Sk8er Boi said he had called a few other girls—his "friends"— and he couldn't understand why they were mad at him. He told me he still had the tissue box I gave him with my message written on it.

I laughed when he told me the news about him having a girlfriend, so hard I teared up.

I sighed, thinking I quite literally dodged a bullet with that guy.

I texted Michael the update.

Ew. I'm so tired of hearing that dude's name.

I laughed.

Yeah. Me too.

"Why are you doing this?" Georgia Boy asked, standing next to me as I washed dishes. "You didn't make the mess."

I looked at him as I scrubbed a pan. "You're not going to be able to hand wash these with your arm." I smiled faintly at the expression on his face. "Don't worry Georgia Boy, I'm restraining myself." I turned off the water and grabbed a towel to dry the pan. "If I were your girlfriend, I'd clean your whole condo."

I made out with him before I left, groaning when I pulled away to put on my shoes. "Ugh. I don't want to leave you and go do this show."

He brushed my hair out of my face, smiling. "I won't be the reason you miss a show." He said, sitting up and wincing. "But I'll damn sure be the reason you're late."

We kissed for a few more minutes. I helped him remove the sling and get comfortable in bed before I left.

Over the next few days, I stopped by every chance I could to make sure he was okay. That Saturday, he wanted to get out of the house so he came to my show at the Taproom.

I wore a white sleeveless dress with a high neckline and flared waist. My shoes were some of my favorites, high heeled wedges with an ankle clasp that looked like multi colored bracelets.

Georgia Boy looked like he was going to pass out in a chair, even with his aviators on.

I motioned to the godfather that it was time for a break and walked up to him.

"Hey sweetie." I said, kneeling down. "Have you eaten today?"

"Mmmm." He stirred. "No."

"And you took your pain medication, huh?"

"Yeah. I did."

I took his good hand and led him across the street to Amavida coffee. I bought him a granola bar, thoroughly checking the label for his allergen, and made him eat it with me staring at him.

He sighed, chewing. "I feel so much better."

"Yep." I said, standing. "Now come on. My break's over."

I took him to get fish tacos at Finn's from Little Village, then drove him to Kinsaul Park in Lynn Haven where we had kayaked for the first time.

An eagle flew across the water, Georgia Boy's mouth fell open.

"Oh my god." He said, staring at me. "That was an eagle."

I chewed and swallowed. "Yeah. We have a few around here."

He continued staring in the direction of the eagle, eyes wide.

"It's a sign."

"A sign of what?" I asked, collecting my trash and throwing it in a brown bag.

"I saw an eagle before I left for my trip." He said, chewing thoughtfully. "My mom said it was a sign. Now I'm seeing one in the same spot we kayaked at when we first met."

"Mmmmm." I said, putting the car in reverse. He was very high on pain pills.

"Sandi. Look." He pointed out the window. "Butterflies."

I froze, staring.

"What is it?" He asked. "You like them right? You're always pointing them out and you have that big painting."

"Yeah…" I said, shaking my head slightly. "Yeah. I do like them."

He accompanied me to my 80s show later that night at Hangar 67.

Georgia Boy was still a little loopy. He got a twenty dollar bill in ones and made it rain on the stage.

I had never had anyone be so enthusiastic about me. He didn't care who was looking, he openly celebrated me, screaming my name and clapping after every song.

The bar had a good crowd. I wandered over and danced with a few people, mostly the men were interested. I tried not to look at Georgia Boy and focused on doing my job.

On one of my breaks he complimented my performance and seemed to pick up on how it made me uncomfortable that he witnessed me dance with other men.

"You know what I saw when I saw you dance with them?" He said.

I shrugged.

"An entertainer, Sandi MarLisa. And a damn good one. Someone who knows how to help people have a good time."

I turned away. "I work with a lot of men, I perform in front of a lot of men and I'm friends with a lot of men. It's made people mad before."

He gently turned my face back towards his. "I'll learn how to do this dance with you, Sandi MarLisa. I'll probably fuck something up along the way, but I'll figure it out eventually."

Near the end of my final set, I walked down with my cordless mic and sat across the table from him.

I sang Kiss by Prince and looked deeply into his eyes. We stared at each other for the whole song.

My bandmate wandered over, cleared his throat and said we could absolutely end the night there, telling Georgia Boy never to sit in the front row again.

Georgia Boy wanted to go to the dock behind Buster's Beer Bait & Tackle again. A large white egret sat in the middle of the dock, the stars were out that night brightly shining over the bay.

"The first time I saw the Milky Way was after the hurricane." I said as we walked.

Georgia Boy appeared agitated and fiddled with his sling.

"The power was out for a hundred miles." I continued, looking up at the sky. "It's amazing how many colors there were, not just white glowing stars. No wonder humans looked up at the sky every night and wondered if there was a Master Designer."

"I saw an eagle today, Sandi." Georgia Boy said abruptly.

"Mmmmm." I said, sitting down on a bench and crossing my legs. I patted my hand on the space beside me.

He turned to me but refused the seat. "When you were singing that Prince song, the rest of the world faded away and I could only see you."

I ran a hand through my hair and rubbed my eyes. I was so tired after a long day of performing.

"You took care of me when I was hurt." He began again. "You made me go to the hospital and stayed with me. I kept coming back to check, but there you were just… just waiting."

"Mhm." I said, nodding.

"You took me to get a granola bar because I was about to pass out."

I sighed impatiently. "Yes, Georgia Boy, of course I did."

"Why?" He said, taking my hand and inviting me to stand up. "Why would you do those things for me?"

I looked up at him and said exasperatedly, "Because I love you, Georgia Boy."

"You love me." He repeated.

"You always going to repeat what I say?"

"Sandi MarLisa loves me." He backed away, taking his eyes off me and looking at the sky. "She really does."

"Yes, Georgia Boy. Yes she does."

"And of course your name would be Sandi!"

"What are you talking about?"

"I mean." He brushed his hair with his free hand. "I mean my family always vacationed here from Georgia. I remember coming down here with my brother and saying, 'One day, I'm going to live in Panama City Beach and play music.'"

He started pacing. "I made that happen. Moved here and then with the pandemic I lost my job, then my wife cheated on me. She was my high school sweetheart, Sandi, like your ex was to you. She never liked me doing music, she thought it was a waste of time. I had to hide it from her. But all I wanted was to be a musician. I settled for the music shop, but when I lost that and my wife I figured, what the hell do I have to lose? Then… I was talking to my mom and I saw this eagle!" He winced slightly. He had tried to throw both hands up when he said 'eagle.'

"So I took a trip." He stopped pacing, rubbing his arm in the sling and looking at me. "The eagle was a sign. That's an animal that symbolizes a lot to me. It means freedom."

I watched him, letting him speak.

He was so much like me, looking for signs and symbolism, making decisions based on gut feelings and intuition and just because he felt like doing it.

I always hated that part of myself. I learned to do things only based on logic and reason.

But some things… some things you just felt in your soul. Some things you just knew down deep in your bones.

Listening to Georgia Boy, I understood that he was mirroring key parts of me back to myself, reminding me of who I was at my core.

I wondered why I ignored those parts of me for so long. I admired how Georgia Boy embraced them.

He was an artist. Just like me. He saw things differently and experienced the world in color.

387

I wanted to embrace that like he did.

I wanted to embrace him until I absorbed his soul into mine.

"The eagle flew west and that's where I went." He continued. "I went all the way to the west coast because Sublime and Dirty Heads sang about it and I saw their beaches. They're nice, but they've got nothing on the Gulf Coast."

I smiled.

"Then I came back. I'd been back in town for a month—a single month, Sandi—officially divorced one month, and I'm at Little Village. All I want to do is be a musician. That's all I want. And then I see this… this beautiful… talented woman doing exactly what I want to do."

I tried not to let tears come to the surface, I pinched the inside of my palm.

"And I say, 'Shit!'" He tilted his head towards the sky. "Shit!"

I laughed.

"Did I really just meet her in the first month of me being divorced! How is that possible? How do things like that happen?"

He knelt down and grabbed my waist with his good hand. "And I knew then, I knew you were it. But I wasn't ready. So I tried to stay away. I didn't want to fuck it up, Sandi."

He let go of my waist and stood, pacing again. "Then we hook up that first time and I thought, 'fuck.'" He stopped and looked down. "I thought I fucked it all up. I wanted to be friends with you. Because I knew I wasn't ready for you. Not in the way I wanted you. The way I've always wanted you." He turned his eyes back to me. "So… I tried to stay away."

Georgia Boy reached out to me with his good hand and I took it, standing up. He touched my face, stroking my cheek with his thumb. "And your name's Sandi. Sandi like the sand on the beach I always wanted to live on. And she's from Florida and she loves her town. And she's a musician. And she has to get out and explore the world when something's bothering her. And she's so much like me. And she's an Aries and I don't know what the fuck that means, but I know you are one."

He released my face to swing me around until I was up against a post on the dock.

"And she's kind. And she's patient. And she's an amazing lover. And... she loves me."

He kissed my cheek, then my forehead.

"I want to wake up next to you. I want to play music with you. I want to grab coffee with you in the mornings. I want to do everything and nothing with you. I..." He looked down at his arm. "...hold on a minute. Stay there."

He backed up and hastily took off his sling and baseball cap, throwing them both to the side, assuming his position again in front of me.

"Sandi MarLisa." He breathed, looking me in the eyes. "I love you. I loved you from the first moment I saw you. I don't want to see you with anybody else. And I can't see anybody else."

I stared into his eyes. I didn't blink, couldn't think.

"Sandi MarLisa." He said my name like a prayer. "Will you be my girl?"

My heart thawed in the radiance of his warmth.

"Yes." I said.

And we kissed, long and slow, fast and hard.

Then, I started jumping up and down. As Georgia Boy likes to put it, I became "giddy."

I dragged him from the dock and straight to his bed.

Maybe, like his arm, our hearts were never broken.

Just dislocated.

And they clicked into place that night on the dock.

Chapter 32

That self love shit

"I think I fell in love with you when I finally fell in love with myself." I tell Georgia Boy over the phone.

I'll see him in less than thirty six hours. I only have a couple stories left to write until I close the book on *Fire Flurries*, looking forward to what comes next.

"Why do you say that?" He asks.

"Because." I begin. "You're so much like me and our goals in life are so similar." I pause, thinking. "I think I was always searching for something else, but when I fell in love with who I am and what I have to offer the world… I could see you. And then I'd never felt anything like it before in my life. You give me butterflies."

I could feel him smile through the phone. "You fell in love with me when you fell in love with yourself. I like that."

"I think that's what I've had time to discover on this trip. This whole book is about love. Losing love and finding it again, realizing love never really actually left. Love for what you do, love for your friends, love for your town, familial love, love for who you are and where you're going. All the different contexts and expressions of it. It's really quite something."

"Are you ready to be home, Sandi?" He asks, his voice deepening in that way that makes my stomach drop.

I long for him. His touch, his voice, his everything.

"Yes. I really am ready to be home."

Because that was him.

He is a home I have never known but spent my whole life searching for.

He is a home for my soul, a soul I have finally learned to embrace and love… just like my friends love me, just like my children love me, just like my family loves me.

Just like he loves me.

And I can't see the end from the beginning. I can't see anything but where I am right now.

But… I think love is worth the risk. Over and over and over again, I will choose love over pain.

Because this?

I'd live through all the pain a thousand times over again. Just for a moment of it.

Don't blow it up

I want to blow up my life.

I do. I really do.

Things are going way too well. Surely something terrible is about to happen.

I have this sense of impending doom riding on my chest at all times. I steal away to private corners to calm myself down.

Is this really my life? Is this really happening?

5 years ago my life looked so different. There was so much to cry about I stopped crying.

And every year there was some new terror.

I drank the dregs of mental illness. I watched how something you can't control can ravage a mind, a family, a home.

A Hurricane came and destroyed the last shred of hope I had left. Then a pandemic directly after that.

I've yelled at God a lot these past few years. Me and that guy go way back to when I would lock myself in my closet as a child and pray for Him to give me a shot at happiness.

"If you're looking for somebody to go. I'll go. I'll do whatever. Just please get me out of here."

There was a place I'd go inside my mind where reality couldn't touch. I learned that I could take the worst situations imaginable and turn them into something beautiful.

I wrote about it everyday. This alternate reality I created in my head.

I spun helpless situations into hopeful narratives. I kept dreaming of a day where everything got better.

Until then, I worked. I worked from sunup to sundown. My coping mechanisms never consisted of substances that helped my brain deal with my reality.

High productivity was my method of coping. I eventually worked as a social media marketer and copywriter, taking on clients and working up to 60 hour weeks. I raised my children at home, bouncing them on my knee as I wrote; eating lunch standing up as I pushed them on swings at the park.

I always gave my mind somewhere to go so it didn't wander too much into the reality of my situation. Reality was not my friend. Reality could kill me.

Then one day, I was offered a gig to start singing 80s music and get into performing again. I had to step away from music for a long time due to trauma.

And God. When I said yes to that gig, reality hit me square in the face.

I realized I had been alone for a long time. For 6 years I worked from home. The most human interaction I really had were on zoom calls, except for my two children.

All of a sudden I was standing before people again who wanted to know me. I was confronted with a new understanding and appreciation for how introverted I actually am.

I had to learn how to be in society again. How to manage more than the handful of friendships I had.

Reality was pulling me down out of the clouds. As if God was taking me out of my safe place in another world and telling me it was time to do the real work now.

I've fought it big time. I realized I had checked out as much as I could from the world. Became as hermit as possible.

Everything rearranged. I got divorced. My kids didn't need me as much anymore. And I physically could no longer distract myself with my ridiculous amounts of high productivity.

In fact, for a few months the only thing I could do was take care of my kids, perform and then lie down in the bed.

I had a lot of processing to do. And it was painful. For so long I dealt with reality by transforming and spinning it into a narrative that was beautiful. It didn't matter how painful something was, with words I could construct meaning. I turned pain into beauty.

But now, it was time to sit with my pain. Rather, I laid with it. Got to know it on an intimate level.

Little by little I spent less time in the bed. I had an epiphany.

As a child, I learned to deal with cold reality by managing what I could control; my inner self. Life could be as harsh as it wanted to me, because I had a secret inner world that would be unaffected by its cruelty.

It served me when I was a child and had little to no control over my external world.

But I'm an adult now. And I have a larger measure of control.

Yet, I continued to let certain negative external experiences happen because it was "okay." I could adjust my inner world to paint over the crappy parts. I could take the shit life threw at me and let my inner world make it beautiful.

I don't have to do that anymore. This changed my life.

Sure, there's stuff I can't control. But there's a lot that I can now.

What if I didn't have to reinterpret or reimagine the shitty stuff that happened to me? What if I could just say, "to hell with it" and create a life that was ACTUALLY beautiful instead of REIMAGINED as beautiful.

That would take me getting out of my head quite a bit, trusting others, saying no, recognizing how I allowed my trauma to isolate me, understanding that I had checked out as much as I could from the world because the world never seemed to like me or treat me well.

Over the past several months I've taken the beauty of my inner world and transferred it to the outer word. I've completely overhauled my life and now there's beauty everywhere I turn.

It's so good it's terrifying me.

Because this can't be real, right? People can't actually be treating me this well. There has to be ulterior motives, right? There's no way there's this many good people in my life.

Everyone secretly hates me, right? I need to retreat back into my own head, play it safe. People always end up hurting you in the end.

Instead of lying with my pain, I'm sitting in my joy. I'm relishing in my happiness and letting it permeate my soul.

I'm allowing it to wash away the years of sadness. I'm making myself sit here in this goodness until it doesn't feel so weird anymore.

I'm recalibrating.

But all I want to do is run. I want to hide. I want to blow up everything. I want to do something to sabotage this whole thing.

There's no way life can be this wonderful. I've never had this feeling. I don't know what to do with it.

I'm going to stand here though. I'm going to stay in this place until it doesn't feel so weird anymore.

I observe my kids and how extraordinary they are. They don't know anything else but security in their own identities. I wonder how different their lives will be from mine.

I don't know if happiness will always be a second step for me. I don't know if I'll ever get used to feeling good because things actually ARE good.

I really don't know. And I'm scared. I'm scared that this is all a dream and it will all go away. After all, I've been living in a dreamworld so much of my life. I'm not used to reality feeling like a friend.

I just know I'm going to keep standing here. I'm going to keep basking in this sunlight for as long as I can.

And if bad times come? That's okay.

After all, that's nothing new to me. Been there and done that over and over again.

But I'm not going to let my past dictate how I enjoy my future. I'm not going to allow previous horrors to rob my present joy.

No. I'm going to stay here. I am. I'm not going to blow it up on purpose when I know life is more than capable of taking care of that on its own if that's what's to come.

Life is already hard. Why would I make it harder for myself?

So as difficult as it is to not pull the trigger and blow everything up, I'm just going to stand here.

That's it.

I'm just going to stand right here.

The balloons

"I need them." I said to Georgia Boy. "I need those balloons. The universe demands that I have them."

It was the ninth anniversary of the Salty Goat Saloon. My son's ninth birthday just happened to be that next day.

And I had... well... I had taken edibles.

It was Georgia Boy's idea!

But there we sat and there were two balloons on the stage shaped like the number nine.

Sons of Saints played. Georgia Boy drank Jack and Coke, I sipped on a Gin and tonic.

Jack and Gin.

"We need a plan." Georgia Boy said.

"No." I said, shaking my head. "No plan. They're mine. They were always supposed to be mine."

"Let me talk to Mason first."

I shook my head vigorously. "No. Because they could say no. There are two number nine balloons. They don't need both of them."

He insisted on speaking with Mason. Our friend agreed to speak with the bar manager after the show.

I shook my leg, agitated.

"Sandi." Georgia Boy said. "We'll get you those balloons."

"I say we grab them and jump out that window." My arms were crossed and I nodded toward one of the open windows. "Then we run like hell."

"Sandi. My parents are here tonight." He turned in his seat to look at them.

"Stop looking suspicious!" I said, slapping his arm.

"Ow. The godfather was right."

Mike Thompson walked up to us. "Hey Sandi. You always look different every time I see you. Love the look."

I smiled at him. "Thank you, darling." I had what I considered to be a bright idea. "Will you cover for us if we steal those balloons?"

"Uhhhh…"

"Don't listen to her, Mike. Great show."

They made conversation while I continued staring at the balloons, sipping my Gin.

The band took the stage again, Georgia Boy still speaking with the band as they prepared to start their next set.

I had made my decision.

I walked up to the stage and grabbed the balloons, handing them to Georgia Boy.

"I'm taking these balloons. Are you in or out?"

He jumped out the window and I ran after him. We walked as nonchalantly as we could past the security guard.

I thought we had made it. I really, really thought we had.

"Hey. You can't take those." The security guard said.

I screamed. "Run!" And took off running.

After a few strides I looked behind me and saw that Georgia Boy was still talking to the security guard, holding the balloons.

I hid behind a car and popped up behind it, motioning for him to run.

Georgia Boy hung his head and started walking back to where he had ran.

I rolled my eyes, standing up and stomping back to the bar. The security guard laughed as I passed him.

I found Georgia Boy inside the bar. He had chucked the balloons at Mike through the window and the whole band was laughing hysterically. His parents were shaking their heads and hiding their faces.

I walked up to him meekly, an apologetic smile on my face.

"Oh. Hello Sandi." He said.

"H-Hey."

He grabbed my elbow, leading me out of the bar. "Why don't we go have a nice talk by my truck."

"Yes. I think that's fair."

We didn't stop until we reached his truck. He turned me to face him and grabbed my chin firmly.

"Sandi MarLisa."

"Georgia Boy."

"You. Ran. From Me."

I shut my eyes.

"Oh no. No no no no no woman. Open your eyes and look at me."

I opened one eye.

"You gave me the balloons and then ran away. I had to put them back in front of the entire bar."

I shut my eye and screwed up my face. "I thought you'd run, too."

"I don't run, woman." Georgia Boy let go of my chin. "And you did."

I caught sight of Mason walking out of the bar and towards the truck. He stopped beside us and said...

"So... uh... that was..."

"Yeah." Georgia Boy said. "We know."

We stood outside in the parking lot for a while until Georgia Boy had the weed induced idea to change his shirt so people wouldn't recognize him.

We believed this would work.

We made out at the bar, drinking and laughing, though Georgia Boy occasionally side eyed me and shook his head.

I tried to make him forgive me by laying it on him thick. I roamed my hands all over his body. He turned to face the bar to give us more privacy.

Georgia Boy pulled away suddenly, laughing. "Oh my god that security guard just looked me dead in the eyes and down. Then he smiled." He cackled, already starting to stand. "Let's get out of here."

We told Mason we were headed out, him promising to try and get the balloons after the show.

Arriving in the parking lot of his condo, Georgia Boy walked me toward the entryway in silence, side-eyeing me the whole way.

"Whatttt?" I said the -t with a bite.

"You ran from me."

"I thought you were behind me!"

"You ran from me, Sandi MarLisa." He didn't look at me. "You gonna run from me again? You gonna run when it's something more serious?"

My insides burned. "I thought you were behind me." I repeated.

"No." Georgia Boy finally looked at me with steely eyes. "Because unlike you. I. Don't. Run."

He kept walking and I watched him go.

Tears welled up in my eyes. I had run. I wanted to run again.

I wanted to run every day still. The closer we got, the more my instincts said "run."

But I stood. I stood and let him love me.

And now he was walking away.

I turned on my heel and began walking towards the road. I passed several cars before stopping, hugging myself.

I wanted to just walk home. I wanted to run away from the fact that I had run away and I didn't even mean to.

I had a flashback of Georgia Boy holding the balloons and speaking with the security guard. I should have gone and stood by him.

But I thought he'd run, too.

"I don't run." He said.

I had just decided to turn back and find him when I looked up and I saw someone walking towards me.

It was Georgia Boy. Because of course it was. He had out paced me, cutting around the cars and looping back.

I smiled and then it quickly faded. I looked down and away.

He didn't stop until he was right in front of me. He grabbed my chin again and pointed in my face.

"You're going to stop walking away from me."

I jerked my chin out of his hand and turned away. Pride kept me from doing anything else.

"Sandi MarLisa. Do you really want to walk away? Is that really what you want?"

I didn't answer.

He walked around me until he was in front of me again. "I'm not possessive. I'm not. You can do what you want. But you are *mine*. And I will leave if you want me to. Just like that night of the hurricane. But I ain't running towards the door."

I lifted my chin at the tone, making myself meet his eyes.

"Says the man who couldn't call me beautiful until he was drunk. Couldn't tell me he loved me until he was mad at me. Then he took it all back as soon as he said it!" I stepped back. "Even our first kiss was at the Salty fucking Hobo for Christ's sake! So don't preach to me about holding back or running away."

He paused, searching my face.

"Our first kiss wasn't at the Hobo."

Every thought went out of my head.

"Wait. What?"

He shook his head slightly, thinking. "Our first kiss was at the Taproom."

My breath caught and I blinked hard, searching myself for a memory.

"We were outside the front doors, on Beck Avenue. You said, 'We're all going to the Hobo. Wanna come?' And you kissed me."

Yes. Oh my god yes. That sounded exactly like me.

And for all I had said about Georgia Boy being drunk during critical turning points in our relationship, I had been drunk and couldn't even remember our first kiss.

Our story…

It was messy. It was questionable. It was complicated.

It was exquisite.

It was love.

Happiness filled every chasm pain had ever left in my soul.

"Our first kiss was at the Taproom." I whispered.

"Yes, Sandi." He said, all anger forgotten. "It was at the Taproom."

I grabbed his shirt, bringing him towards me.

"I want to learn to please you a thousand different ways." I breathed, running my mouth up his jawline and to his ear. "And do each of those ways a thousand times." I kissed him and pulled away, framing his face with my hands. "And it will never be enough."

We stood there looking at one another.

With something like forever in our eyes.

"I love…" He bent his head toward my ear and whispered. "...my guitars."

We burst out laughing in the parking lot, the first feeling of Fall in the air.

"You know what, Georgia Boy?"

"What, Sandi MarLisa?"

I looked at his face, glowing under the moon. "I think you're exquisite."

He put his good arm around me. "I told you, woman. We're gonna fuck this town up." He kissed the top of my head. "Now let's go home."

One who chose it, the other born into it.

But home.

Bay County was home—our home—nonetheless.

Chapter 33

Taproom

I sat at the bar with my sister, my boyfriend and Beanie.

The odd conglomerate of companions began with a full moon.

"You boys ready?"

It was the night of the Letdowns debut at the Taproom. We were sweating in October.

We had practiced in my living room for a couple months and even did a test run at Play Music on the Porch Day.

Our sound was great and I was incredibly excited to work with Georgia Boy. The godfather was finally on the drums. Plus, Beanie's voice was smooth like butter and he was an incredible bassist.

Things were coming full circle.

"Did your son like his balloons, Sandi?" Beanie asked.

I laughed. "Yes. Mason did good. I picked them up the next morning before Judah's birthday party."

"Because if my girl wants something." Georgia Boy bent over his pedals. "And I can't get it for her? I've got friends who can." He winked at me.

"Team effort." I said, smiling.

I walked around to the full tables. Friends of mine had taken off work specifically for the event. Sierra, Lauren, Greg, Michelle and Michael all said they would try to be there as soon as they could.

We had all come a long way from that first gathering in my backyard last year.

Local musicians waited to check the new project out. The energy was electric.

I had personally worked all year for this. The boys had worked hard, too, and this meant different things to each of them.

I wanted a big band. That was always the goal.

And here it was.

We played the first song, Drops of Jupiter of course.

The crowd cheered when we were finished.

"That's the most cheers I've gotten at a show." I heard the godfather say.

We were good. Really good.

We played Let's See How Far We've Come by Matchbox Twenty. I felt chills all over my body as I played the keys. I stopped playing, letting the band take it, and grabbed my cordless mic, walking around the bar.

It was then I saw Boss Man coming towards the stage with a familiar look on his face.

The neighbors were complaining.

"Not tonight." I thought to myself.

After the song I spoke with him. He explained the situation.

"They're doing a play at Oaks by the Bay. They can't hear the performers. And, well, you already know the neighbors are complaining."

The cops showed up then. Bartender tried to mitigate the situation.

I called for a break.

I walked to the center of the stage to speak with the boys about how to move forward. Beanie sat, holding his bass and looking down. Georgia Boy stared at me, bracingly, the godfather putting his drumsticks in a case.

"I don't know why you booked us here, Sandi." The godfather said, not looking at me.

Jacqueline was already at the stage, beer in hand.

I kept looking at him, stung.

"What?" I said.

But he didn't answer me. He ignored that I existed.

I had felt that things had been tense lately. He couldn't play a big festival with me in Mexico Beach, Stronger than the Storm—a festival that happened every year on the anniversary of Hurricane Michael—because he was booked with Jacqueline on that day.

So... I asked Georgia Boy to play it with me.

We had an amazing time figuring out a setlist for the hour show. We even tried our hand at writing songs together.

Georgia Boy would play a riff on the guitar and sing a single line.

"...Jack and Gin..." He sang.

I smiled. Our alter egos.

He kept strumming his guitar, humming a melody.

"What are they doing?" He asked. "What are Jack and Gin doing?"

I'd smile, nodding my head to the rhythm, closing my eyes and feeling the music.

"Jack and Gin went up the wind to catch a pair of clouds..."

"I like it!" Georgia Boy said, grinning.

I paused, letting the progression start over.

"Jack and Gin went up the wind to catch a pair of clouds. Jack fell through a sea of stars and Gin came tumbling down."

"Yes!" He said, sticking the guitar pick in his mouth. "O. M. G. I have to record this." He pulled his phone out, giddy. He found the voice recorder and pressed the red button, setting the phone in front of me and grabbing his pick again. "Okay. Do that again."

I'd play around with lyrics and he'd encourage me to try a different direction. He added new verses.

"Jack told Gin I like to fly with the wind. Don't be surprised if I take you too far. Two worlds collided, Jack and Gin decided. They crash landed on a shooting—SHIT!"

"A shooting shit?"

"No!" He'd stopped playing, looking off into space. "Okay okay okay. What if we added this riff here?"

And we... played. I realized I could do that with him for hours and hours.

We rocked Stronger than the Storm together, helping raise funds for hurricane victims. Having two singers opened up a wider array of songs. My favorite song he sang was Beast of Burden by the Rolling Stones.

The crowd loved us.

I approached Matt Larson, the organizer for the event.

"You were the only band today that didn't play country. Nothing against Country, but it's refreshing!" He mopped his brow with the back of his hand. "I can't believe it's been three years since the storm."

I nodded. "I know." I looked off towards the beach I knew well. "It's amazing that you put on this event."

"Thank you for coming." He said. "I'll go grab your checks."

I walked with Georgia Boy, searching for food.

"V.I.P." Georgia Boy waved his badge before bending and grabbing a beer out of the cooler. "God I love saying that."

I smiled and looked off towards the Gulf again.

"You okay?" Georgia Boy asked, cracking open his beer.

"Yeah… just thinking."

"This day holds a lot of memories for you."

"Yeah." I looked towards the sky and then back at Georgia Boy. "You know, it took the Federal Government almost a year to approve a federal relief package for Hurricane Michael victims? Meanwhile my people were living in tents."

Georgia Boy sipped his beer, looking at me.

"At the end of the day." I sighed. "It was my neighbor who cut fallen trees out of the road with a chainsaw, rescuing me and my family. Not the government." I looked towards Matt Larson. "At the end of the day, it was my people who came together and saved our town. People like Matt Larson. People like the St. Andrews business owners."

Georgia Boy touched my hand.

"Everybody looks to the government for answers, or to the church, or to God, the universe… whatever. Something bigger than themselves… they want to change the world. But everybody wants to change the world." I squeezed Georgia Boy's hand. "Nobody wants to change their town. And don't you think it starts there?"

Georgia Boy smiled, still gripping my hand as he led me to the beach.

We walked the shore, holding hands and sipping our drinks.

The Forgotten Coast was beautiful.

Seagulls sang their out-of-tune song. Pelicans dived for fish. A sailboat reflected the light of the setting sun over the Emerald Coast.

Dolphins jumped in the distance and I took it as a sign.

"What do you say we go make out in that boat?" Georgia Boy asked, jerking his chin in the direction of a large rubber boat left on the shore by a rental company.

I rolled my eyes.

He threw his head back and laughed. "What are you gonna do with me, woman?"

I looked at him confidently, throwing my hair behind my shoulder. "I'm gonna make you a man."

He dropped his voice. "Well, I'm gonna make you a woman!"

I rolled my eyes again. "I'm already a woman, Georgia Boy." And I turned to walk to the boat.

"Wait..." I heard him say behind me. "...dammit."

I smiled to myself while I climbed in the boat.

He found me and climbed on top of me, shaking his head before tickling me.

I giggled and he stopped, gazing into my eyes.

"Well how about this, Sandi MarLisa."

"Hm?"

"I'm gonna teach you what it means to be loved by a man."

I swallowed hard, my eyes roaming his face. "Yeah. Yeah you could do that."

"You gonna stay with me, Sandi MarLisa? You gonna do this thing with me?"

I sat up a bit. "I'll stay as long as you treat me well."

"And what is treating you well?"

"You already do it."

"I want to do more of it." He said, sitting up and looking at me expectantly.

"What, do you want a list?"

"Yes."

Oh.

I thought about it for a moment, looking off toward the Gulf.

"Buy me flowers sometimes." I turned to him. "I like them. If we move in together at some point in the future, clean. Do housework. It doesn't take that long and it means the world to me." I gazed towards the sky. "If you're mad about something, just tell me. Don't be passive aggressive. I want to make you happy. So I'll do my best to be accommodating and work with you towards a compromise if it's needed… that's all I've got right now… wait!"

"Hm?"

"Sex. Lots of sex."

He smiled, nodding. "I want to fuck you every day. And yes. I can do all those things."

Georgia Boy put his arm around my waist at the Taproom. "You okay, Sandi?"

"Yeah." I said, not looking at him. I was staring at the godfather who was seated at a table just outside the courtyard. "I need to talk to the godfather."

I approached his table and looked at the godfather. He wouldn't meet my eyes.

"Hey. So. What's the plan?"

"I'm not getting back up there."

And I should have yelled at him. I shouldn't have let him off so easily.

Except for one thing. I could see he was already gone.

"Okay." I said, and walked away.

The godfather packed up his drum set on our break and loaded it into his car, the whole Taproom watching.

When we took the stage again, Georgia Boy and I spotted the godfather skipping off to the Hobo with Jacqueline and Jacob.

Beanie sat down for a bit, discouraged. So Georgia Boy and I kept up the energy as best we could, walking around the bar with my wireless mic and his wireless guitar.

"What a letdown" was the joke. We had people laughing and shaking their heads. They stayed to watch the whole performance erupt in flames.

It was entertainment in its rawest form.

So, we embraced it. I ran out of the courtyard gates to sing into the neighbor's window who constantly called and complained. I heard Georgia Boy say into his mic, "And then there was one letdown left."

Megghan took a picture of me, my back to the camera and fist in the air.

"That was punk." Georgia Boy said. "What the godfather did wasn't punk. What you did, singing into the neighbor's window with your fist in the air, that was punk."

So we sang Let's See How Far We've Come again, and I screamed the title over and over again, jumping up and down.

That's when I noticed someone limping into the courtyard.

"Hey Sandi." Georgia Boy said, pointing the neck of his guitar in the direction of the limping stranger. "Isn't that your sister?"

Oh my god.

"Yes… yes it is."

We sat at the bar after the show, going over the night's events. My sister had twisted her ankle in one of her sports leagues. Even in her state, she checked on Georgia Boy's arm and scolded him for not following her instructions properly.

Georgia Boy took me aside.

"Are you okay?"

I shrugged.

"Your friend walked out on you today."

My eyes filled with tears. I wiped them away.

"Are you… are you crying?"

I shrugged again and looked away.

"I'll kill him."

I laughed and shook my head.

"I've never seen you cry before."

I turned away for a minute, drying my eyes, and turned back to face him.

"I'm sorry. I don't know why but that really affected me. I just thought we both wanted the same things. A big band. And this was our first show."

He paused, considering. "You know that day on the creek? You told me I was one of three men you ever loved."

I nodded, remembering what he had told me.

"Well. You listed them."

I cocked my head.

"One of them was your ex." He began. "One of them was me. And the other… was the person who just walked out on you tonight."

I processed what he said, and then I couldn't stop the tears from rolling. "Why didn't you tell me?"

"You weren't ready for it yet." He said, grabbing my waist. "You're my woman, Sandi MarLisa." He tucked his hand under my chin. "You know I hold that in high esteem?"

I nodded, my eyes shining like stars. "You're my second chance."

He tipped my chin more towards himself. "No Sandi MarLisa. A fresh chance."

And the man who loved me pulled me into a hug.

Chapter 34

One last coffee

I pour myself another cup of coffee. It's 11:14pm Alaska time the night before I leave for home. It's 2:14am back in Panama City.

My boyfriend tried to stay up with me as best he could, texting me encouragement. My parents were up watching a Lynyrd Skynyrd documentary, petting Boo Bear and complaining about his salmon breath.

But now… I'm on my own.

This ends tonight.

Begins… really. It begins tonight.

I spent my last full day in Alaska in downtown Anchorage with my parents. We ate crab sandwiches and mussels at F. Street Station and then went to the Anchorage Museum.

I wandered around the museum, taking in the spectacular artwork by local artists.

Alaska isn't something that you can encapsulate in a photo.

But maybe you can get close with a painting.

I could feel the artists' souls and love for their home in every brushstroke, could feel the same magic I felt when looking at Denali as I stared at a painting depicting it.

I walked through a room that displayed traditional Native tools, clothing and even art. Puffin beaks adorned their coats and even the teeth of animals made beautiful necklaces.

The Native's used every part of the animal and honored the life that gave them life.

I learned about their pain due to colonization as I admired photographs of fishermen and children laughing around fires.

The Lynyrd Skynyrd documentary my parents were watching earlier covered the topic of the band using the confederate flag as a branding tool. Many of the surviving band members of the infamous plane crash insist that they simply didn't think too deeply into what the flag symbolizes to people of color, and ultimately regret their past association with it.

I watched for a minute, taking in their words.

I'm going sledding tomorrow. My final hurrah in Alaska until we meet again.

No Northern Lights. They remained ever elusive.

"Aw." My boyfriend had said. "I know you wanted it for poetic justice in your book. I've enjoyed reading what you have."

"I think I got my poetic justice."

"What do you mean?"

"I mean... I think people spend a lot of their lives hoping for what they want to happen... and then they miss the beauty that does happen. I didn't see the Northern Lights, but I did so many other things that are worth celebrating. I've seen and experienced so many things that few people get the opportunity to enjoy. And I wrote a freaking book!"

He laughs.

"I... you know... I thought my life was going to turn out one way and then it took a complete 180 degree turn. I thought I'd be with one person and never imagined a future without them... now I'm happier than I've ever been because I knew something needed to change or I was going to wither away."

"Mmmm."

"And now.... yeah... it's like missing the Northern Lights. I thought that's what I wanted, but if I had spent this whole trip trying to search for them, I would have missed out on so many other opportunities, plus I still wouldn't have seen the lights. The lights do what they want and I don't get a say in it! Nobody does!"

"Sandi MarLisa."

"Yes?"

"Come home to me."

I pause in my writing to shoot him a text, knowing he won't see it until the morning.

I know you won't see this until morning. But I finished the book! When you wake up, read the final word of the book. Then I want you to ask me why. Don't read anything else until you've asked me yourself.

You asked me what I learned on this trip and now I can finally tell you in my way. And I just hope you understand it.

Georgia

"Are you asking me to quit my job and run away with you?" Georgia Boy asked, holding me.

"Yes." I said.

"Okay. Done."

I wanted to go to Asheville to visit Jessica and see the changing leaves, but Georgia Boy's work at the dispensary kept him from being able to go.

"You're a musician!" I said, shaking him. "It's time to level the fuck up and embrace it!"

But it wasn't until we were lying in bed, doing what lovers do, and I asked him sweetly.

"Run away with me."

"This is how you ask me, woman." He stroked my back. "Whenever you want something from me, ask me just like this."

He stood in the frame of my bedroom—I had finally taken over the master—and watched me pack for our trip.

"Sandi MarLisa is home again." He said.

I took a deep breath. My room was still a mess and needed some serious organizing, but it was indeed mine once more. "Yes. Yes she is."

Georgia Boy walked over to me and grabbed me from behind, pushing me stomach down over the bed.

"Mmmmm." I moaned.

He took my hips and grinded into me, giving me a slap on the ass. "I can't wait to break in this bed."

"Knowing us." I said, standing and turning to face him. "We'll probably just break it."

"What am I gonna do when you go to Alaska for a month, huh?" He nuzzled my neck and bit my ear.

"I guess you'll just have to come with me." I said, hopefully.

He allowed a few seconds to pass. "You know this isn't my journey. But… I wanted to ask you something."

"What is it?"

"I want to stop over at my home in Georgia on our way up. It's halfway to Asheville."

I paused, searching his face. "You want me to see your home?"

He framed my face with his hands. "I want you to see where I come from." He paused. "I have a bridge, too."

I closed my eyes and kissed the palm of his hand, then I pulled his hands down from where they held my face and gazed up at him. "Does Georgia have fireflies?"

He stepped closer to me. "First of all, they're lightning bugs, not fireflies. And yes. Yes we have them."

"Two completely separate creatures." I said.

He rolled his eyes. "What are you talking about, woman?"

"It's obvious." I turned back to my packing. "Fireflies have fire and lightning bugs have lightning." I bumped him with my butt. "Understand?"

He turned me back to him and gazed down at me, smiling. "Yes ma'am."

"Runaway, runaway, runaway with me…"

We sang a song we wrote called All the Colors on our way to Georgia. I looked out the window and spotted a confederate flag and made a face.

"What is it?" Georgia Boy asked.

"I just don't understand why people insist on flying those."

He paused. "They consider it cultural."

"There are better elements of southern culture to celebrate. Things we can actually be proud of. "

He rolled down the windows, the breeze rushing in. Astrovan by Mt. Joy played through the speakers of his truck. "Most people in Georgia would disagree with you."

"I'm Floridian! I'll scream it out of this window!"

He sighed, looking over at me. "I'm excited to take you to my favorite spots today."

"I'm excited to see them!"

He took me to the covered bridge in his town and showed me where they used to rope swing into the river. Georgia Boy pointed out the street signs named after his own family.

"I'm starting to believe you're a country girl, Sandi MarLisa. You look right at home."

I smiled, taking in the beauty around me. The trees seemed to whisper old things, ancient things.

Oh, the stories they would tell.

"Yes. My family originates in Jackson County, Florida." I turned to look at him as we walked to the pond on his family's property. His favorite spot. "There are streets named after my family as well."

"Sandi MarLisa, a country girl." He nudged me. "But you sure don't let that accent fly." Georgia Boy put his arm around me. "Until I smack that ass."

I brushed him off, laughing. "Yes. My father was born in Chicago and is a speech language pathologist. He was especially concerned with our diction." I paused, a memory surfacing.

"That thought you just had, woman." Georgia Boy pointed at me. "I want to know it."

I laughed. "He took care of my voice in many ways. I was prone to sinus infections. I stayed sick. So I had to get my tonsils taken out. They typically remove the adenoids as well." My eyes glazed up towards the sky. "I think I was maybe ten? And my father sat me down in front of the doctor and told me I had a decision to make. He explained that if they took out my adenoids, it might affect the quality of my singing voice. He said he was leaving the decision up to me."

"Wow. What did you decide?"

"I told the doctor I didn't want my adenoids taken out."

"I'm learning so much about you right now." Georgia Boy pointed, indicating the pond was close by. "What about your mom?"

I smiled. "She was born in Jackson County. My parents met at a bank she worked at. My father always said he was supposed to start his life in Maine, but then he met my mother. And he stayed in Florida twenty five years."

Georgia Boy made a slow whistling sound. "But he didn't like Florida?"

"He didn't like the heat." I answered. Then I had a thought and laughed. "We Floridians are bred in the fire and we don't settle for smoke."

He rolled his eyes. "So proud."

"Yes."

413

We arrived at the pond and sat down beneath a pole barn Georgia Boy himself had built. I thought of his history on the land and thought I'd offer up some of my own.

"My mother's father was a musician." I said with fondness. "He… he was a good man. He died when I was seven, but he would play music for the nursing homes and invite me to sing. He'd always joke that I stole the show from him. I thought he was really mad at me for the longest time!"

Georgia Boy laughed.

"I shared a birthday with his mother. She… she would never tell her family who his father was. She claimed he was a Native. My Papa's last name she gave him didn't ever even really exist before him. He didn't even have a middle name. They were both shunned by her family and society."

Georgia Boy touched my knee and waited.

"But he fell in love with my Mema and she loved that man. That side of the family has its roots deep in Florida… but it's a tainted past. My Mema's father, the man who fed me cheese puffs from his rocking chair, was a member of the local KKK." I spit out the name, disgusted. "I was recently made aware of this information."

"Oh my god." Georgia Boy hung his head.

"Growing up, people always asked me what I was. I always told them my family's story of what my Papa's mother told everyone. But then I was working towards my Bachelors in Sociology… and I read a few interesting papers about how Southerners would claim Native roots during the Civil War in order to justify their ties to the South."

I looked around at the pole barn, thinking.

"It made sense to me. So I kept it in my heart… but still these random people would come up to me and pepper me with questions. 'What are you? What are you? What are you?' Racially ambiguous is what I've been dubbed… so the question always stayed in the back of my mind, especially when I had children.'"

I paused, wondering how to continue.

"It started with my son, Judah. I called my mom one day and asked her if it was normal for his little butt cheeks to have blue spots on them."

Georgia Boy chuckled.

"They looked like bruises. I was really concerned… but my mother assured me immediately and said that I had the same marks when I was a baby. They're called Mongolian birthmarks and they disappear usually within the first year of a child's life. They're present in people with Asian, African or Native descent."

I stood up and looked around the pole barn, my hands on my hips. "Everything was fine until the day I took him to a church nursery and was accused of abusing my child."

Georgia Boy's mouth dropped open.

"I learned to thoroughly explain Mongolian birthmarks to anyone who watched my children after that. I even pulled out my phone and showed proof with pictures that it was a real thing. Just so there was no confusion."

My boyfriend continued listening patiently.

"Anyway, I took a DNA test eventually. Basically I'm a mosaic, that's how I like to think of it anyway… with a list too long to name." I smiled. "All the colors."

"And your great grandfather was a member of the KKK."

I sighed. "Exactly." I finally made eye contact with him. "I'll never know the history of why people ask me 'What are you?' And I will never be able to answer them in full. I think what bothers me the most is that my own family hated a part of who I am. Of who made me."

I sat back down on the bench, deep in thought.

"I do know that I'm Floridian." I looked at him then and smiled. "If there is anything I am… it's that."

"Yes ma'am." He said, pulling me close. "You are that."

My phone buzzed. It was a text from Bartender.

She had sent a video. It simply said: *I did it. I did it for you.*

Georgia Boy and I gathered around the phone to watch.

Bartender was yelling, yelling at the Taproom neighbor who liked to call and complain.

You always have to cause problems! Why don't you just go home?

The neighbor said something unintelligible.

Just go! Go you fucking Brussels sprout!

Georgia Boy and I looked at each other and lost it, practically weeping with our laughter.

Asheville, North Carolina

We arrived in Asheville the next day with one goal. We wanted to do one single gig together.

"What should we tell people is our band name?" Georgia Boy asked.

I thought about it. "Lavender Soul?"

"You're gonna have to explain that one to me."

I laughed. "It was Jessica's response when I told her my soul is black. She said, 'Sandi. If your soul was a color, it'd be something like lavender.'"

Georgia Boy threw his head back and laughed. "Hmmm... I could get on board with that... but..." He drummed the steering wheel. "What about Jack and Gin?"

"What?" I asked.

"It's what we drink! Our alter egos!"

I considered it. "It's kinda catchy!"

We arrived at a trail head, we were hiking to see a waterfall. Georgia Boy carried a guitar on his back, the same one he used to write songs with when he traveled the country.

We found a boulder and sat down. Georgia Boy straddled me, putting his arms around my shoulders, humming in my ears the tune to All the Colors. We added some verses.

"We drank from a waterfall, and danced in the stream, made love by the trees in a bed of vibrant leaves..."

He readjusted and pulled his guitar out, the waterfall creating an entirely new instrumental moment.

"Oooooo girl!" He smiled, hugging his guitar to his chest. "That's it. We're going to a recording studio while we're here!"

I laughed, readjusting my sweater.

"Come on." Georgia Boy said, standing up. "Let's go fulfill the lyrics."

We approached a path that led to the top of the waterfall, caution tape partially blocking it off.

"That way." Georgia Boy pointed. He began climbing the large rocks.

I watched him for a moment before shaking my head and shouting, "Georgia Boy! This is how you die!"

He turned to me and smiled.

And all my fears died like stars in his eyes.

A stranger comes up the path, trudging through the snow. They reach out a hand and help pull me out of the snowbank I had fallen into.

The German Shepherd releases Boo Bear's neck. We continue down the path on our skis until we reach a high hill. I take my aim and pull up my sticks, bending my knees and soaring down the incline.

"Hey hey!" My father calls. "You did it!"

The snow tube lands on the other side of the snow barrier. I roll out into four feet of snow so I don't keep cascading down the mountain.

"I'm okay!" I call to my parents.

I dry my tears, remembering my children slept through the earthquake, just as they laughed during the worst of a thousand year storm.

I reach shore, dragging my daughter along the ice with me. We all laugh and leave the frozen lake to go to the North Pole.

My father and I clink glasses, and then I laugh with my bonus mom as he tries to scoop the fly out of his wine.

I hold my son and we slide and slide and slide across the snow, coming to a halt at the base of the sled hill. My son opens his eyes.

"Mom? Where's the sled?"

I tip back my head and laugh loudly. My son joins in with me.

Georgia Boy meets me at the Emerald Coast airport.

"There she is!" He says, exiting the truck. "There's my girl! I almost didn't recognize you with that hat on!"

I grin and take off the red hat I bought from a brewery in Alaska. I put it on his head backwards and kiss him. Toast peeks out of my backpack.

My bandmate and I sit at a bar called Jack of the Wood in Asheville. The booking manager asks us our band name.

"The name of the bar is a sign." He says. So Georgia Boy answers, "Jack and Gin."

And now he's inviting me to come with him to the top of the waterfall and make love.

"No, Sandi MarLisa." He reaches out his hand.

And I see all the colors.

All of them.

And they are bright and vivid.

They are full of hope and promise.

"This is how you live."

So I take his hand and he leads me to the top of the waterfall.

I lie down when we reach the peak and he's on top of me, kissing me, loving me, holding me.

"Oh God." I sigh into his ear.

"Who? No, Sandi MarLisa." He says my name like a song. "What's my name?"

Georgia Boy. My Boyfriend. River Boy. Mr. Love is Overrated.

The Boy Who Makes Trees Sing. My Friend. My Bandmate. My Fresh Chance. Jack.

My Partner. One to Call My Own. My One Fucking Person.

My Lover.

My Love.

"Eli."

Acknowledgements

It's 1:47am in the morning four days before I'm supposed to have my book signing and this is it! I have to be done!

All I can say is, thanks to everyone who has supported me over the years in my various artistic pursuits.

Thanks to Sara Griffith for the drop-dead-gorgeous book cover and Fire Flurries logo. It was my goal to feature a Bay County artist on the cover and she rose to the challenge!

To every St. Andrews artist, I see you and I love you.

To every Bay County business owner, artist—and yes—every creature of the night… we built this city. Actually we resurrected it out of what Hurricane Michael left us and made a beautiful mosaic from the pieces. I think we did a damn good job and there's still work to be done! #850Strong

Kids, I love you more than my life. It was important for your mom to make this book about her own personal journey. But, Lorelai, you gave me a damn good title. And, Judah, I hope I do, in fact, make you rich.

To my friends, I hope I do indeed give in equal measure.

Dad and Selena, thank you so much for allowing me to stay in your home in Alaska for a whole month. I hope the end product is worth it, but maybe Selena should screen the book for you dad!

Mom, thanks so much for helping me get to Alaska. Kelli, thank you so much for supporting your big sister in her wild ideas. Luke, I know I need to answer your phone calls more, but I love you baby bro and I'm so proud of you.

Thank you to all who donated to help me make the trip to Alaska possible. Thanks for supporting independent artists!

Eli, my love. Without you… what can I say? I'm still learning us, it's all so new and beautiful. Thanks for helping me fund this first round of books and believing in me and my dreams.

And to the rest… well… just know that love always has the final word.

Connect

Sandi MarLisa considers herself a modern day Renaissance Person. She doesn't believe you have to be "just one thing."

Her two favorite mediums, however, are expressing herself through music and the written word.

Sandi currently resides in Lynn Haven, Florida with her two children.

You can connect with her at **SandiMarLisa.com** or on social media.

Sandi MarLisa and Jack and Gin now streaming everywhere!

You can also find the *Fire Flurries* playlist on Spotify and Apple Music to enhance your experience.

Made in the USA
Columbia, SC
26 September 2024

42409403R00230